THE WAY TO NICAEA

THE FORMATION OF CHRISTIAN THEOLOGY
VOLUME I

The Way to Nicaea

by

JOHN BEHR

ST VLADIMIR'S SEMINARY PRESS
CRESTWOOD, NEW YORK

Library of Congress Cataloging-in-Publication Data

Behr, John.
    The Way to Nicaea / by John Behr.
        p. cm. — (The formation of Christian theology; v. 1)
    Includes bibliographical references and index.
    ISBN 0-88141-224-4 (alk. paper)
        1. Theology, Doctrinal—History—Early church, ca. 30-600.   2. Theology,
    Doctrinal—History—Middle Ages, 600-1500.   I. Title   II. Series

    BT23.B47 2001
    230'.13—dc21

                                                              2001019386

The Way to Nicaea
The Formation of Christian Theology: Volume 1

ST VLADIMIR'S SEMINARY PRESS
575 Scarsdale Road, Crestwood, NY 10707
1-800-204-2665

ISBN 0-88141-224-4 (paper)
ISBN 0-88141-230-9 (hard)

PRINTED IN THE UNITED STATES OF AMERICA

CONTENTS

For Fr Thomas

Abbreviations

Primary Sources

The following abbreviations are used in the course of this work. The numeration of the editions cited in the Bibliography is followed.

AH	*Irenaeus, Against the Heresies* (in the numeration of Massuet—PG and SC)
Ap.	Justin Martyr, *First Apology*
App.	Justin Martyr, *Second Apology*
Bibl.	Photius, *Bibliotheca*
CC	Origen, *Contra Celsum*
CN	Hippolytus, *Contra Noetum*
ComJn.	Origen, *Commentary on John*
ComMatt.	Origen, *Commentary on Matthew*
Comp.	Theodoret of Cyrus, *Compendium of Heretical Fables*
Dem.	Irenaeus, *Demonstration of the Apostolic Preaching*
Dial.	Justin Martyr, *Dialogue with Trypho*
FP	Origen, *On First Principles*
EH	Eusebius, *Ecclesiastical History*
Eph.	Ignatius, *Letter to the Ephesians*
HomJer.	Origen, *Homilies on Jeremiah*
Magn.	Ignatius, *Letter to the Magnesians*
Phld.	Ignatius, *Letter to the Philadelphians*
Phil.	Origen, *Philokalia*
Ref.	"Hippolytus," *Refutation of all Heresies*
Rom.	Ignatius, *Letter to the Romans*
Smyrn.	Ignatius, *Letter to the Smyrneans*
Strom.	Clement of Alexandria, *Stromata*
Trall.	Ignatius, *Letter to the Trallians*

Journals and Series

ACO	*Acta Conciliorum Oecumenicorum*, ed. E. Schwartz (Berlin and Leipzig: De Gruyter, 1927-44).
ACW	Ancient Christian Writers
ANF	Ante-Nicene Fathers

CH	*Church History*
CSCO	Corpus Scriptorum Christianorum Orientalium
FC	Fathers of the Church
GCS	Die griechischen christlichen Schriftsteller der ersten drei Jahrhunderte
GNO	Gregorii Nysseni Opera (Leiden: Brill)
GOTR	*Greek Orthodox Theological Review*
HTR	*Harvard Theological Review*
JBL	*Journal of Biblical Literature*
JECS	*Journal of Early Christian Studies*
JEH	*Journal of Ecclesiastical History*
JRS	*Journal of Roman Studies*
JTS	*Journal of Theological Studies*
LCL	Loeb Classical Library
NPNF	Nicene and Post-Nicene Fathers
NTS	*New Testament Studies*
OCP	*Orientalia Christiana Periodica*
OECT	Oxford Early Christian Texts
PG	Patrologia Graeca
PL	Patrologia Latina
PO	Patrologia Orientalis
PTS	Patristische Texte und Studien
RSPhTh	*Revue des Sciences Philosophiques et Théologiques*
RSR	*Recherches de Science Religieuse*
SC	Sources Chrétiennes
St. Patr.	*Studia Patristica*
SVF	*Stoicorum Veterum Fragmenta*, ed. J. Von Arnim
SVTQ	*Saint Vladimir's Theological Quarterly*
TS	*Theological Studies*
TU	Texte und Untersuchungen zur Geschichte der altchristlichen Literatur
VC	*Vigiliae Christianae*
ZAC	Zeitschrift für antikes Christentum: Journal of Ancient Christianity
ZNTW	*Zeitschrift für die neutestamentliche Wissenschaft und die Kunde der Urchristentums*

Foreword

Orthodoxy has a problem with theology. The reasons for this problem are mainly historical. The science of theology developed in the medieval universities, and then passed through the waves of cultural history that swept through the West: Renaissance, Reformation, Enlightenment, Romanticism. But by the time the universities began to develop, in the twelfth century, Christendom had divided, and these developments all took place in a world from which Orthodoxy was estranged. In the twentieth century Orthodoxy encountered the West, and also theology as it had developed in that period of estrangement (earlier encounters, through the discussions connected with the union councils in the Middle Ages, and the establishment of theological academies and later theological faculties in universities in Orthodox countries, only compounded the problem by subjecting Orthodox theology to the "pseudomorphosis" so deplored by Fr Georges Florovsky). Most Orthodox are critical of the development of theology in the West, in particular the way theology had developed as an academic discipline, remote from the life of prayer (a complaint already heard in the West from the fourteenth century onwards), and yet the fruits of critical scholarship, which have led, among other things, to a rediscovery of the riches of the theology of the Fathers, can hardly be ignored. This has led to an uneasy coexistence between traditional theology and the critical spirit, one result of which has been Orthodox seeking refuge in historical scholarship focused on the period (from the fourth century onwards) when the dogmatic tradition had established itself (in this way shadowing the phenomenon in the Roman Catholic Church between the condemnation of Modernism in the papal decree *Lamentabili* in 1907 and the Second Vatican Council). Biblical scholarship has not, on the whole, attracted the best Orthodox minds in the twentieth century, and there has been a tendency in such scholarship (especially perhaps in the case of the New Testament) to look to conservative Protestant and Catholic scholarship, with the consequent danger of confusing conservatism and Orthodoxy.

There are signs, however, that this uneasy relationship between Orthodoxy and critical theology is being transcended in some of our younger Orthodox theologians. The most striking, and hopeful, example is this work by John Behr. His academic background was initially in philosophy; he then went on to study Christian theology with Bishop Kallistos of Diokleia in Oxford, concentrating on the formative period of Christian theology, and gaining a doctorate which was published in revised form as *Asceticism and Anthropology in Irenaeus and Clement* (2000). The title suggests something more than an ordinary patristic monograph, and indeed there is more: for the book attempts a *theological* engagement with the social anthropological and sociological approach to Early Christian asceticism, associated especially with the names of Michel Foucault and Peter Brown. Through such a theological engagement, Professor Behr maintains, and demonstrates in his book, that it is possible to rescue early Christian thinkers from what has come to be called "late antiquity" and listen to them once again as Fathers of the Church. In that first book, it was Irenaeus with whom Professor Behr found a deep affinity. His study of Irenaeus has continued since completing his doctoral studies, during which time he has been teaching theology at St Vladimir's Seminary, and he has published a translation of Irenaeus' *On the Apostolic Preaching* (1997), from Armenian, the only ancient language in which this precious work survives.

Irenaeus also guides the steps taken in the early chapters of this present book. This is a book, easy to characterize in general terms, but which still, perhaps, needs some introduction. In general terms, this is the first in a series on the formation of Christian theology in the formative period of the seven Ecumenical Councils, that is, up to the Second Council of Nicaea, held in 787, at which the veneration of icons was upheld, a decision that set its seal on the visual aspect of Orthodoxy, and which has been celebrated, since its reaffirmation in 843, on the First Sunday of Lent each year as the "Triumph of Orthodoxy." With the choice of that period for this introduction to Christian theology,

Professor Behr sets out his credentials as a theologian of the Orthodox tradition.

His method, however, is radical (for Orthodoxy is radical, not conservative): He does not duck the New Testament and the period of what is sometimes called in English "primitive Christianity," nor the historical problems and uncertainties associated with it. Rather, guided by his own understanding of Irenaeus, an understanding for which he carefully and courteously presents his arguments, he takes his account back to Jesus' question to his disciples at Cæsarea Philippi, "Who do you say that I am?" and to the apostolic response to this abiding question, where he finds both the heart of the Christian faith and starting-point of Christian theology. It is this question that he pursues here and in the volumes that follow.

It is important, I think, to be clear about two things, entailed by this starting-point. First, the answer to this question involves two interrelated affirmations: that the one who Christ is is Christ crucified and risen, the person of the Paschal mystery, and also that Christ is the Word of God, meaning by this that he is the meaning of God's utterance in the Scriptures (a term that primarily means what Christians came to call the Old Testament: Professor Behr argues that this primary meaning is not set aside by the later Christian extension of the term "Scripture" to include the New Testament). Both these assertions have radical consequences for the approach to theology taken here: the former means that the Paschal mystery is the focus of theology, not something displaced by an emphasis on the "Incarnation" (Professor Behr notes how the Nativity is seen by both Orthodox iconography and Orthodox liturgical song in terms of the Passion), the latter keeps at the centre of Christian theology the Pauline (and credal) emphasis on "according to the Scriptures," with all that entails for the Christian use of Scripture (something Orthodox constantly encounter in their liturgical texts). Both these affirmations prevent theology from detaching itself from prayer, in which Christ is encountered as the crucified and risen Lord, and also from liturgical prayer, in which we stand together before God as the Body of Christ.

Secondly, since it is people, men and women, who respond to Christ, this work focuses on particular Christian thinkers. The formation of Christian theology is not the development of Christian doctrine

(Orthodox theologians ought to have more problems with that idea, a fruit of Romanticism, popularized by Cardinal Newman, than they often seem to): We can never pass beyond the apostolic confession of Christ. Rather the formation of Christian theology is the result of sustained, and prayerful, thinking and meditation by those who sought to grasp what is entailed by the Paschal mystery. Thought does not exist apart from thinkers, and Professor Behr, as he seeks to understand the formation of Christian theology, is as much, if not more, interested in the thinking that went on, rather than the thoughts that resulted. This does not elide the difference between Orthodoxy and heresy, but it does qualify the distinction between Orthodox thinkers and heretics. Origen, therefore, receives immensely sympathetic attention here, and even Paul of Samosata comes over as a genuine theological thinker, rather than the buffoon with which Eusebius presents us.

Throughout this book, and those that follow, the account of the formation of Christian theology is presented, drawing on the best of modern scholarship and in engagement with the critical issues raised by such scholarship. Professor Behr does not take refuge in easy answers and, as we have seen, his Orthodoxy is radical, not conservative. Moreover, while being thoroughly Orthodox, it is written in the theological idiom of contemporary academic theology, which thereby also enables Orthodoxy to have an authentic voice in current theological debates. In order to concentrate on theology, relatively little space is devoted to historical background, whether institutional, cultural or intellectual. Nonetheless, it is very clear that Professor Behr is aware of all these aspects, and brings out its significance where it is relevant. It is not true of this account of the formation of Christian theology, as has been said of some other accounts, that it all might have taken place on the moon! This is, therefore, a demanding book, requiring of its readers careful attention: but such attention will be richly repaid.

Andrew Louth

Introduction

"Who do you say I am?" (Matt 16:15). This question, posed by Jesus Christ, is the one that Christian theology seeks to answer. This series provides an introduction to the reflection provoked by this question in the formative years of the history of the Christian Church. This was not an archaeological enterprise then, nor is it merely so now. The identity of Christ is not explained by the bare details of his biography, but by the interpretation of these particulars, by understanding the significance of the person and work of Jesus Christ. This task was initiated by the apostles and evangelists, thus establishing the tradition of such reflection once for all, but it still requires the engagement of all those who would respond to the challenge. This interpretative engagement raises many difficult issues, but it is unavoidable for "disciples," or more accurately "students" (μαθηταί), "learning Christ" (cf. Eph 4:20), the knowledge of whom is eternal life (cf. Jn 17:3).

There are certain landmarks in the history of this reflection, and certain systematic issues, which no student of theology can avoid. At the most fundamental level are the questions of how Christ is known and what, if any, are the criteria for assessing the interpretations offered. These issues lie at the heart of the debate concerning the role of Scripture and the formation of the New Testament, and the relationship between Scripture, tradition, and ecclesial authority. This whole nexus of themes is also intrinsically related to the assertion that Christ is the Word of God. Further questions then need to be answered: how does Jesus Christ relate to God, his Father, and to us—is he both God and man, and if so, how is he "one Lord" (1 Cor 8:6)? Moreover, if he is "the image of the invisible God" (Col 1:15), what implications does this have for depicting God, and, conversely, for understanding those created "in the image" of God (Gen 1:27)?

None of these issues can be separated from the others; in order to understand how any given writer understood a particular topic it is necessary to see how the whole complex of themes is brought together. Nevertheless, the order of these questions, as raised above and discussed in this volume and those to follow, charts the history of theological reflection up to the time of the Seventh Ecumenical Council. This series explores that history by focusing on certain figures, the debates they were involved in and the settlements reached. Yet by concentrating on these contributions to the topic at issue, while trying to set it in a broader context, this work not only presents a history, but a systematic analysis of essential elements of the theological project, as they were discussed, and resolved, at decisive moments in history. The "formation" with which this series is concerned is both that of the formative periods in the history of theological reflection and also the structure of the resulting theology.

Comprehensiveness, both in the range of figures treated and in the scope of the presentation of their theology, has been sacrificed to allow room for greater depth. This volume treats the first three centuries of the Christian era, examining how the basic elements of the theological project came together and how certain questions and issues came to the fore. Part One looks primarily at the work of Irenaeus, to see how the elements of Scripture, canon, apostolic tradition and succession, were brought together to maintain the proclamation of the Gospel "according to the Scriptures." With these elements settled, the portrait of the Scriptural Christ is then sketched. Part Two examines Ignatius, Justin and Irenaeus, to see how, during the course of the debate described in Part One, a particular understanding of Christ as the Word of God was articulated. Finally, Part Three turns to Rome, Alexandria and Antioch, from the end of the second century to the end of the third, to consider the issues being debated in these centers and the theological vision of their protagonists, and to see how, as a result of their reflection, particular attention came to be focused on the question of the eternity and independent subsistence, the divinity and the humanity of Jesus Christ, the Son of God, so raising the problems which would dominate the following centuries. Subsequent volumes will treat these controversies, and their affirmation that Jesus Christ is indeed truly God and truly human, the image of the invisible God.

There are some striking omissions from this work, both of figures included and subjects treated. On the one hand, a number of important writers are treated only in passing, if at all: Clement of Alexandria is referred to a couple of times, Tertullian and Novatian only tangentially, and many others not at all. Subsequent volumes will also have to be selective. This is not meant in any way as a comment on the value of the work of those authors not included. Nor, for that matter, is the decision to stop with the Second Council of Nicaea, meant to suggest that what follows is of no importance. It is doubtful whether even a more extensive multivolume series than the one begun here could do justice to the wealth of theological reflection over the last two millennia, and certainly not one written by a single author! But it was never the intention simply to provide an exhaustive survey. Rather, the object has been to consider, in some depth, the structure and elements of the Christian confession, as articulated at key moments in the history of theological reflection. On the other hand, even in the case of those writers who are treated here, only a part of their overall theological vision is explored. This is significant—what is presented here is only part of the task of theology. The theological elements and structures discussed here are not *themselves* the answer to Christ's question. At most they provide the framework or parameters within which the interpretative task can be carried out, an engagement in which students of theology are also interpreted by the Word of God, coming to understand themselves in the light of Christ and in relation to God. This ascetic dimension is too important to the theological endeavor to be neglected, but to do it justice requires another study.

Thus this work does not present, as did the grand Histories of Dogma, an overarching narrative of theological development, or, as Harnack considered it, the transformation of the primitive Gospel into Greek metaphysics.[1] Neither does it simply survey the various Christian writers, their lives, literary remains and key points of their theology, as did the manuals of patrology. Nor, finally, is this work a handbook of patristic doctrine, like the staple of all students of the

---

1 As A. McGrath points out, "From its beginnings, the history of dogma has been written about by those concerned with its elimination." (*The Genesis of Doctrine: A Study in the Foundation of Doctrinal Criticism* [Grand Rapids, Mich.: Eerdmans, 1997], 138).

early Church, J. N. D. Kelly's *Early Christian Doctrines*, which gathers together, thematically, what different writers have to say about any given number of topics, with the result that the reader is not introduced to how these different aspects fit together in the thought of any one writer.[2]

The decades since the publication of such classic works have seen a burgeoning of studies devoted to the life and thought of the writers of the early Christian period. Our appreciation of their theological endeavors has been considerably deepened through innumerable monographs and articles devoted to particular writers or specific themes. The reverse side of this is, perhaps inevitably, that scholarship has tended to focus in ever-greater detail upon smaller themes, while at the same time setting them in broader contexts. Attempts to gather the fruit of this research into comprehensive surveys have either become mammoth multivolume projects, encyclopedic histories of theology or works such as A. Grillmeier, *Christ in Christian Tradition*, treating the history of a single theme, or alternatively unwieldy single volumes covering a more restricted period, such as R. P. C. Hanson, *The Search for the Christian Doctrine of God*, which devotes some nine hundred pages to (only!) fourth-century trinitarian theology.[3]

An equally important phenomenon of the last century has been the growing recognition that the theological reflection of the writers of antiquity cannot be divorced, as pure dogmatic speculation, from the ecclesial, social, and political situations and struggles in which they were immersed. This development provides, in turn, the context for the increasing interest in, and skepticism of, the claims of certain groups of Christians to be "right" while others are "wrong," accused of having deviated from the right faith even if they profess to be Christian. It is now frequently assumed that the real causes of this polarization into "orthodox" and "heretical" lie in any area apart from theology. The discovery of the Nag Hammadi material provided fresh

2 J. N. D. Kelly, *Early Christian Doctrines*, 5th ed. (San Francisco: Harper, 1978 [1958]).
3 A. Grillmeier, *Christ in Christian Tradition*, vol. 1, trans. from the 2nd rev. ed. by J. Bowden (London: Mowbrays, 1975); subsequent volumes were written with the help of T. Hainthaler. R. P. C. Hanson, *The Search for the Christian Doctrine of God* (Edinburgh: T. and T. Clark, 1988).

fodder for the reconsideration of such claims and stimulated many imaginative reconstructions of early alternative "Christianities." And thus the previous, almost universal presupposition that "orthodoxy" preceded "heresy," so dramatically challenged by Bauer,[4] has mutated into a general presupposition of cynicism regarding the very possibility of there being a catholic, orthodox, or, more simply, normative Christianity.

A further effect of the growing interest in and sensitivity to the various contexts in which theology was written is that the specifically theological dimensions of its reflection have often been displaced. Without wishing to minimize the importance of the various contexts within which the works studied here were written, they have nevertheless not been addressed, partly for the practical reasons of economy of space, but also from a conviction that theological reflection is worth studying for its own sake. There is no denying that, however elevated, theology is only ever undertaken within the "real world," that there were many other agendas operative in the various controversies, and in our modern interpretations of them, but to assume that these other agendas *explain* the theological points made is to overlook deliberately what are the stated concerns of the subjects under investigation and to presume to know them better.[5] Without wishing to minimize the importance of the broader contexts, this work focuses on the central issues of theology, examining how they are bound up with the Gospel itself, in such a manner that there is a standard or canon that both enables meaningful theological reflection and facilitates the evaluation, on theological grounds, of this reflection.

The prolific scholarship on the early Church over the last century has been beneficial in a manner perhaps unexpected. It has meant that more attention has been given to understanding earlier writers on their own terms, rather than as stages on the way to later landmarks, such as

---

4 W. Bauer, *Rechtglaübigkeit und Ketzerei im ältesten Christentum* (Tübingen: Mohr, 1934); trans. of second edition (1964, ed. by G. Strecker) by R. Kraft et al., *Orthodoxy and Heresy in Earliest Christianity* (Philadelphia: Fortress, 1971).

5 As the sociologist J. Elster points out, "There is no reason to suppose that beliefs that serve certain interests are also to be explained by those interests." ("Belief, Bias and Ideology," in M. Hollis and S. Lukes, eds., *Rationality and Relativism* [Cambridge, Mass.: MIT Press, 1982], 143).

ie. corellation ≠ causation ... logical falacy

Nicaea and Chalcedon, or simply as proof-texts for modern dogmatic systems or for a "neo-patristic synthesis." Unless the process of reflection on the Gospel which led to Nicaea and Chalcedon is grasped, any statements of faith such Councils formulated will not be adequately understood. As Eric Osborn succinctly put it, "Conclusions are ambiguous without the argument which leads to them."[6] Detached, by their very familiarity, from the Gospel that inspired them, theological formulae can too easily become spectacles by which the Gospel is retold to different effect. Thus the title of this volume, *The Way to Nicaea*, should not be taken as implying that Nicaea is the definitive moment to which all prior theological reflection and debates were inevitably tending. When this is done, as it often is, the earlier period is to all intents and purposes overlooked, being considered only insofar as it appears to anticipate later formulae. But an answer cannot stand alone, without being an answer to a specific question; the question provides the context within which the answer has its meaning. The theological contemplation and controversy of previous centuries provides the background for Nicaea, and without the study of this period, on its own terms, Nicaea itself will not be properly understood.

That we all stand within a tradition has been emphasized enough within recent scholarship not to need repeating here.[7] Tradition, like canon, is not a paralyzing constriction, but a stimulus for fruitful reflection, requiring us to think creatively; it is a challenge, a task, and, ultimately, liberating. The tradition within which this book is written is that of the Orthodox Church. That certain writers, the Fathers of the Church (though not exclusively), and certain councils, the Ecumenical Councils, have been chosen rather than others, is evidence of this. Yet, as I hope to show, what we will find in the Fathers studied here is a reflection on and within the Gospel of Jesus Christ. It is not the transformation of the primitive Gospel into Greek metaphysics, the development of something not there from the beginning, but is rather the

---

6   E. Osborn, *Tertullian: First Theologian of the West* (Cambridge: Cambridge University Press, 1997), 6.
7   Cf. Esp. H. G. Gadamer, *Wahrheit und Methode*, 5th edn. (Tübingen: Mohr, 1986), trans. J. Weinsheimer and D. G. Marshall, *Truth and Method* (New York: Continuum, 1997); A. Louth, *Discerning the Mystery: An Essay on the Nature of Theology* (Oxford: Clarendon, 1983); A. McGrath, *The Genesis of Doctrine*.

deepening understanding of what is given once and for all. Theological reflection, both in antiquity and today, must continually return, as Polycarp urged his readers in the early second century, to "the Word delivered to us in the beginning."[8]

---

8   Polycarp, *Letter to the Philippians*, 7.2.

PART ONE

The Gospel of Jesus Christ

~

"Who do you say I am?" Before we can even begin to answer Christ's question, we must consider the background against which this question is raised and the framework within which it can be answered. The first subject inevitably raises issues concerning the historical background, and the delicate subject of the relation between history and faith, while the latter immerses us in the divisive topic of the relation between Scripture and tradition and the complex problem of canon. All these topics were debated in the first couple of centuries, and settled in a manner which thereafter (at least for the period considered in this series) became normative.

Concerning the issues surrounding historicity, much has been written on "the scandal of particularity," the fact that God revealed himself uniquely through his Son, a first century Jew. Many volumes have also been devoted to describing the social, political, economic, and cultural setting of first century Palestine. In a similar vein, there have been many attempts, especially in the last decades of the twentieth century, to reconstruct the "historical Jesus" through the supposedly objective methods of historical-critical research. It must be clearly noted, however, that such endeavors, the speculativeness and arbitrariness of which are amply demonstrated by the bewildering variety of "real" Jesuses they fabricate, are neither an answer to Christ's question nor, consequently, are they of the order of knowledge upon which the Christian Church is based.[1] Christ's question calls for interpretation, to explain the meaning and significance of this person, his life and works. To say that Jesus was born of Mary and was crucified under Pontius

---

1 For a devastating critique of recent works devoted to the "historical Jesus," and for a sensitive handling of the relation between faith and history, see Luke Timothy Johnson, *The Real Jesus: The Misguided Quest for the Historical Jesus and the Truth of the Traditional Gospels* (San Francisco: Harper, 1997).

Pilate is to make an assertion concerning the order of history, about an event, possibly verifiable, possibly not; to say that he is the incarnate Word of God, the crucified and risen Lord and Savior, is an interpretation and explanation of who he is and how he stands in relation to those seeking to respond to him—a confession. The writings of the New Testament are already such interpretations, written in the context of faith in the one whom God raised from the dead. Their status as interpretations cannot be bypassed in an effort to seek the supposed historical core and then subject it to other interpretative frameworks. The "real Jesus" inscribed in the writings of the New Testament is already interpreted, and to understand him more deeply, we must turn primarily to the symbolic world of Scripture, in and through which Christ is, from the first, understood and explained—revealed.

However, to speak of a collection of writings known as the New Testament presupposes certain developments, raising further difficult issues. Most immediately, why these writings and not others? Although it seems probable that the letters of Paul began to be gathered into collections towards the end of the first century, and a fourfold Gospel collection soon thereafter,[2] the crucial battles lay ahead in the following century, and it is really only by the end of the second century that a recognizable New Testament came into use, and along with it an appeal to apostolic tradition, apostolic succession, and the canon or rule of truth. The importance of these debates cannot be overstated; through them these elements are brought together into one coherent whole. The New Testament has its place within a larger constellation. If we are to understand the particular contours of this debate and its resolution, we must avoid reading its terms in the manner set by the polemics of the Reformation and Counter-Reformation, in which Scripture is opposed to tradition, as two distinct sources of authority.[3] Separating Scripture

2   Cf. H. Y. Gamble, *Books and Readers in the Early Church: A History of Early Christian Texts* (New Haven and London: Yale University Press, 1995), 58-65; T. C. Skeat, "The Oldest Manuscript of the Four Gospels?" *NTS* 43 (1997), 1-34; G. N. Stanton, "The Fourfold Gospel," *NTS* 43 (1997), 317-46.

3   In its official pronouncement, the Council of Trent (1545-63) affirmed, somewhat ambiguously, that the truth and rule are contained in written books and unwritten traditions (*in libris scriptis et sine scripto traditionibus*), Session 4, 8 April 1546; a draft of the decree submitted on 22 March 1564, suggests a greater independence of these two mediums, referring to the truth contained "partly (*partim*) in written books and partly (*partim*) in

and tradition in this way introduces an inevitable quandary: if the locus of authority is fixed solely in Scripture, and "canon" is understood exclusively in the sense of a "list" of authoritative books, then accounting for that list becomes problematic;[4] if, on the other hand, Scripture is subsumed under tradition, on the grounds that the Church predates the writings of the New Testament (conveniently forgetting, in a Marcionite fashion, the existence of Scripture—the Law, the Psalms and the Prophets), then again a problem arises from the lack of a criterion or canon, this time for differentiating, as is often done, between "Tradition" and "traditions"—all traditions are venerable, though some more so than others, yet the basis for this distinction is never clarified.

With regard to the establishment by the end of the second century of catholic, orthodox or normative Christianity, the most important question must be: on what basis was this done? Was it a valid development, intrinsic to the proclamation of the Gospel itself, or an arbitrary imposition, dictated by a male, monarchical, power-driven episcopate suppressing all alternative voices by processes of exclusion and demonization, or however else the history might be written? The picture of an originally pure orthodoxy, manifest in exemplary Christian

unwritten traditions." Text cited and discussed in Y. M. J. Congar, *Tradition and Traditions: An Historical and a Theological Essay* (New York: Macmillan, 1967), 164-9.

4   R. Pfeiffer points out that the term "canon" was first used to designate "list" (the πίνακες drawn up by the Alexandrian literary critics) by David Ruhnken in 1768, and that "His coinage met with worldwide and lasting success, as the term was found to be so convenient; one has the impression that most people who use it believe that this usage is of Greek origin. But κανών was never used in this sense, nor would this have been possible. From its frequent use in ethics κανών always retained the meaning of rule or model." (*History of Classical Scholarship: From the Beginnings to the End of the Hellenistic Age* [Oxford: Clarendon, 1968], 207). Despite this recognition, Pfeiffer himself a few lines later describes the list of biblical books as its "canon," appealing to passages where κανών could equally be taken in the sense of "rule" (Origen *apud* Eusebius *HE* 6.25.3; Athanasius, *On the Decrees of Nicaea*, 18), cf. G. A. Robbins, "Eusebius' Lexicon of 'Canonicity,'" *St. Patr.* 25 (Leuven: Peeters, 1993), 134-41. Most of the studies treating the canon of Scripture note that "canon" primarily meant "rule," yet presuppose that it should mean "list," and so devote most attention to cataloguing when, where and by whom, the various writings were accepted as Scripture. For a more considered discussion of the issues concerning canon and Scripture, see, J. Barton, *Holy Writings, Sacred Text: The Canon in Early Christianity* (Louisville, KY: Westminster John Knox Press, 1997) and W. J. Abraham, *Canon and Criterion in Christian Theology* (Oxford: Clarendon Press, 1998).

communities, from which various heresies developed and split off, as it
was presented for instance in the book of Acts and, in the fourth century, in the *Ecclesiastical History* of Eusebius of Caesarea, has become
increasing difficult to maintain, especially since the work of Walter
Bauer, *Orthodoxy and Heresy in Earliest Christianity*.[5] And rightly so:
the earliest Christian writings that we have, the letters of Paul, are
addressed to churches already falling away from the Gospel which he
had delivered to them.

Yet the Gospel was delivered. Debates certainly raged from the
beginning about the correct interpretation of this Gospel; it is a mis-
take to look back to the early Church hoping to find a lost golden age
of theological or ecclesiastical purity—whether in the apostolic times
as narrated in the book of Acts, or the early Church, as recorded by
Eusebius, or the age of the Fathers and Church Councils, or the
Empire of Byzantium. Nevertheless, the Gospel was delivered, once for
all. However, the Gospel of Jesus Christ is the Gospel of the Coming
One (ὁ ἐρχόμενος, cf. Matt 11:3; 21:9; 23:39) and accordingly the cit-
izenship of Christians is not on earth but in heaven, from which they
await their Savior, the Lord Jesus Christ (Phil 3:20). In like manner the
Gospel is not located in a specific text; what came to be recognized as
"canonical" Gospels are always described as "The Gospel *according
to...*" The Gospel is not fixed in a particular text, but, as we will see, in
an interpretative relationship to the Scriptures—the Law, the Psalms
and the Prophets.

Inseparable from the debates about which works were to count as
Scripture, was the issue of the correct interpretation of Scripture. Not
only was there a commitment to a body of Scripture, but there was also
the affirmation that there is a correct reading of this Scripture, or more
exactly, that there is a correct canon for reading Scripture, a canon
expressing the hypothesis of Scripture itself. Even if it was expressed in
many different ways and its articulation continued to be refined, a process which continues today, nevertheless there was a conviction that
there is *one right faith*; and this conviction that there is one right faith,
one right reading of the one Scripture, is intimately tied to the

---

5   First published in German in 1934; trans. of second edition (1964, ed. by G. Strecker) by
    R. Kraft et al. (Philadelphia: Fortress, 1971).

confession that there is one Jesus Christ, the only Son of the one Father, who alone has made known (ἐξηγήσατο, "exegeted," Jn 1:18) the Father. The assertion that there is such a thing as right faith came to be expressed, by the end of the second century, in terms of the canon (rule) of faith or truth, where canon does not mean an ultimately arbitrary list of articles of belief which must be adhered to, or a list of authoritative books which must be accepted, but is rather a crystallization of the hypothesis of Scripture itself. The canon in this sense is the presupposition for reading Scripture on its own terms—it is the canon of truth, where Scripture is the body of truth.

It is often said that Christianity (along with Judaism and Islam, though these are not dealt with here) is a "religion of the book," and this is usually taken in a very weak sense, that somehow, somewhere, for whatever reason, Christianity involves a book. But what is established as normative Christianity in the second century takes this in a much stronger sense: If God acts through His Word, then that Word needs to be heard, to be read, to be understood—the relationship with God is, in a broad sense, *literary*. As such, it requires the full engagement of all the intellective faculties to understand and accomplish, or incarnate, God's Word. It was no accident, as Frances Young observes, that what came to be orthodox or normative Christianity was "committed to a text-based version of revealed truth."[6] *This* Christianity, one might say, is an interpretative text-based religion. She further points out, concerning the question of historicity touched on earlier, that it would be anachronistic to suppose that in antiquity God's revelation was thought of as located in historical events behind the text, events to which, it is claimed, we can have access by reconstructing them from the text, treating the texts as mere historical documents which provide raw historical data, subject to our own analysis, rather than in the interpreted events as presented in Scripture, where the interpretation is already given through the medium of Scripture.[7] What is recognized, by the end of the second century, as normative Christianity is committed to understanding Christ by engaging with Scripture on the basis of the canon of truth and in the context of tradition (παράδοσις).

6 Frances Young, *Biblical Exegesis and the Formation of Christian Culture* (Cambridge: Cambridge University Press, 1997), 57.
7 Ibid., 167.

But if this is the basis for what is established as normative Christianity by the end of the second century, it is no less the very dynamic of the Gospel itself. One of the earliest formulae for proclaiming the Gospel is that Christ was crucified and raised "according to the Scriptures":

> I delivered (παρέδωκα) to you as of first importance what I also received that Christ died for our sins according to the Scriptures, that he was buried and that he was raised on the third day according to the Scriptures. (1 Cor 15:3-4)

The Gospel which Paul delivered ("traditioned") is from the first "according to the Scriptures." Clearly the Scriptures to which Paul is referring here are not the four Gospels, but the Law, the Psalms and the Prophets. The importance of this written reference, repeated twice, is such that the phrase is preserved in later Creeds; Christians who use the Nicene-Constantinopolitan creed still confess that Christ died and rose according to the (same) Scriptures. The point of concern in this basic Christian confession is not the historicity of the events behind their reports, but that the reports are continuous with, in accordance with, Scripture; it is a textual, or more accurately an "intertextual" or interpretative confession. And this scriptural texture of the Gospel is, as we will see, the basis of both canon and tradition as articulated by what emerges as normative Christianity. If "orthodoxy" is indeed later than "heresy," as Bauer claimed and as is commonly assumed, it is nevertheless based on nothing other than Gospel as it was delivered at the beginning.

Heresy first, then orthodoxy, but an orthodoxy that appeals to Scripture and arises from an apostolic canon of truth that subsequently became the N.T.

I

The Tradition and Canon of the Gospel According to the Scriptures

Before examining the scriptural texture of the Gospel, and its relation to both the canon and tradition, it is worth considering the two main challenges against which it was worked out. The first is that of Marcion, a rich ship owner from the Black Sea, who arrived in Rome in the middle of the second century and donated a large sum of money to the church there, for its charitable works, which was soon after returned to him when his particular teaching became known and rejected. His teaching, however, found adherents, and a Marcionite church existed around the Mediterranean for several centuries. Marcion is infamous for having drawn a sharp distinction between the God of the Jewish Scriptures, on the one hand, a spiteful, vengeful and malicious deity, and, on the other hand, the newly revealed God, the Father of Jesus Christ, a loving God who redeems us from the God of the Old Testament. His major written work, the *Antitheses*, was a series of juxtaposed statements from the Old Testament and the Gospel demonstrating the contrast between their depictions of the ones whom they call God. He claimed that not only had the Old Testament proclaimed another God, but that all the apostles apart from Paul had misunderstood Jesus Christ in terms of the expected Messiah of the God of the Old Testament, and so had distorted his message—as Paul had said, there is only one Gospel which false brethren were perverting (Gal 1:6-7). According to Marcion, only Paul had fully understood Jesus Christ, but, even then, Marcion had to excise passages from Paul's letters.[1] The only Gospel in which Marcion had any confidence

1   See now U. Schmid, *Marcion und sein Apostolos* (Berlin: De Gruyter, 1995).

is supposed to have been that of Luke, the disciple of Paul, though this again required some editorial work.

It is what led Marcion to such a position that is of particular interest. Tertullian, writing at the beginning of the third century, gives us an indication:

> The separation of the Law and Gospel is the primary and principal exploit of Marcion.... For such are Marcion's *Antitheses*, or Contrary Oppositions, which are designed to show the conflict and disagreement of the Gospel and the Law, so that from the diversity of principles between those two documents they may argue further for a diversity of gods.[2]

That is, it is his particular *exegetical* concerns—the perceived opposition between the Law and Gospel—that led Marcion to postulate two different gods. Marcion denied the legitimacy of reading the Law allegorically, as speaking of Christ,[3] preferring rather to sever the Gospel from the Law, and to introduce instead a previously unknown god. The complete separation of the Gospel from Scripture (the Law, the Psalms and the Prophets) is dramatically repeated by Adolf von Harnack in what remains an indispensable study of Marcion. He concludes his monumental work by asserting, in highlighted text:

> The rejection of the Old Testament in the second century was a mistake which the great church rightly avoided; to maintain it in the sixteenth century was a fate from which the Reformation was not yet able to escape; but still to preserve it in Protestantism as a canonical document since the nineteenth century is the consequence of a religious and ecclesiastical crippling.[4]

While there were no doubt many other factors at work (that both were disowned as Christians by their own fathers is perhaps not irrelevant),[5] both Marcion and Harnack exemplify a continuing reluctance to see

---

2   Tertullian, *Against Marcion*, 1.19.
3   This effectively demoted the Jewish Scriptures from their status as sacred, and raises the intriguing possibility that "Trypho," in Justin Martyr's *Dialogue with Trypho the Jew*, might be modeled on Marcion. Cf. J. Barton, *Holy Writings*, 53-62.
4   A. von Harnack, *Marcion: Das Evangelium vom fremden Gott*, 2nd ed. (Leipzig: Hinrichs, 1924), 217; (partial) trans. by J. E. Steely and L. D. Bierma, *Marcion: The Gospel of an Alien God* (Durham, N.C.: Labyrinth Press, 1990), 134.
5   What this might have meant in each case is, of course, different. The report concerning Marcion comes from Hippolytus' lost *Syntagma*, and subsequently Epiphanius' *Panarion*, 42; for Harnack, see A. von Zahn-Harnack, *Adolf von Harnack* (Berlin: De Gruyter, 1951), 104-5.

the Gospel as related in any way to the Scriptures, a problem which becomes exacerbated when the writings comprising the New Testament are recognized as themselves Scripture and treated with increasing independence from the Law, the Psalms and the Prophets.

Marcion's solution of postulating another god might seem to us to be rather drastic. After many centuries of monotheism, understood from a philosophical rather than a scriptural perspective, it is today more likely to be assumed that if there is a God, there is only one God, and that while Scripture speaks about him, it is also possible to be in an independent or direct relationship with him; that one can believe in God before he is encountered through Scripture, and the one already known (or thought to be known) is then identified with the God of Abraham, Isaac and Jacob, the Father of Jesus Christ. And so, if a discrepancy were to be perceived, as Marcion thought, between what is said of God in the Old Testament and what is said in the New Testament, the response would probably be to claim that it is one and the same God operating in two different modes, historicizing the difference, and God himself.

But how can one be sure that the God already thought to be known is the same one spoken of in Scripture? There are, as Paul warns, many gods (1 Cor 8:5). Marcion's route seems to follow the opposite direction. His theology is derived from exegetical concerns: that our knowledge about God depends upon his revelation, which is mediated through Scripture, so that God is bound up with his Scripture. The same perspective is presupposed by Tertullian. And, as Northrop Frye concludes in his study of the nature and workings of scriptural language, it also seems to be the approach presupposed by Scripture itself: "We could almost say that even the existence of God is an inference from the existence of the Bible: in the *beginning* was the Word."[6] Beginning from what God has in fact revealed of himself, the Christian confession is certainly that the God of Abraham, Isaac and Jacob, the Father of Jesus Christ, is alone the one true God, who, together with his Son and his Spirit, created all things, and besides whom there is no other. But this is a confession, derived from his revelation, from his

6   Northrop Frye, *The Great Code: The Bible and Literature* (New York: Harcourt Brace Jovanovich, 1982), 61.

Scripture, not a metaphysical presupposition with which Scripture is approached and understood.

2 The second challenge is provided by the figures and writings grouped together, in modern times, under the general rubric of "Gnosticism."[7] What "Gnosticism" actually is, and how it relates to Christianity, has been the subject of intense debate, especially since the discovery of a large cache of works at Nag Hammadi (in 1945-6). One of the key figures in the second century was Valentinus, a native of Egypt, who, his disciples claimed, had been taught by Theodas, a pupil of Paul. Like Marcion, Valentinus also ended up in Rome, sometime in the middle of the second century, where he led a group of more speculative Christians. It is possible that as Valentinus came to recognize the increasing distance which lay between himself, and his followers, and other Christians, he began to differentiate between the faith of those in the Church, who have remained at the "psychical" level of understanding, and the deeper *gnôsis*, possessed by those like himself who were truly "spiritual."[8] What is particularly interesting about Valentinus, and brought out well by David Dawson, is his use of Scripture.[9] Unlike Marcion, Valentinus did not feel the need to close a body of fixed authoritative writings, but rather continued to reuse, imaginatively and creatively, texts and images from Scripture in much the same way that the New Testament had used the Old Testament, so producing his own works, such as the *Gospel of Truth* (if it is indeed by him), a work which echoes much of Scripture (Old Testament and New Testament) yet is not at all tied to the text of Scripture. For Valentinus, the things spoken of in Scripture are expressions of the truth that is most authentically perceived in the heart, and as such, they are truths also

7   On the difficulty of the category of "Gnosticism," see Michael A. Williams, *Rethinking "Gnosticism": An Argument for Dismantling a Dubious Category* (Princeton: Princeton University Press, 1996).

8   As argued by S. Pétrement, *A Separate God: The Origins and Teachings of Gnosticism*, trans. C. Harrison (San Francisco: Harper Collins, 1990), 133, 192, 370-8. C. Markschies basing himself solely on the fragments, rather than the works attributed to Valentinus (such as the *Gospel of Truth*), draws a figure much closer to Alexandrian teachers such as Clement rather than the later "Valentinians" such as Ptolemy (*Valentinus Gnosticus?* [Tübingen: Mohr, 1992]).

9   D. Dawson, *Allegorical Readers and Cultural Revision in Ancient Alexandria* (Berkeley: University of California Press, 1992).

seen in other places, in the writings of the philosophers and elsewhere, enabling him to draw diverse sources into his amalgam. As Valentinus put it:

> Many of the things written in publicly available books [i.e. Classical Greek literature] are found in the writings of God's church [Christian literature]. For this shared matter is the utterances that come from the heart, the law that is written on the heart.[10]

The encounter with God takes place in the interiority of the heart, and it is this experience which comes to expression in diverse writings. This vision alone, according to Valentinus, is the origin of all truth, knowledge and wisdom. As Dawson comments:

> Valentinus relies on his own heart's visionary experience. There alone is the true origin of the wisdom that others routinely attribute to authoritative texts... One does not need to go to derivative sources, for the truth originally lies in the very interior of one's being.[11]

One has direct access to truth itself, that which has inspired what is true in various writings. Having such direct access to wisdom, Valentinus no longer recognized any distinction between Scripture and commentary, between source and interpretation. Rather, he reconfigured the language and images of Scripture in the light of his experience, and the results are themselves new compositions: "The visionary possesses those insights from which the shared wisdom of classical and Christian literature is derived; he or she is enabled not merely to comment (like Philo or Clement)... but to create (like... Philo's Moses or Clement's *logos*)."[12] The goal for Valentinus was to attain the *gnôsis*, the higher knowledge, which enables its possessors to draw the truth out of various ancient writings and redeploy them in new myths. The important point here is, as Frances Young puts it, that "Gnostic doctrine is revelatory, rather than traditional, textual or rational."[13] It is Valentinus's own vision or understanding that is determinative,

10 From Clement of Alexandria, *Stromata* 6.52.3-4; trans., as Fragment G, in B. Layton, *The Gnostic Scriptures: Ancient Wisdom for the New Age* (New York: Doubleday, 1987), 243; my insertions, following Dawson, *Allegorical Readers*, 167.
11 Dawson, *ibid.*
12 Dawson, *ibid.* 168.
13 Young, *Biblical Exegesis*, 61.

around which he reconfigures whatever he finds in Scripture and elsewhere, to produce his own myth. Not only is there no canon for
Valentinus (either as a rule of right belief, or as a specific body of literature), but Scripture itself is no longer sacrosanct, it is superseded by the
visionary's own experience and the new literary creation, and so there
is, finally, no interpretative engagement with Scripture. What is fash-
ioned by such reading of Scripture is, as Irenaeus puts it, the reader's
own fabrication (πλάσμα), rather than the handiwork (πλάσμα) of
God, flesh formed in the image and likeness of his Son.[14] Irenaeus's accusation that the Valentinians project their own inner states onto the
heavens[15] is reiterated by Dawson when he comments that Valentinus
turns the drama of Scripture into a "psychodrama": "In the end, this
state of being [wrought by the *Gospel of Truth*] is the speaker's own; as
visionary, Valentinus's ultimate concern is neither for textuality nor
language in general, but for the personal subject or self."[16] While Williams is right to point out that the diverse figures characterized as
"Gnostic" do not share a distinctive approach to the Scriptures, or
method of interpretation,[17] this very individualizing freedom is itself
the common feature uniting those who did not share in the emerging
consensus concerning Christ "according to the Scriptures."[18]

A similar lack of concern for engagement with the Scriptures is
shown by the *Gospel according to Thomas*, a collection of the sayings of
Jesus presented with no narrative structure. Some of these sayings parallel those in Matthew and Luke, so prompting speculation concerning
its relationship to the hypothetical Synoptic Sayings Source, "Q." The
date of *Thomas*, and its relationship to "Gnosticism" are extremely
problematic and extensively debated. However, whatever its date and
provenance, and even if it really does preserve some authentic sayings
of the "historical Jesus," the *Gospel according to Thomas* makes no

14 Cf. Irenaeus, *AH* 1.8.1; 3.16-18.
15 Irenaeus, *AH* 2.13.3.
16 Dawson, *Allegorical Readers*, 171, 165.
17 Williams, *Rethinking "Gnosticism"*, 59.
18 Cf. Dawson, "It is precisely this revisionary freedom towards one's precursors that marks
    the presence of an authentically 'Gnostic' Spirit. Conversely, deference to the past, whether
    canonical texts or other traditional authorities, marks the domestication of *gnôsis*." (*Allegor-
    ical Readers*, 131).

attempt to present these sayings, or its picture of Christ, in a form "according to the Scriptures." There is not even any mention in it of the basic Christian proclamation concerning the Crucifixion and Resurrection, though it is possible that this is presupposed.[19]

Alongside such positions, there were also, of course, writers who espoused what was explicitly acknowledged, by the end of the second century, to be the orthodox position, figures such as Ignatius of Antioch, who was led under guard from Asia to Rome to be martyred at the beginning of the century; Justin Martyr, a Christian teacher in Rome in the middle of the second century; and later Irenaeus of Lyons, a bishop in Gaul, all of whom will be examined in depth in Part Two. In their own ways, these all maintained a text-interpretative framework for revelation, the point that Christ was preached by the apostles as having been crucified and risen "according to the Scriptures." So, what sense does it make to say that Christ is proclaimed "according to the Scriptures"? What is the relationship between Christ, the Gospel, and the Scriptures?

The place and function of literature in the ancient world, and especially the idea of *mimêsis* or emulation, provides the context in which this relationship is best understood. To be cultured in the ancient world, to have acquired a *paideia*, meant to be versed in the classics. The classics provided not only models of sublime style and speech, but also supplied moral exemplars, encouraged virtue and piety, and provided the material in which to learn to think and on which to hone one's critical skills.[20] In a word it meant providing a context, a "symbolic world," in terms of which one understood oneself and the events of one's life. The same also goes for the Scripture of Israel.[21] Throughout its history, the writers of

---

19 See, for instance, *The Gospel according to Thomas*, saying 55, which refers to carrying the Cross as Jesus himself does. As such it seems doubtful whether *Thomas* can be taken to represent a trajectory of Christianity which focuses solely on the interpretation of Jesus' words, circumventing any reference to, or participation in, the Passion of Christ, as argued by R. Valantasis, *The Gospel of Thomas* (New York: Routledge, 1997), 21-2 and *passim*.

20 On early Christian appropriation of literary critical skills from classical education, see F. Young, *Biblical Exegesis*. Gregory Nazianzus, specifically attributes his acquisition of the principles of inquiry and contemplation (τὸ ἐξεταστικόν τε καὶ θεωρητικὸν) to his studies in Cappadocia, Alexandria and above all Athens (*Panegyric on St Basil*, Oration 43.11).

21 Cf. N. Frye, *The Great Code*; M. Fishbane, *Biblical Interpretation in Ancient Israel* (Oxford: Clarendon Press, 1985), esp. 350-80; J. L. Kugel and R. A. Greer, *Early Biblical Interpreta-*

Israel used images and figures of earlier events and figures to understand, explicate and describe the events and figures at hand. For example, Noah, in Genesis 9:1-7, is blessed to preside over a renewed world which is described in the vocabulary and imagery of Genesis 1:26-31: Noah is presented in terms which make him a new Adam, establishing a typological relation between them. And what has been established with Noah, then becomes a paradigm for understanding subsequent events. So, for instance, after referring to the overflowing wrath which resulted in Israel being forsaken, in exile, Isaiah adds the following oracle:

> "For this is like the days of Noah to me;
> as I swore that the waters of Noah should no more go over the earth,
> so I have sworn that I will not be angry with you and will not rebuke you.
> For the mountains may depart and the hills be removed,
> But my steadfast love shall not depart from you,
> and my covenant of peace shall not be removed."
> Thus says the Lord who has compassion on you. (Is 54:9-10)

The description of the divine wrath of the flood followed by the covenant of natural order established with Noah is used to explain the divine wrath of the exile that will give way to eternal covenant of divine grace. And so, again, a typology is created between the two episodes.

A similar typology is created by Isaiah between Abraham and the post-exilic situation of Israel. Isaiah encourages the despairing people, and urges them to "look to Abraham your father, and Sarah who bore you; for he was one when I called him, but I blessed him and made him many" (Is 51:2). However small the remnant has become, the people are a promised national renewal if only they imitate the patriarchal action and return to their ancestral land: Abraham is a "type" both of the required action and of the promised outcome. And again, this invocation of Abraham as a type for the new exodus seems to be based upon an earlier typology already at work in the description of Abraham, this time between Abraham and the original exodus. Genesis 12 describes how Abram was forced to leave Canaan, when the land was struck by

tion (Philadelphia: Westminster Press, 1986); J. L. Kugel, *The Traditions of the Bible: A Guide to the Bible as it was at the Start of the Common Era* (Cambridge, Mass.: Harvard University Press, 1998).

famine, and migrate to Egypt. When Pharaoh made amorous advances towards Sarai, believing her to be Abram's sister, the Lord brought a plague against Pharaoh and his household, prompting Pharaoh to send the patriarch away from his land. The typological parallelism is clear: Abraham is described as foreshadowing in his life the destiny of his descendants.[22]

This process, reemploying images to understand and explain the present in terms of the past, and so as being anticipated by the past, which is evident throughout the Scriptures, continues in the New Testament and its presentation of Christ "according to the Scriptures." For instance, Christ's Passion is described in terms of being the true and primary Pascha (now etymologized as "Passion"), of which the Exodus Pascha is but a type; Christ is the true Lamb of God. Or, according to another typology, in John 3:14: "Just as Moses raised the snake in the wilderness, so must the Son of man be lifted up, so that those who believe in Him may have eternal life." This refers back to Numbers 21, where the Israelites were complaining to Moses that it was folly to remain in the desert—the wisdom of the world arguing that it is preferable to go back to Egypt. God then struck the people with the deadly bites of serpents, and at the same time provided a remedy, the bronze serpent lifted up on a pole: by looking upon the serpent, the people regained life. Paul also appeals to this concatenation of images, when he points out to those in his Corinthian community who were seduced by wisdom, that the folly of God (Christ lifted on the Cross, as the bronze snake lifted on the pole) overcomes the wisdom of the world, and, as such, Christ is the true power and wisdom of God (1 Cor 1:22-5). In another vein, but using the same scriptural, literary or intertextual technique, Matthew describes Christ as a new Moses, going up a mountain to deliver the law, while Paul describes Christ as the new Adam, correcting the mistakes of the first Adam, whom Paul explicitly describes as being "a type of the One to come" (Rom 5:14).

The relationship between Scripture, the Gospel and Christ is not a subject of direct reflection for Paul, as it will be in the second century,

---

22 Cf. Fishbane, *Biblical Interpretation*, 375-6.

examined in Part Two. However, the dynamics of this relationship is intimated by Paul, in a complex passage which merits being cited at length:

> Since we have such a hope, we are very bold, not like Moses, who put a veil over his face so that the Israelites might not see the end of the fading splendour. But their minds were hardened; for to this day, when they read the old covenant, that same veil remains unlifted, because only through Christ is it taken away. Yes to this day whenever Moses is read a veil lies over their minds; but when a man turns to the Lord the veil is removed. Now the Lord is the Spirit, and where the Spirit of the Lord is, there is freedom. And we all, with unveiled face, beholding the glory of the Lord, are being changed into his likeness from one degree of glory to another; for this comes from the Lord who is the Spirit.
>
> Therefore, having this ministry by the mercy of God, we do not lose heart. We have renounced disgraceful, underhanded ways; we refuse to practice cunning or to tamper with God's word, but by the open statement of the truth we would commend ourselves to every man's conscience in the sight of God. And even if our gospel is veiled, it is veiled only to those who are perishing. In their case the god of this world has blinded the minds of the unbelievers, to keep them from seeing the light of the gospel of the glory of Christ, who is the likeness of God. For what we preach is not ourselves, but Jesus Christ as Lord, with ourselves as your servants for Jesus' sake. For it is the God who said, "Let light shine out of darkness," who has shone in our hearts to give the light of the knowledge of the glory of God in the face of Christ. (2 Cor 3:12-4:6)

In this very dense passage, Paul begins to address the interconnected relationships between Moses and Christ, the Scriptures and the Gospel. According to Paul, the "same veil" that Moses placed over his own head remains to this day upon those who read "Moses"—now a text.[23] But this veil is removed for those who have turned to the Lord and can now understand Scripture aright. That the veil was removed by Christ means that it is only in Christ that the glory of God is revealed and that we can discern the true meaning of Scripture, and that

---

23 R. Hays points out the "metaphorical fusion... in which Moses *becomes* the Torah... Moses the metaphor is both man and text, and the narrative of the man's self-veiling is at the same time a story about the veiling of the text" (*Echoes of Scripture in the Letters of Paul* [New Haven and London: Yale University Press, 1989], 144-145). My reading of this passage is indebted to that of Hays.

these two aspects are inseparable. The identity between Moses the man and Moses the text, whose face and meaning were hidden by the same veil, is paralleled by the identity between Christ, in whose face is revealed the glory of God, and the Gospel which proclaims this. So, behind the veil is nothing other than "the light of the Gospel of the glory of Christ," himself the image of God, though this remains "veiled" to those who reject the Gospel. What this means, as Hays points out, is that, ultimately, "Scripture becomes—in Paul's reading—a metaphor, a vast trope that signifies and illuminates the gospel of Jesus Christ."[24]

This is not to imply that the Gospel itself is, as Ricoeur claimed, simply "the rereading of an ancient Scripture."[25] The proclamation of the death and resurrection of Christ is not straightforwardly derivable from Scripture. Rather, the death and resurrection of Christ acts as a catalyst. Because God has acted in Christ in a definitive, and unexpected, manner, making everything new, Scripture itself must be read anew. The "word of the Cross," the preaching of "Christ crucified" may be a scandal for the Jews and folly for the Gentiles, but it alone is the "power of God" making known "the wisdom of God" (1 Cor 1:18-25). This preaching, the *kerygma*, provides what Hays describes as "the eschatological *apokalypsis* of the Cross," a hermeneutical lens, through which Scripture can now be refracted with "a profound new symbolic coherence."[26] Read in the light of what God has wrought in Christ, the Scriptures provided the terms and images, the context, within which the apostles made sense of what happened, and with which they explained it and preached it, so justifying the claim that Christ died and rose "according to the Scriptures." It is important to note that it is Christ who is being explained through the medium of Scripture, not Scripture itself that is being exegeted; the object is not to understand the "original meaning" of an ancient text, as in modern historical-critical scholarship, but to understand Christ, who, by being

---

24 Hays, *Echoes*, 149.
25 P. Ricoeur, *Essays on Biblical Interpretation* (Philadelphia: Fortress Press, 1980), 51. See the comments by J. Barr, *Holy Scripture: Canon, Authority, Criticism* (Philadelphia: Westminster Press, 1983), 70.
26 Hays, *Echoes*, 169.

explained "according to the Scriptures," becomes the sole subject of Scripture throughout.[27]

And this interpretative engagement with Scripture is indeed what we find in the canonical Gospels, where, in the descriptions of Christ and his activity, culminating in the Passion and always told from that perspective, there is constant allusion to scriptural imagery. The very "beginning of the Gospel of Jesus Christ" in Mark is illustrated by the citation of a passage from Isaiah (Mk 1:1-3; Mal 3:1; Is 40:3). In Matthew, the same engagement with Scripture is found throughout, in terms of prophecy-fulfilment structuring the narrative. While in Luke it appears as the hermeneutic, the principle of interpretation, taught by the risen Christ and so enlightening his disciples: "Beginning with Moses and all the prophets, he interpreted to them in all the Scriptures the things concerning himself" (Lk 24:27, cf. Lk 24:44-49). This literary enlightening of the disciples is paralleled in John when Christ breathes on his disciples the Holy Spirit, the one he had promised, who would remind them of all things concerning Christ, leading them into all truth (cf. Jn 20:22; 14:26); Word and Spirit can never be separated, and both are at work in the task of interpretation. It is also in John where the relationship between the Scriptures and Christ is stated most emphatically, by Christ himself: "If you believed Moses, you would believe me, for he wrote of me" (Jn 5:46).

The writers of the second century who were later recognized as orthodox by those of the "Great Church," to use the expression of the second-century pagan Celsus,[28] were sensitive to this relationship between Scripture and the Gospel: not only does Scripture speak of Christ, but everything that is said in the apostolic writings is found already in Scripture. For instance, Justin Martyr asserts categorically:

27 J. Barr makes a pertinent comment when he notes that "large elements in the text [of the Genesis story of Adam] cannot be made to support Paul's use of the story without distortion of their meaning." This is simply because "Paul was not interpreting the story in and for itself; he was really *interpreting Christ* through the use of images from this story." (*The Garden of Eden and the Hope of Immortality* [Minneapolis: Fortress Press, 1993], 89). For the problems which arise when the synchronic character of Scripture, as the product of one author or as speaking of a single subject throughout, is replaced by a diachronic study of the text, attempting to reconstruct the "original meaning" of its various parts, see J. D. Levenson, "The Eighth Principle of Judaism and the Literary Simultaneity of Scripture," *Journal of Religion*, 68 (1988), 205-25.

28 Cf. Origen, *CC* 5.59-61.

In these books, then, of the prophets, we found foretold as coming, born of a virgin, growing up to man's estate, and healing every disease and every sickness and raising the dead, and being hated and unrecognized, and crucified, Jesus our Christ, and dying, and rising again and ascending into heaven, and being and being-called the Son of God, and certain persons being sent by him to every race of men proclaiming these things, and [that] from among the Gentiles, rather, people would believe in him.[29]

The point of importance for Justin is clearly *not* the "historical Christ," in our modern sense of the word "historical," but rather to demonstrate the scriptural texture of what is said of Christ, and the scriptural texture of the Christ thus described, the Word of God. There is, as Greer puts it, a twofold dynamic at work in this relationship between Scripture and the Gospel. On the one hand, "the earliest Christian attempts to explain Christ are in great measure exegetical in character. What is said of Christ is rooted in the details of Scripture." And on the other hand, "what gives form to the exegetical work is the Christian story." It is in this sense that Christ, the Word of God, is often said to be the key to Scripture.[30]

The ways in which Ignatius, Justin and Irenaeus understood Christ to be the Word of God will be dealt with in Part Two. The concern in this chapter is with the relation between the symbolic coherence of Scripture, effected by the word of the Cross, and the appeal to canon and tradition—the key elements in the self-identification of orthodox or normative Christianity. The coherence of Scripture—the Law, the Psalms and the Prophets—in the apostolic preaching of Christ is shown most clearly in the short, nonpolemical, and perhaps catechetical treatise of Irenaeus devoted to the topic, *The Demonstration of the Apostolic Preaching.*[31] That Irenaeus is concerned with the preaching *of the apostles*, rather than the authentic words of the "historical Christ," is significant, and shows a development over earlier works, such as the *Didache*, the subtitle of which is "The Lord's Teaching to the Gentiles by the

29 Justin Martyr, *First Apology*, 31.7.
30 Greer, "The Christian Bible and Its Interpretation," in J. Kugel and R. Greer, *Early Biblical Interpretation* (Philadelphia: Westminster Press, 1986), 133.
31 Cf. *St Irenaeus of Lyons: On the Apostolic Preaching*, trans. J. Behr (New York: St Vladimir's Seminary Press, 1997).

Twelve Apostles."[32] Although Irenaeus clearly knows the apostolic writings,[33] the substance of his exposition is drawn exclusively from Scripture: that Jesus was born from a virgin and worked miracles is shown from Isaiah and others; while the names of Pilate and Herod are known from the evangelists, that Christ was bound and brought before them is shown by Hosea; that he was crucified, raised and exalted is again shown by the prophets. In the first part of the work (3b-42a), Irenaeus recounts the scriptural history of God's salvific work which culminates in the apostolic proclamation of Christ. In the second part of the work (42b-97), Irenaeus demonstrates how all the things which have come to pass in Jesus Christ, were spoken of by the prophets, both so that we might believe in God, as what he previously proclaimed has come to pass, and also to demonstrate that Scripture throughout does in fact speak of Jesus Christ, the Word of God, as preached by the apostles.

This coherence of Scripture, the scriptural texture of the apostolic preaching of the Gospel in its interpretative engagement with Scripture, is the basis for Irenaeus' appeal to canon and tradition, and the full use of the apostolic writings as themselves Scripture, in his work *Against the Heresies*.[34] This text is the earliest extant work to employ all the elements of apostolic Scripture, tradition, succession and canon, and it does so in confrontation with those who "speak the same, but think otherwise" (*AH* 1.Pref.2). After beginning with a description of some of the Valentinian myths, Irenaeus turns to an analysis of their use of Scripture, and discusses the role of canon and tradition:

---

32 A point made by B. Reynders, "Paradosis: Le progrès de l'idée de tradition jusqu'à saint Irénée," *Recherches de Théologie Ancienne et Médiévale*, 5 (1933), 179, n. 146.

33 He refers to the apostles seven times (*Dem.* 3, 41, 46, 47, 86, 98, 99); cites Paul three times, twice referring to him as "his [Christ's] apostle" (*Dem.* 5, 8, 87), and also cites "his [Christ's] disciple John" (*Dem.* 43, 94). Moreover, when Irenaeus cites a verse from the Scriptures, attributing it to its original source, it is often given in the form used by the New Testament (e.g., *Dem.* 81, referring to Jeremiah, though citing Matt 27:9-10).

34 Although the penultimate chapter of the *Demonstration* refers to *Against the Heresies*, it would seem preferable, on the basis of its more primitive use of Scripture and certain stylistic points of the Armenian translation, to regard the last two chapters as an interpolation and *Against the Heresies* as the later work. Cf. *St Irenaeus of Lyons: On the Apostolic Preaching*, trans. J. Behr, 118.

Such is their hypothesis (ὑπόθεσις) which neither the prophets preached, nor the Lord taught, nor the apostles handed down. They boast rather loudly of knowing more about it than others do, citing it from non-Scriptural [works] (ἐξ ἀγράφων)[35]; and as people would say, they attempt to braid ropes of sand. They try to adapt to their own sayings in a manner worthy of credence, either the Lord's parables or the prophets sayings, or the apostles' words, so that their fabrication (πλάσμα) might not appear to be without witness. They disregard the order (τάξις) and the connection (εἱρμός) of the Scriptures and, as much as in them lies, they disjoint the members of the truth. They transfer passages and rearrange them; and, making one thing out of another, they deceive many by the badly composed fantasy of the Lord's words that they adapt. By way of illustration, suppose someone would take the beautiful image of a king, carefully made out of precious stones by a skillful artist, and would destroy the features of the man on it and change it around and rearrange the jewels, and make the form of a dog or of a fox out of them, and that rather a bad piece of work. Suppose he would then say with determination that this is the beautiful image of the king that the skillful artist had made, and at the same time pointing to the jewels which had been beautifully fitted together by the first artist into the image of the king, but which had been badly changed by the second into the form of a dog. And suppose he would through this fanciful arrangement of the jewels deceive the inexperienced who had no idea of what the king's picture looked like, and would persuade them that this base picture of a fox is that beautiful image of the king. In the same way these people patch together old women's fables, and then pluck words and sayings and parables from here and there and wish to adapt these words of God to their myths (μύθοις). (*AH* 1.8.1)

The terms used by Irenaeus to critique his opponents all have a very precise meaning within Hellenistic epistemology and literary theory. And indeed, after further examples of his opponents' exegesis, Irenaeus continues by using a literary example. In *AH* 1.9.4, he describes how some people take diverse lines from the work of Homer and then rearrange them to produce homeric-sounding verses which tell a tale not to be found in Homer. While these centos can mislead those who have only a passing knowledge of Homer, they will not deceive those who are well versed in his poetry, for they will be able to identify the lines and restore them to their proper context.

---

35 This could also refer to unwritten, oral, traditions.

Irenaeus' basic charge against the Valentinians is that they have dis-
regarded "the order and the connection of the Scriptures," the body of
truth, so distorting one picture into another. They have not accepted
the coherence of the Scriptures, as speaking about Christ, but have preferred their own fabrication, created by adapting passages from Scripture to a different hypothesis, attempting to endow it with persuasive
plausibility. The terms used by Irenaeus, "fabrication" (πλάσμα) and
"myth" (μῦθος), are terms which, in Hellenistic literary theory, describe
stories that are, in the first case, not true but seem to be so, and in the
latter case, manifestly untrue.[36] In doing this, according to Irenaeus,
the Valentinians have based their exegesis of Scripture upon their own
"hypothesis" (ὑπόθεσις), rather than that foretold by the prophets,
taught by Christ and delivered ("traditioned") by the apostles. In Hellenistic times, the term "hypothesis" (ὑπόθεσις) had a variety of meanings, one of which, again in a literary context, was the plot or outline of
a drama or epic (what Aristotle, in the *Poetics*, had termed the μῦθος).[37]
It is what the poet posits, as the basic outline for his subsequent creative
work. It is not derived from reasoning, but rather provides the raw
material upon which the poet can exercise his talents. The Valentinians
have used the words and phrases from Scripture, but have creatively
adapted them to a different hypothesis, and so have created their own
fabrication.[38]

In the other arts, it is similarly the hypothesis, as that which is posited,
which facilitates both action and inquiry, and ultimately knowledge itself.
Hypotheses are, as Aristotle puts it, the starting points or first principles (ἀρχαί) of demonstrations.[39] The goal of health is the hypothesis
for a doctor, who then deliberates on how it is to be attained, just as
mathematicians hypothesize certain axioms and then proceed with

---

36 Cf. Sextus Empiricus, *Against the Grammarians*, 12 (252-68). Cf. R. Meijering, *Literary and Rhetorical Theories in Greek Scholia* (Groningen: Egbert Forsten, 1987), 72-90.
37 Cf. Meijering, *Literary and Rhetorical Theories*, 99-133.
38 When Irenaeus, in *AH* 3-5, turns to examining "the scriptural demonstration of the apos-
    tles who also composed the Gospel" (*AH* 3.5.1), the term πλάσμα is used primarily to de-
    scribe the "fabrication of God," the flesh fashioned by the Hands of God, to which the
    Word is finally united, manifesting the image and likeness of God. The background here is
    clearly Gen 2:7, Is 29:16 and Rom 9:20, though the two uses of πλάσμα should not be
    completely separated: the issue is, who is the ποιητής, the poet/creator?
39 Aristotle, *Metaphysics*, 5.1.2 (1013a17).

their demonstrations.[40] Such hypotheses are in both cases tentative; if the goal proves to be unattainable or if the conclusions derived from the supposition turn out to be manifestly false, then the hypothesis in question must be rejected. The aim of philosophy, however, at least since Plato, has been to discover the ultimate, non-hypothetical first principles.[41] But even here, as Aristotle concedes, it is impossible to demand demonstrations of the first principles themselves; the first principles cannot themselves be proved, otherwise they would be dependent upon something prior to them, and so the inquirer would be led into an infinite regress.[42] This means, as Clement of Alexandria points out, that the search for the first principles of demonstration ends up with indemonstrable faith.[43] For Christian faith, according to Clement, it is the Scriptures, and in particular, the Lord who speaks in them, that is the first principle of all knowledge.[44] It is the voice of the Lord, speaking throughout Scripture, that is the first principle, the (nonhypothetical) hypothesis of all demonstrations from Scripture, by which Christians are led to the knowledge of the truth.

These first principles, grasped by faith, are the basis for subsequent demonstrations, and are also subsequently used to evaluate other claims to truth, acting thus as a "canon." Originally this term simply meant a straight line, a rule by which other lines could be judged: "by that which is straight, we discern both the straight and the crooked; for the carpenter's rule (ὁ κανών) is the test of both, but the crooked tests neither itself nor the straight."[45] Epicurus' *Canon* seems to have been the first work devoted to the need to establish "the criteria of truth,"[46] a need which, in

---

40 Cf. Aristotle, *Eudemian Ethics*, 1227b, 28-33; Meijering, 106.

41 Cf. Plato, *Republic*, 6.20-1 (510-11).

42 Aristotle, *Metaphysics*, 4.4.2 (1006a, 6-12).

43 Clement, *Strom.*, 8.3.6.7-7.2; cf. E. Osborn, "Arguments for Faith in Clement of Alexandria," *VC* 48 (1994), 12-14.

44 Cf. Clement, *Strom.*, 7.16.95.4-6: "He, then, who of himself believes the Lord's Scriptures and voice (τῇ κυριακῇ γραφῇ τε καὶ φωνῇ), which by the Lord acts for the benefit of men, is rightly faithful. Certainly we use it as a criterion in the discovery of things. What is subjected to criticism is not believed till it is so subjected, so that what needs criticism cannot be a first principle. Therefore, as is reasonable, grasping by faith the indemonstrable first principle, and receiving in abundance, from the first principle itself, demonstrations in reference to the first principle, we are by the voice of the Lord trained up to the knowledge of the truth."

45 Aristotle, *On the Soul*, 1.5 (411a, 5-7).

46 Diogenes Laertius, *Lives of Eminent Philosophers*, 10.31.

the face of the Sceptical onslaught, made it almost obligatory in the Hellenistic period to begin any systematic presentation of philosophy with an
account of "the criterion."[47] Without a canon or criterion, knowledge is
simply not possible, for all inquiry will be drawn helplessly into an end-
less regression. It was generally held in Hellenistic philosophy that it is
preconceptions (προλήψεις—generic notions synthesized out of repeated
sense perceptions, later held to be innate) that facilitate knowledge and act
as criteria. The self-evidence (ἐνάργεια) of the sense-perceptions for the
Epicureans, and the clarity of the cognitive impressions for the Stoics, provide the infallible criterion for examining what truly exists. But again
Clement points out how even Epicurus accepted that this "preconception
of the mind" is "faith," and that without it, neither inquiry nor judgement
is possible.[48]

In the same manner in which Hellenistic philosophers argued
against the infinite regression of the Sceptics by appealing to a canon or
criterion of truth, Irenaeus, Tertullian and Clement of Alexandria
countered the constantly mutating Gnostic mythology (Irenaeus
claims that the Gnostics were obliged to devise something new every
day. *AH* 1.18.1; 1.21.5), by an appeal to their own canon of truth.[49]
Using similar terminology to the philosophers, Irenaeus asserts that
"we must keep the canon of faith unswervingly and perform the commandments of God" in faith, for such faith "is established upon things
truly real" and enables us to have "a true comprehension of what is"
(*Dem.* 3). After criticizing the Gnostics for their distortion of Scripture
according to their own hypothesis and giving the example of the
Homeric cento, as described above, Irenaeus continues:

> ... anyone who keeps unswervingly in himself the canon of truth (τὸν
> κανόνα τῆς ἀληθείας) received through baptism will recognize the names

47 Cf. G. Striker, "Κριτήριον τῆς ἀληθείας," *Nachrichten der Akademie der Wissenschaften
in Göttingen*, Phil.-hist. Kl. (1974), 2:47-110; M. Schofield, M. Burnyeat, and J. Barnes,
eds., *Doubt and Dogmatism: Studies in Hellenistic Epistemology* (Oxford: Oxford University
Press, 1980); P. Huby and G. Neals eds., *The Criterion of Truth* (Liverpool: Liverpool University Press, 1989).

48 Clement, *Strom.* 2.5.16.3. Cf. S. R. C. Lilla, *Clement of Alexandria: A Study in Christian
Platonism and Gnosticism* (Oxford: Oxford University Press, 1971), 120-31.

49 Cf. E. Osborn, "Reason and the Rule of Faith in the Second Century AD," in R. Williams
ed., *The Making of Orthodoxy: Essays in Honour of Henry Chadwick* (Cambridge: Cambridge University Press, 1989), 40-61.

and sayings and parables from the Scriptures, but this blasphemous hypothesis of theirs he will not recognize. For if he recognizes the jewels, he will not accept the fox for the image of the king. He will restore each one of the passages to its proper order and, having fit it into the body of the truth, he will lay bare their fabrication and show that it is without support. (*AH* 1:9:4)

This is followed, in *AH* 1.10.1, by the fullest description, given by Irenaeus, of the faith which was received from the apostles: "the faith in one God the Father Almighty, Creator of heaven and earth...; and in one Jesus Christ, the Son of God, who was enfleshed for our salvation; and in the Holy Spirit, who through the prophets preached the economies"[50] that is, his coming (τὴν ἔλευσιν), the birth from a Virgin, the Passion, Resurrection and bodily ascension into heaven, and his coming (παρουσία) from heaven, to recapitulate all things, bringing judgement to eternal separation or life. In *AH* 1.9.4, Irenaeus described the canon of truth as having been "received through baptism," and what he presents in *AH* 1.10.1 is indeed structured upon the same three central articles of belief found in the interrogatory baptismal creeds from the earliest times and going back to the baptismal command of Christ himself (Matt 28:19). Elsewhere, in the context of discussing the rule of truth, Irenaeus also affirms that "the baptism of our regeneration takes place through these three articles" (*Dem.* 7). Despite this connection with baptism, the rule of truth is not given in a declarative form, as are the creeds used in baptism from the fourth century onwards.[51] The canons of truth remained much more flexible in their wording than the later declaratory creeds, and seem to have been used differently, as a guide for theology rather than as a confession of faith.

The point of the canon of truth is not so much to give fixed, and abstract, statements of Christian doctrine. Nor does it provide a narrative description of Christian belief, the literary hypothesis of Scripture.[52] Rather, the canon of truth expresses the correct hypothesis of

50 "Economy" (οἰκονομία) is another literary term, referring to the arrangement of a poem, or the purpose of a particular episode within it. Cf. Meijering, *Literary and Rhetorical Theories*, 171-81.

51 For a recent discussion see W. Kinzig and M. Vinzent, "Recent Research on the Origin of the Creed," *JTS* ns 50:2 (1999), 535-59.

52 As argued by P. M. Blowers, "The *Regula Fidei* and the Narrative Character of Early Christian Faith," *Pro Ecclesia* 6:2 (1997), 199-228. If this were the case, then the canon of truth would include a full narrative description of "salvation history," from the creation and fall

2nd-3rd — The faith with which we believe — subjective
4th-5th — The faith we believe — objective

Scripture itself, that by which one can see in Scripture the picture of a king, Christ, rather than a dog or fox. It is ultimately the presupposition of the apostolic Christ himself, the one who is "according to the Scripture" and, in reverse, the subject of Scripture throughout, being spoken of by the Spirit through the prophets, so revealing the one God and Father. As a canon it facilitates the demonstration of the incongruous and extraneous nature of the Gnostic hypotheses. By means of the same canon of truth the various passages, the "members of truth" (*AH* 1.8.1), can be returned to their rightful place within "the body of truth" (*Dem.* 1), Scripture, so that it again speaks of Christ, while exposing the Gnostic fabrications for what they are. The canon of truth is neither a system of detached doctrinal beliefs nor a narrative. Based upon the three names of baptism, the canon of truth is inextricably connected, for Irenaeus, with "the order (τάξις) and the connection (εἱρμός) of the Scriptures" (*AH* 1.8.1) for it presents the one Father who has made himself known through the one Son by the Holy Spirit speaking through the prophets, that is, through the Scripture—the Law, the Psalms and the Prophets. It is striking that in the fullest canon of truth outlined by Irenaeus, in *AH* 1.10.1, all the economies of Christ, the episodes recounted in the Gospels, are presented under the confession of the Holy Spirit, who preached these things through the prophets, Scripture when read according to the Spirit, rather than under the second article, as in the later declaratory creeds, where what it is that the Spirit "spoke through the prophets" is left unspecified. For Irenaeus, the canon of truth is the embodiment or crystallization of the coherence of Scripture, read as speaking of the Christ who is revealed in the Gospel, the apostolic preaching of Christ "according to Scripture." It is along these lines that Clement of Alexandria attempts to define the canon:

> The ecclesiastical canon is the concord and harmony of the law and the prophets in the covenant delivered at the coming of the Lord.[53]

Understood in this way, the canon is not an arbitrary principle used to exclude other legitimate voices or trajectories. Rather it expresses the

---

onwards. Cf. F. Young, *The Art of Performance: Towards a Theology of Holy Scripture* (London: Darton, Longman and Todd, 1990), 48-53.

53 Clement, *Strom.* 6.15.125.3: κανὼν δὲ ἐκκλησιαστικὸς ἡ συνῳδία καὶ ἡ συμφωνία νόμου τε καὶ προφητῶν τῇ κατὰ τὴν τοῦ κυρίου παρουσίαν παραδιδομένη διαθήκη.

hypothesis of Scripture, enabling the demonstrations from Scripture to describe, accurately, the portrait of a king, Christ; it is a mode of interpretation delivered by the apostles in their proclamation of Christ.[54] This certainly excludes other pictures or fabrications, but then, other pictures do not present the Christ spoken of by the apostles, the Christ presented "according to the Scriptures."

The key elements of the faith delivered by the apostles are crystallized in the canon of truth. This canon expresses the basic elements of the one Gospel, maintained and preached in the Church, in an ever-changing context. The continually changing context in which the same unchanging Gospel is preached makes it necessary that different aspects or facets of the same Gospel be drawn out to address contemporary challenges. However, whilst the context continually changes, the content of that tradition does not—it is the same Gospel. So, after stating the rule of truth in *AH* 1.10.1, Irenaeus continues:

> The Church ... though disseminated throughout the world, carefully guards this preaching and this faith, which she has received, as if she dwelt in one house. She likewise believes these things as if she had but one soul and one and the same heart; she preaches, teaches and hands them down harmoniously (συμφώνως), as if she possessed one mouth. For though the languages of the world are dissimilar, nevertheless the meaning of tradition (ἡ δύναμις τῆς παραδόσεως) is one and the same. To explain, the churches which have been founded in Germany do not believe or hand down anything else; neither do those founded in Spain or Gaul or Libya or in the central regions of the world. But just as the sun, God's creation, is one and the same throughout the world, so too, the light, the preaching of the truth, shines everywhere and enlightens all men who wish to come to a knowledge of the truth. Neither will any of those who preside in the churches, though exceedingly eloquent, say anything else (for no one is above the Master); nor will a poor speaker subtract from the tradition. For, since the faith is one and the same, neither he who can discourse at length about it adds to it, nor he who can say only a little subtracts from it. (*AH* 1.10.2)

54 Although the connection is not explicitly made, the unity of Scripture—the Law and the Prophets—in the coming of Christ as expounded by the apostles clearly forms the fabric of early Christian worship and the celebration of the Eucharist as exemplified in the homily by Melito of Sardis, *On Pascha* (c.160–70 A.D.). Though little hard evidence remains, the study of which goes beyond the scope of this work, the importance of worship for the formation of normative Christianity was undoubtedly important.

As the faith is the same, those who can speak endlessly about it do not add to it, any more than those who are poor speakers detract from it, for the meaning or the content of tradition is one and the same. It is clear, then, that for Irenaeus "tradition" is not alive, in the sense that it cannot change, grow or develop into something else.[55] The Church is to guard carefully this preaching and this faith, which she has received and which she is to preach, teach and hand down harmoniously.

However, as we saw above, the point of a canon is not to stymie inquiry and reflection, but rather to make it possible.[56] So, although Irenaeus specifies that the content of the apostolic tradition remains one and the same, in the next section, *AH* 1.10.3, he nevertheless gives directions to those who desire to inquire more deeply into the revelation of God. Here Irenaeus reiterates his basic perspective: theological inquiry is not to be carried out by changing the hypothesis itself (thinking up another God or another Christ), but by reflecting further on whatever was said in parables, bringing out the meaning of the obscure passages, by placing them in the clear light of the "hypothesis of truth."

Irenaeus further examines the relation between Scripture and tradition in the opening five chapters of his third book *Against the Heresies*, this time to counter the claim of the Gnostics to possess secret, oral traditions. He begins by affirming categorically that the revelation of God is mediated through the apostles. It is not enough to see the "Jesus of history" to see God, nor to imagine God as a partner with whom one can dialogue directly, bypassing his own Word. Rather the locus of revelation, and the medium for our relationship with God, is precisely in the apostolic preaching of him, the Gospel which, as we have seen, stands in an

---

55 W. W. Harvey, in his edition of *Against the Heresies*, printed twelve years after Newman's *Essay on the Development of Christian Doctrine*, pointed out, in a footnote to *AH* 1.10.2: "At least here there is no reserve made in favour of any theory of development. If ever we find any trace of this dangerous delusion in Christian antiquity, it is uniformly the plea of heresy." (Cambridge, 1857), 1.94. This is noted by D. Minns, who also comments appositely on the use of Irenaeus made by the Second Vatican Council in its statement on tradition, *Irenaeus* (London: Geoffrey Chapman, 1994), 119, 133-4.

56 Cf. E. Osborn, "The rule did not limit reason to make room for faith, but used faith to make room for reason. Without a credible first principle, reason was lost in an infinite regress." ("Reason and the Rule of Faith in the Second Century AD," 57).

interpretative engagement with Scripture. The role of the apostles in delivering the Gospel is definitive. As Irenaeus puts it:

> We have learned from no others the plan of our salvation than from those through whom the Gospel has come down to us, which they did at one time proclaim in public, and at a later period, by the will of God, handed down (*tradiderunt*) to us in the Scriptures, to be the ground and pillar of our faith... Matthew issued a written Gospel among the Hebrews in their own dialect, while Peter and Paul were preaching in Rome, and laying the foundations for the Church. After their departure, Mark, the disciple and interpreter of Peter, did also hand down in writing what had been preached by Peter. Luke also, the companion of Paul, recorded in a book the Gospel preached by him. Afterwards, John, the disciple of the Lord, who had leaned upon his breast, did himself publish the Gospel during his residence at Ephesus in Asia. These have all declared to us that there is one God, Creator of heaven and earth, announced by the Law and Prophets; and one Christ the Son of God. (*AH* 3.1.1-2)

It is the apostles alone who have brought the revelation of Christ to the world, though what they preach is already announced by Scripture—the Law and the Prophets. The Gospels composed by those who were not apostles, Irenaeus claims, are interpretations of the preaching of those who were apostles. Irenaeus further emphasizes the foundational role of the apostles by asserting, in the passage elided from the above quotation, that the apostles did not begin to preach until they were invested with the fullness of knowledge by the risen Lord. That the apostles preached the Gospel and then subsequently wrote it down is important for Irenaeus, as it will later enable him to appeal to the continuous preaching of the Gospel in the Church, the tradition of the apostles. It is also important to Irenaeus to specify that what they wrote has been handed down ("traditioned") in the Scriptures, as the ground and pillar of our faith. While Paul had spoken of the Church as being the pillar and foundation of the truth (1 Tim 3:15), in the need to define more clearly the identity of the Church Irenaeus modifies Paul's words so that it is the Scripture which is the "ground and pillar" of the faith, or, he states later, it is the Gospel, found in four forms, and the Spirit of life that is "the pillar and foundation of the Church" (*AH* 3.11.8). It is by their preaching the Gospel that Peter and Paul lay the foundations for the Church, and so the Church, constituted by the Gospel, must preserve this deposit intact.

Having specified the foundational character of Scripture and the Gospel, Irenaeus turns to the mechanics of his debate with his opponents:

> When, however, they are confuted from the Scriptures, they turn round and accuse these same Scriptures as not being correct, nor of authority, and that they are ambiguous, and that the truth cannot be derived from them by those who are ignorant of tradition. For [they allege that] the truth was not delivered by means of written documents, but through a living voice, for which reason Paul says "we speak wisdom among those that are perfect, but not the wisdom of the world" (1 Cor 2:6). And this wisdom each one of them alleges to be what is found by them, that is, a fabrication; so that, according to them, the truth properly resides at one time in Valentinus, at another in Marcion, at another in Cerinthus, then afterwards in Basilides, or has even been indifferently in any other disputant, who could say nothing salvific. For every one of these, being completely perverted, distorting the canon of truth, is not ashamed to preach himself. (*AH* 3.2.1)

According to Irenaeus, his opponents' response to the charge that their teaching is not to be found in Scripture is simply to assert that these Scriptures are not authoritative, that they are inadequate for full knowledge, that they are ambiguous and need to be interpreted in the light of a tradition which is not handed down in writing but orally. That is, they appeal to a dichotomy between Scripture and tradition, understanding by the latter the oral communication of teaching derived from the apostles, containing material not to be found in the Scriptures yet which is needed to understand Scripture correctly.[57] As we have seen, the apostles certainly delivered a new manner of reading the Scriptures, proclaiming Christ "according to the Scriptures," but, according to Irenaeus, what they handed down, both in public preaching and in writing, remained tied to the Scripture. Rather than standing within this tradition of the apostolic engagement with Scripture, in which Christ is revealed, the Word

---

57 For such a statement, see the *Letter to Flora*, by Ptolemy, a Valentinian writing around 160, in which Flora is encouraged in this way: "If God allows, you will learn later on the beginning and birth of them [the various Gnostic aeons], if you are granted the apostolic tradition which we also received from a succession together with the regulation [τοῦ κανονίσαι] of all [our] words by our Savior's teaching." Text preserved in Epiphanius, *Panarion*, 33.7.9; ed. G. Quispel, *Ptolémée: Lettre à Flora*, SC 24 (Paris: Cerf, 1966); following, and modifying, the translation of R. Grant, *Second-Century Christianity: A Collection of Fragments* (London: SPCK, 1946), 36. For a further example of Ptolemy's teaching, see his comments on the prologue of John preserved by Irenaeus in *AH* 1.8.

which is not man's but God's, those who distort this canon think that the truth resides in their own interpretations, their own fabrications, and so end up preaching themselves.

Irenaeus continues his rhetorical argument, by making an appeal to the apostolic tradition as he understands it:

> But, again, when we refer them to that tradition from the apostles which is preserved through the successions of the presbyters in the churches, they object to the tradition, saying that they themselves are wiser not merely than the presbyters, but even than the apostles, because they have discovered the unadulterated truth. For they maintain that the apostles intermingled the things of the Law with the words of the Saviour; and that not the apostles alone, but even the Lord himself, spoke at one time from the demiurge, at another time from the intermediate place, and yet again from the pleroma; but that they themselves, indubitably, unsulliedly, and purely, have knowledge of the hidden mystery... Therefore it comes to this, that these men do now consent neither to Scripture nor to tradition. (*AH* 3.2.2)

Irenaeus clearly believes that an appeal to tradition is legitimate. And just like his opponents, Irenaeus claims that the tradition to which he appeals derives from the apostles, though this time it is one which has been maintained publicly, by the succession of presbyters in the churches. As we saw, Irenaeus began his argument by asserting the identity between what the apostles preached publicly and subsequently wrote down. Just as Irenaeus's opponents object to his use of Scripture, so also they object to the tradition to which he appeals, for the tradition to which Irenaeus appeals, in both its written and oral form, has elements of Scripture, the Law, mixed up with what comes from the Saviour himself. Moreover, according to his opponents, even the words of the Lord have to be carefully discerned, to determine whence they derive.[58] Not surprisingly, those who set themselves above Scripture in this manner have little use for tradition as understood by Irenaeus.

Irenaeus continues in chapter three by developing his allusion to the apostolic tradition being preserved by the successions of presbyters in

58 According to Ptolemy, in the *Letter to Flora*, the Pentateuch, was not decreed by one author, rather some parts belong to God, some to Moses and others to the elders. The part derived from God is also to be divided into three categories, that which is itself holy, that which is fulfilled by the Saviour and that which was removed by him. For Irenaeus' attempts to deal with the different aspects of Scripture, see *AH* 4.12-13.

Apostles → canon → Scripture → tradition → creed

Valentinus had apostolic succession, no? (p.20)

∴ not sufficient standard

the churches. As we have seen, the apostolic tradition is nothing other than the Gospel proclaimed by the apostles as the foundation for the Church. Insofar as the Gospel, proclaimed in public, has been preserved intact, it is possible to appeal, as a point of reference for what has been taught from the beginning, to the succession of presbyter/bishops who have taught and preached the same Gospel. In this way, apostolic succession becomes an element, alongside Scripture, canon and tradition, in the self-identification of orthodox or normative Christianity. So Irenaeus begins:

> Thus, the tradition of the apostles, which is manifest throughout the whole world, is clearly to be seen in every church by those who wish to see the truth. And we are able to list those who were appointed by the apostles as bishops in the churches and their successions until our own times. They have neither taught or known the gibberish spoken by these people. For if the apostles had known secret mysteries, which they taught "the perfect" privately and apart from the rest, they would have delivered them especially to those to whom they were also committing the churches themselves. For they desired that these men should be perfect and blameless in all things, who they were leaving behind as successors, delivering up their own place of teaching. (*AH* 3.3.1)

The tradition of the apostles is manifest in all the churches throughout the world, preserved by those to whom the apostles entrusted the well-being of the churches founded upon the Gospel. To demonstrate this, Irenaeus next turns to list the succession of bishops at Rome, as being the preeminent example of an apostolic church. When considering this passage, it is important to remember that monarchical episcopacy was not established in Rome until at least the end of the second century, and perhaps later.[59] The Church in Rome was primarily composed of house churches, each with its own leader. These communities would have appeared like philosophical schools, groups gathering around their teachers, such as Justin and Valentinus, studying their scriptures and performing their rites. Thus the purpose of enumerating "those who were appointed by the apostles as bishops in the churches," is not to establish the "validity" of their individual offices and the jurisdiction pertaining to it, but, as Irenaeus puts it, to make possible the discovery "in every church" of

---

59 P. Lampe, *Die stadtrömischen Christen in den ersten beiden Jahrhunderten*, 2nd rev. edn. (Tübingen: Mohr, 1989); A. Brent, *Hippolytus and the Roman Church in the Third Century: Communities in Tension before the Emergence of a Monarch-Bishop* (Leiden: Brill, 1995).

Roman Catholics trace back to Peter?

the "tradition of the apostles" manifest in the whole world, that is, the truth taught by the apostles, insofar as it has been preserved, in public, intact. Similarly, although Irenaeus describes the apostles as leaving these men behind as their successors, they are not themselves described as "apostles." A firm distinction is made between the "blessed apostles" and the first "bishop" of Rome (*AH* 3.3.3). More important than the office itself is the continuity of teaching with which the successors are charged.[60] After listing the various presbyter/bishops up to his own time, Irenaeus concludes by again emphasizing the point of referring to such successions: "In this order and by this succession, the ecclesiastical tradition from the apostles and the preaching of the truth have come down to us" (*AH* 3.3.3). It is the preaching of the truth, preserved by the presbyter/bishops throughout their successions, that is the ecclesiastical tradition deriving from the apostles. Finally, after establishing this to be the case in Rome, Irenaeus turns briefly to speak of the churches in Asia, at Smyrna and Ephesus, both of which for him are "true witnesses to the tradition of the apostles" (*AH* 3.3.4).

In the following chapter, after again emphasizing the completeness and exclusivity of the revelation made by the apostles, who deposited "all things pertaining to the truth" in the Church, Irenaeus continues with an interesting hypothetical case:

> Suppose there arise a dispute relative to some important question among us, should we not have recourse to the most ancient Churches with which the apostles held constant intercourse, and learn from them what is certain and clear in regard to the present question? For how should it be if the apostles themselves had not left us writings? Would it not be necessary in that case to follow the course of tradition which they handed down to those to whom they did commit the Churches?

> To which course many nations of the barbarians who believe in Christ do assent, having salvation written in their hearts by the Spirit, without paper

---

60 A. Brent points out the background of this language of succession (διαδοχή), in works such as the *Lives of Eminent Philosophers* by Diogenes Laertius, which describes the succession of the heads of the philosophical schools (προιστάμενος τῆς σχολῆς), who were responsible for the transmission of the teachings of their founders, and incorporates into these successions incidents from the lives of the heads and short epitomes of their teachings; Irenaeus similarly describes events from the life of Clement and aspects of his teaching. ("Diogenes Laertius and the Apostolic Succession," *JEH* 44.3 [1993], 367-89).

and ink, and, carefully preserving the ancient tradition, believing in one God, the Creator of heaven and earth and all things therein, by means of Christ Jesus, the Son of God; who because of his surpassing love towards his creation, condescended to be born of the virgin, he himself uniting man through himself to God, and having suffered under Pontius Pilate, and rising again, and having been received up in splendor, shall come in glory, the Savior of those who are saved and the Judge of those who are judged, and sending into eternal fire those who transform the truth, and despise his Father and his advent. Those who, in the absence of written documents, have believed this faith, are barbarians so far as regards our language; but as regards doctrine, manner and tenor of life, they are, because of faith, very wise indeed, and they do please God ordering their conversation in all righteousness, chastity and wisdom. (*AH* 3.4.1-2)

Here Irenaeus goes even further than his appeal to tradition in *AH* 3.2.2; not only can one appeal to tradition in the sense of the Christian revelation delivered by the apostles, and now preserved and preached by the Church, but even if the apostles had not left behind anything written, we should "follow the course of the tradition which they have handed down to those to whom they did commit the churches," as do the barbarians, who believe in Christ, having salvation written in their hearts by the Holy Spirit, "preserving the ancient tradition, believing in one God..."[61] So that "by means of the ancient tradition of the apostles," true believers will not be swayed by those who teach anything else. Although it is not actually called a canon of truth, what Irenaeus describes as being believed by these illiterate people written upon by the Spirit, is very much like his descriptions of the canon elsewhere. The content of tradition, what it is that these barbarians believe, it is important to note, is nothing other than what is written in the apostolic writings, themselves "according to Scripture." Again, the apostolic writings and tradition are not two independent or complementary sources, but two modalities of the Gospel "according to the Scriptures."

---

61 For the new writing of the covenant established by Christ, see Clement, *Strom.* 6.16.131.4-5: "Further, Isaiah the prophet is ordered to take 'a new book and write in it' [Is 8:1] certain things: the Spirit prophesying that through the exposition of the Scriptures there would come afterwards the sacred knowledge which at that period was still unwritten, because not yet known. For it was spoken from the beginning to those only who understand. Now that the Savior has taught the apostles, the unwritten [interpretation] of the written (ἡ τῆς ἐγγράφου ἄγραφος) has been handed down also to us, inscribed (ἐγγεγραμμένη) by the power of God on hearts new, according to the renovation of the book."

So, for Irenaeus, both the true apostolic tradition maintained by the churches, and the apostolic writings themselves, derive from the same apostles, and have one and the same content, the Gospel, which is itself, as we have seen, "according to the Scriptures." "Tradition" for the early Church is, as Florovsky put it, "Scripture rightly understood."[62] Irenaeus' appeal to tradition is thus fundamentally different to that of his opponents. While they appealed to tradition precisely for that which was not in Scripture, or for principles which would legitimize their interpretation of Scripture, Irenaeus, in his appeal to tradition, was not appealing to anything else that was not also in Scripture. Thus Irenaeus can appeal to tradition, to establish his case, and at the same time maintain that Scripture cannot be understood except on the basis of Scripture itself, using its own hypothesis and canon.[63]

Having established, in principle, that the tradition delivered by the apostles is a current reality in the church, Irenaeus turns, however, to Scripture to examine what it says about God and Christ:

> Since, therefore, the tradition from the apostles does exist in the Church, and is permanent among us, let us revert to the demonstration from the Scriptures of the apostles who wrote the Gospel (*ad eam quae est ex Scripturis ostensionem eorum qui evangelium conscripserunt apostolorum*), in which they recorded the doctrine regarding God, pointing out that our Lord Jesus Christ is the truth, and that there is no lie in Him. (*AH* 3.5.1)

Scripture, as written, is fixed,[64] and though the tradition maintained by the succession of presbyters is similarly fixed in principle, in practice it is much less secure, and, in any case, it can never be, for Irenaeus, a point of reference apart from Scripture. The doctrine concerning God, and the truth that is Christ, is to be found in the exposition of the Scriptures as interpreted by the apostles, who alone proclaimed the Gospel, handing it down in both Scripture and tradition.

---

62 G. Florovsky, "The Function of Tradition in the Early Church," *GOTR* 9.2 (1963), 182; repr. in idem. *Bible, Church, Tradition* (Vaduz, Büchervertriebsanstalt, 1987), 75.

63 Cf. *AH* 3.12.9: "the demonstrations [of things contained] in the Scriptures cannot be demonstrated except from the Scriptures themselves."

64 Though see B. Ehrman, *The Orthodox Corruption of Scripture: The Effect of Early Christological Controversies on the Text of the New Testament* (New York and Oxford: Oxford University Press, 1993).

But this is inevitable since they must all be legitimated by apostolic authority.

The vital point established in all this is the affirmation that there is indeed one Gospel, a Gospel which is of God, not of man (cf. Rom 1:1; Gal 1:11-12). This point is equally an affirmation that there is one Lord Jesus Christ. The one Christ, the Son of God, proclaimed by the apostles in the one Gospel "according to the Scriptures," makes known (cf. Jn 1:18: ἐξηγήσατο, "exegeted") the Father, just as the one God has made himself known through his one Son by the Holy Spirit who speaks about him through the prophets. Yet, as noted in the beginning of this chapter, this Gospel proclaims the Coming One (ὁ ἐρχόμενος), and so it is not fixed in a text, but is found in an interpretative engagement with Scripture, based upon its own hypothesis, not man's, and in accordance with the canon and tradition delivered by the apostles. Equally important is that, despite the great variety of positions against which this basis was articulated, and even if not manifest clearly and continuously from the beginning, it is nevertheless based upon what was delivered at the beginning. The order and structure of the Christian Church, its ordained ministers and its liturgy, all underwent many developments and modifications in subsequent centuries, which it is beyond the scope of this present work to examine. Because of these changes, care needs to be taken to ensure that later understandings of the Church, her ministers and her tradition, are not projected back into the use that was made of the appeal to apostolic succession and tradition in the earliest debates concerning the basis of normative or orthodox Christianity.

Heresy

This very success entailed certain consequences in the realm of ecclesiology. The reverse side of the affirmation of truth is the recognition of error. And so, the very proclamation that Christians are united in their faith throughout the whole world introduces, in fact, division and exclusion. However, it must be remembered that in this period the Church did not have the authoritarian powers, or the financial basis enabling such powers, that would later be bestowed upon it. In this context, excommunication was a self-chosen affair. According to Ignatius, it is the one who refuses to come to the common assembly that separates himself (*Ephesian* 5.3). Similarly, Irenaeus describes how Cerdo sometimes taught secretly and at other times confessed openly, but when refuted for his false teaching "he separated himself from the assembly of the brethren" (*AH* 3.4.3). Rather than share in the common teaching, Cerdo preferred to break with the other communities in Rome, probably symbolized by the refusal to exchange the *fermentum*, the common symbol of eucharistic communion.[65] Even though these communities which preferred to separate from others were outwardly similar to them, such a decision was described pejoratively by Irenaeus as the founding of a "school" with its own succession of teaching (Ptolemy from Valentinus, *AH* 1.Pref.2; Marcion from Cerdo, *AH* 1.27.2), all ultimately deriving from Simon Magus (*AH* 1.23), and so not part of the succession of teaching which was traced back to the apostles (*AH* 3.3).[66] The unity of the Church established in this way, in the late second century, was perceived by Christians themselves, such as Avircius Marcellus, the bishop of Hierapolis in Phrygia, who on his own epitaph describes how he has traveled from Nisibis to Rome and found the same faith, serving the same nourishment, everywhere,[67] and also acknowledged by pagans, such as Celsus, who differentiated between the various sects and "the Great Church."[68]

That there is indeed one Christ made known through the one Gospel, means that the question, "Who do you say I am?" is meaningful, one to which an answer is possible. As we have seen, inquiry is only possible on the basis of a hypothesis and a canon, and in this case the hypothesis is that of Scripture itself, and the canon is found in the interpretative engagement with Scripture according to which Christ was preached by the apostles, an engagement in which the student of the Word is also "interpreted" by the Word as he or she puts on the identity of Christ. This scriptural engagement cannot be avoided; even when John the Baptist was imprisoned and sent his disciples to ask Jesus "Are you he who is to come (ὁ ἐρχόμενος) or shall we look for another?" Jesus did not give a straightforward answer, but directed him to signs—the blind seeing, the lame walking—which can only be

---

65 Cf. Brent, *Hippolytus*, 420-1.
66 Such genealogical claims should perhaps not be understood too literally; the figure of Simon Magus seems to be modeled on Paul himself, so that the point being made is that, despite their claims to be disciples of Paul, they have in fact misunderstood Paul, as did those mentioned in 2 Peter 3:15-16. Cf. Pétrement, *A Separate God*, 233-46.
67 Translation in J. Stevenson, *A New Eusebius* (London: SPCK, 1963), 143.
68 Cf. Origen, *Contra Celsum*, 5.59-61. For other, more sociological reasons, for the consolidation of the Great Church in the early centuries, see especially, R. Stark, *The Rise of Christianity: A Sociologist Reconsiders History* (Princeton: Princeton University Press, 1996).

understood as "messianic" through the interpretation of them by
Scripture (Matt 11:2-5). This hypothesis and canon calls for continual
reflection, and the centuries that followed did so reflect and used all the
means at their disposal. There are many monuments to this continual
engagement with the Gospel proclaimed according to the Scriptures—writings of the Fathers and saints, schools of iconography and
hagiography and so on—all of which have a certain authority to the
extent that they point to the same vision of the King, the Gospel image
of Christ. In the light of the canon of truth itself, other elements are
also called "canons," such as the classical liturgical anaphoras, which
epitomize the whole of Scripture; those saints whose lives and teachings embody the truth are "canons" of faith and piety; and similarly the
decisions of the councils concerning the proper order for the Church
and people of God in particular situations are "canons." The Word
grows, as Acts puts it (Acts 6:7), in that as more and more people
believe on it and reflect on it, there are ever new, more detailed and
comprehensive explanations elaborated in defense of one and the same
faith, the faith in what has been delivered from the beginning, the
Gospel according to the Scriptures, the same Word of God—Jesus
Christ, the same yesterday, today and for ever (Heb 13:8).

Organic growth = orthodoxy and apostolicity

2

The Scriptural Christ

The Christ who appears on the pages of the writings recognized as canonical Scripture, the Scriptural Christ, is always the crucified and risen one. By this I do not mean to undermine the historical specificity of the Passion ("once for all," ἐφάπαξ, Rom 6:10; Heb 7:27), but to emphasize *who* it is that these texts describe. That they were all written after the Passion is obvious; that the proclamation, the *kerygma*, that the crucified and risen Jesus is Lord, so clear in the letters of Paul, is also at the basis of the depiction of Jesus in the canonical Gospels is equally evident. And this orientation is vital. The Christian confession is not simply about who a figure of the past *was*, what he did and said, but rather who he *is*; the Christian faith confesses the living Lord: "Jesus Christ, the same yesterday, today and for ever" (Heb 13:8). Similarly, whatever oral reports concerning the sayings and deeds of Jesus there might have been, stemming from those who had contact with him prior to his Passion, these have been recontextualized, in the canonical Gospels, in the light of the Passion and the proclamation of him as Lord and Christ. Moreover, as we have seen, their presentation of Christ has been interpreted through the medium of Scripture, again, in the light of the Cross. The four canonical Gospels are not attempts to preserve accurate historical records, but are witnesses to and Scriptural interpretations, based upon the *kerygma*, of this person Jesus Christ.[1] There may well be authentic,

---

1 This point is also clearly maintained by the canons of Orthodox Iconography, which, for instance, includes Paul with the other apostles in the icon of Pentecost. That the Passion is at the basis for the depiction of Jesus in the Gospels is also echoed in, for instance, the icon for the nativity, where the infant Christ is wrapped in bandages, lying in a manger (to be partaken of), and placed in a cave (as a corpse), following the suggestions of the infancy narratives themselves. Cf. R. E. Brown, *The Birth of the Messiah* (New York: Doubleday, 1993), and, more briefly, *An Adult Christ at Christmas* (Collegeville: Liturgical Press, 1988). The same point could by made from hymnography (compare, for instance, the material for the prefeast of the Nativity to that for Holy Week).

historical material pertaining to Jesus in some of the non-canonical material, such as the *Gospel of Thomas* or *The Infancy Gospel of Thomas*, but in these cases the Cross is almost totally eclipsed and the engagement with Scripture non-existent.[2] In reverse, those attempts to reduce the diversity of the canonical witnesses to Christ to a unified "life of Christ," such the *Diatessaron* of Tatian and *On the Harmony of the Gospels* by Augustine, might produce a coherent and harmonious account, but in so doing they have removed Christ from the canonical Scriptures to a world created, and restricted, by their own imagination.

It would, however, be wrong to separate the canonical material into two independent sources or traditions with two distinct subjects, the oral reports, on the one hand, concerning the "historical Jesus," and, on the other, the *kerygma*, proclaiming the Christ of faith. The letters of Paul, the earliest writings of the New Testament, are certainly almost exclusively concerned with the proclamation of Christ and the formation of the Christian communities; almost, that is, because Paul clearly knows certain key features about Christ,[3] and claims to preach the same Gospel as do the Palestinian witnesses to the risen Christ (Gal 2; 1 Cor 15:3-11). On the other hand, the narrative depictions of Christ in the Gospels are no less concerned to maintain the centrality of the Passion. Indeed, in them the very identity of Christ is intimately connected with the Cross. At the very center of the synoptic Gospels, both in a literary sense and as that to which they are themselves answers, is Christ's question, "Who do you say I am?" When Peter replies, "You are the Christ" (Mk 8:29; Lk 9:20),[4] Christ immediately begins to explain to his disciples how he must go to Jerusalem to suffer and be rejected by the elders, chief priests and scribes, to be killed and rise

2   A separate study would be needed to examine how, in some of the apocryphal material, the expansion of details seems to be based on the scriptural presentation of Christ but extended to other figures in the narrative, for instance Mary in the *Protoevangelium of James* and the various liturgical traditions surrounding her.

3   Paul knows that Jesus was a man (Gal 4:4), descended from David (Rom 1:3); that he taught (1 Cor 7:10; 1 Cor 9:14) and interpreted his last meal in terms of his coming Passion (1 Cor 11:23-5); that was tried before Pontius Pilate (1 Tim 6:13), abused (Rom 15:3), crucified (1 Cor 1:23 etc.), buried and rose again (Rom 6:4; 1 Cor 15:4-8).

4   In Matt 16:16, Peter gives a fuller answer, "The Christ, the Son of the Living God," to have Jesus point out that this was known only through a revelation of the Father, not by human intercourse.

again on the third day. When Peter then tries to put himself between Christ and his Cross, he receives the sharpest rebuke imaginable—"Get behind me, Satan!" Moreover, despite this instruction and the benefit of accompanying Jesus during his ministry, Peter still denied Christ, and is glaringly absent, along with the other apostles and disciples, from the crucifixion scene. It is the resurrected Christ who again instructs his disciples how, according to the prophets, it was necessary for the Christ "to suffer these things and to enter into his glory" (Lk 24:26). The structure of these narratives downplays the things said and done by Jesus prior to his Passion, as any kind of historical base for Christian faith. Rather, on the basis of faith in the living, crucified and risen, Jesus Christ, the Gospels present the words and deeds of Christ as addressed now to the believers, just as the miracles reported in the Pauline proclamation are those worked *now* amongst the Christian communities in which Christ is portrayed as crucified (Gal 3:1-5).

It is in the Gospel according to John that the narrative depiction of Jesus is most thoroughly united to the proclamation of the risen Christ as Lord. Unlike the Synoptics, where the narrative is always told from the standpoint of the Resurrection, but where Jesus has yet to be glorified, John depicts Jesus as the exalted Lord from the beginning: He is the one from above, he is always in control, he suffers no anxiety in the garden, and needs no transfiguration for us to see his glory. Yet this is far from being an incipient docetism. In some ways, Jesus is depicted here as being even more human: only in John does Jesus cry, for his friend Lazarus (Jn 11:35), indeed, only in this Gospel is Jesus said to have friends whom he loves (Jn 11:5, 11) and some more than others (Jn 13:23, etc), and asks for the same in return (Jn 21:15-17).[5] More to the point, John's depiction of Jesus ultimately has an antidocetic thrust, emphasizing that the revelation of God in Christ takes place in the flesh and on earth, when interpreted correctly. John stresses the total identity between the humiliated Jesus and the exalted Christ. In fact, for John, the moment of humiliation on the Cross *is* the moment of exaltation and glorification (Jn 3:13-14; 12:27-36), and in this the work of God is completed or perfected (τετέλεσται, Jn 19:30), just as for Paul the word of the Cross is the definitive revelation of the power, wisdom and glory of God (1 Cor 1-2).

---

5   A point made by L. Timothy Johnson, *The Real Jesus*, 156.

The answer to Jesus' question, given in the Synoptics, "You are the Christ" (Matt 16:16, etc.) immediately relates Jesus to the Law, the Psalms, and the Prophets: Jesus is the Anointed One, the Messiah, the chosen representative of God. Likewise the name "Jesus" (Ἰησοῦς) itself is already an interpretation of who he is (cf. Matt 1:21): the victory or salvation (*yešuʿah*) of God, the one who will lead the people of God to salvation, just as the other Joshua (also Ἰησοῦς in the LXX and Heb 4:8) led his people through the Jordan to the promised land. In the Gospels, Jesus works all the messianic signs: He heals the sick, gives sight to the blind, feeds the people in the wilderness, calms the waters, forgives sins, and raises the dead. Moreover, he does these things in his own name, so provoking the question "what manner of man is this" that can do such things (cf. Matt 8:27)? The Gospels attribute to Jesus what in the Law, the Psalms and the Prophets, belongs to God alone. He is certainly divine, yet he is not the one God of Israel. When Peter further confesses "You are the Son of the living God" (Matt 16:16), this designation "Son of God," in the light of Jesus' divine actions, must be taken in a stronger sense than the manner in which it is applied to Adam (Lk 3:38); Adam was a representative of God on earth, created *in* the image of God, but only Christ, the last Adam (1 Cor 15:45), the man from heaven (1 Cor 15:47), *is* the image of the invisible God (Col 1:15), so making Adam a "type of the One to come" (Rom 5:14).

However, just how Jesus is the Anointed One of God is not revealed simply through the wondrous deeds he wrought, not even by placing these deeds within the context of the fulfillment of the messianic prophecies. In fact, Christ warns against trusting messiahs and prophets who work wonders (Matt 24:23-5), and also suggests that signs such as one arising from the dead are not sufficient grounds for belief if Moses and the prophets are not heard (Lk 16:31). Rather, once Jesus is recognized as the Messiah, what distinguishes his Messiahship, as he himself explains, is that he must be crucified (Matt 16:21) to enter his glory, as the prophets have already announced (cf. Lk 24:26). Christ was clearly not the nationalistic or political messiah hoped for by some (cf. Lk 24:19-21; Acts 1:6); he died the most shameful death imaginable, not only death, but death on a Cross (Phil 2:8), becoming a curse for our

sake (Gal 3:13, cf. Deut 21:23). But through this, the idea of Messiahship was brought together with the image of the Suffering Servant, subverting expectations and revealing the strength and wisdom of God in the weakness and folly of the Cross (1 Cor 1-2).

The Gospels describe Jesus Christ with practically every scriptural image possible. Jesus is the Teacher and the Prophet, bringing God's Word, which he himself is, as well as being the Wisdom of God, in whom are hid all the treasures of wisdom and knowledge (Col 2:3). He is the Savior, bringing us the knowledge of God, in which alone is eternal life (Jn 17:3). He is the Life of those who live in the Light which he is, seeing all things and knowing how to walk according to the ways of God; he is the Author of life (Acts 3:15) as well as the way, the truth and the life (Jn 14:6). He is the image (εἰκών) of the invisible God (Col 1:15), the impress of his Father's hypostasis (χαρακτὴρ τῆς ὑποστάσεως αὐτοῦ, Heb 1:3), and in him the fullness of the divinity dwells bodily (Col 2:9); in him we see God, and it is in him that the glory of God is revealed (Jn 1:14), shining in the face (ἐν προσώπῳ) of Christ (2 Cor 4:6), the Lord of glory (1 Cor 2:8).

Another aspect of the scriptural Christ is described by applying to him the imagery surrounding the temple and worship. Jesus is the High Priest who makes expiation for the sins of the people (Heb 2:17, etc.), yet does so as the one who is offered, the Lamb of God (Is 53; Jn 1:29; Acts 8:32; 1 Pet 1:19; Rev *passim*). He is our Pascha, sacrificed for our sake (1 Cor 5:7). He gives his life as a ransom for many (λύτρον, Matt 20:28; ἀντίλυτρον, 1 Tim 2:6), reconciling all things to God, making peace by the blood of his Cross (Col 1:20), bringing hostility to an end by the Cross (Eph 2:16). All this is achieved by the "one mediator between God and man, the man Jesus Christ" (1 Tim 2:5), who has mediated for us a new covenant (Heb 8:6, 9:15, 12:24). Christians who are crucified with Christ (cf. Rom 6:6, Gal 2:20), buried with him in baptism (Rom 6:4), are now the temple of the living God (2 Cor 6:16), those in whom God dwells (1 Jn 4:12). In another cluster of images, Christ is depicted as the Good Shepherd (1 Peter 2:25, 5:4), who leads his sheep through the door, again Christ himself, to salvation (Jn 10:7-15). He is the one whom God exalted as Leader or Prince (Acts 5:31), the Ruler of the kings of the earth (Rev

1:5), the Lord of lords and the King of kings (Rev 17:14, 19:16). As
the Power of God working salvation, he accomplishes the victory of
God: by voluntarily undergoing death he destroys the power of death,
manifesting life as the firstborn from the dead (Col 1:18); becoming a
curse (Gal 3:13), he empties the curse of its power and brings instead
the peace and blessing of God; becoming sin, yet not knowing sin, he
opens to us the righteousness of God (2 Cor 5:21). That all the terms
and imagery used to describe Christ and his activity are derived from
Scripture, emphasizes the point that Christ is from God (Jn 8:42),
from above not below (Jn 8:23), that he has come down from heaven
to do God's will (Jn 4:34, 5:30, 6:38-9), that in him God is at work,
and in him alone we see God (Jn 1:18, 14:9; Matt 11:27, etc.), just as
he alone has revealed to us the meaning of the Scriptures, which again
is Christ himself (Lk 24:27; Jn 5:46). He is the one seen by Isaiah (Jn
12:41), about whom Moses wrote (Jn 5:46), and who is before Abraham was (Jn 8:58); with God in the beginning (Jn 1:1) he is eternal:
"Jesus Christ, the same yesterday, today, and forever" (Heb 13:8).

The overall effect of applying all these descriptions, from alpha to
omega (Rev 1:8), to Jesus Christ, is to arrive at a figure quite distinct from
the possibilities within any one of the elements which have contributed to
the overall description. There is, as we have seen, a transformation of
meaning that takes place in the light of the Passion and the subsequent
proclamation of him as Lord and Christ. Whatever Jesus might actually
have said about himself, and whatever his followers might have thought of
him, any oral reports that preserved such information were sifted and
re-presented through the medium of Scripture, interpreted on the basis of
the *kerygma*. Similarly, application of all the different scriptural titles to
Jesus, on this basis invests these titles with new meaning, reinterpreting
them: not only is Jesus the Messiah, but he is so as the Suffering Servant;
not only is he the son of David, but he is David's Lord (Matt 22:45); as
son of David he could not be a priest, so he is proclaimed as the High
Priest *par excellence*. Not only is he a son of God, as was Adam, and himself God, in the sense of Psalm verse which proclaims "I said you are gods,
sons of the Most High" (Ps 81:6 LXX), a verse used by Jesus to legitimate
calling "gods" all those to whom the word of God came (Jn 10:34-5), but
he is *the* Son of God, and as divine as God is himself.

evolution of dogma = incarnation

Through this process of selection and reinterpretation, there is a general tendency towards a particular interpretation of Christ, who he is and what he has done. It would be misleading to suggest that this is evident from the pages of the New Testament itself, just as it would be erroneous to suppose that the collection known as the "New Testament" was always a given; but it is clear from the theological discussions, and especially the canon of truth, which precede the appearance of the New Testament as a book. Nor is this to suggest that any particular element of the New Testament mosaic of Christ is submerged or lost; each remains vitally important for understanding Christ and what God has wrought in him. But it does help to understand why, although no particular explanation of the salvific work of Christ has ever been "canonized" in a creed or definition as being the only or exclusively acceptable model, there has been a claim, which became increasingly dominant and exclusive, that there is one right way of understanding who and what Jesus Christ is: the Son of the Father, the Word of God incarnate, both God and man. This is not simply a Greek philosophical approach to the revelation of God in Christ, but is rather a continuation of what is happening within each of the New Testament texts, the continuing reflection, on the basis of Scripture and the *kerygma*, about who Christ is, a reflection which has already reached canonical shape, in the canon of truth, by the time that the New Testament is recognized as such.

That continuing reflection will begin to be traced in Part Two. For now, attention needs to be directed more specifically to how it is that the New Testament texts speak of Jesus Christ, as the Incarnate Word, God and man. This is already a limitation on the overall picture of Christ presented here, yet it is not an arbitrary one, but based on the same canon by which the New Testament is itself recognized as canonical. Other aspects of the description of Christ, briefly and incompletely mentioned above, address more the interpretation of what it is that God has wrought in Christ, but that is a subject for a different work. Of particular importance, in view of subsequent theological reflection, are the terms which express the humanity and divinity of Jesus Christ, especially "man," "God," "Lord," "Word."

The term "man," as the most straightforward, is the best place to begin. That Jesus Christ is a man was not really an issue for the New

Testament writers, for they knew him as a man. From Pilate's exclamation, "Behold the man!" (Jn 19:5), to the Pharisees complaint that Jesus, "being a man," made himself God (Jn 10:33), to the affirmation that the one mediator between God and men is "the man Jesus Christ" (1 Tim 2:5), it was not that Jesus is a man that was problematic. Rather, the New Testament writers had to explain or justify their proclamation that he is also God. They were not yet faced with full-blown docetic thought, though there does appear to be a reaction to what might have been an incipient doceticism in some of the later New Testament texts, in particular the First Epistle of John. We have already seen how the Gospel of John most fully integrates the *kerygma* to the narrative depiction to produce the highest form of Christology in the New Testament, where Jesus is the exalted Lord from the beginning, the Word made flesh. The purpose of this, within the Gospel of John, is actually antidocetic, emphasizing that the revelation of God in Christ takes place in and through his flesh, which, as described in the Gospel of John, needs no transfiguration for us to see the glory of God. However, the profound tension created in this way, also makes it easier to misinterpret. Judging from the First Epistle of John, it seems that some had come to emphasize the divinity of Jesus to such an extent that they overlooked that which would have been unquestionable for earlier Christians, that is, the human, fleshly, being of Jesus Christ, the Son of God.[6] Hence the insistence that the mark of the Spirit of God is the affirmation that Jesus has come in the flesh, the premise which is denied by the antichrist (1 Jn 4:2; sim. 2 Jn 7). This was the given from the beginning, even if the author of the Fourth Gospel had carried his christological reflections to a greater depth than any other writer. The contrasting emphasis, yet profound unity, between the Gospel and the First Epistle, is clear from the opening verses of each: while the Gospel refers to a beginning before creation in which the Word is with God, in First John the beginning refers to the human presence and activity of the Lord:

---

6   This of course assumes that First John was written later than the Gospel. For an attempt to reconstruct the history of the community in which these texts were written, see R. E. Brown, *The Community of the Beloved Disciple: The Life, Loves, and Hates of an Individual Church in New Testament Times* (Mahwah, NY: Paulist Press, 1979).

That which was from the beginning, which we have heard, which we have seen with our eyes, which we have looked upon and touched with our hands, concerning the Word of life—the life was made manifest, and we saw it, and testify to it, and proclaim to you the eternal life which was with the Father and was made manifest to us—that which we have seen and heard we proclaim also to you, so that you may have fellowship with us; and our fellowship is with the Father and his Son Jesus Christ. (1 Jn 1:1-3)

And this is also the position of the Gospel, however some may have been interpreting it. For various reasons the Christology of the Gospel of John has become so identified with the description of the Word in the Prologue, that it almost comes as a surprise that, when the intent of the Gospel is explicitly stated, no reference is made to the Word:

...these things are written that you may believe that Jesus is the Christ, the Son of God, and that believing you may have life in his name. (Jn 20:31)

That is, it is Jesus himself who is the given from the beginning, and the issue for the Gospel, as for the rest of the New Testament, is to convince us that the same one is the Son of God, Lord and Savior.

The divinity of Jesus is expressed in the New Testament primarily by ascribing to him all the activities and properties that, in Scripture, belong to God alone, such as creating (Jn 1:3), bestowing life (Jn 6:35; Acts 3:15), forgiving sins (Mk 2:5-7), raising the dead (Lk 7:14-15), and being the recipient of prayers (Acts 7:59). However, there are also a few places where the divinity of Jesus is indicated more directly, by using the terms "God" and "Lord." In the New Testament, the title "God," with an article (ὁ θεός) is almost without exception reserved for the one God of Israel, the Father of Jesus Christ.[7] Without an article, Scripture applies the term in a much broader sense: according to Psalm 81:6 (LXX): "I said you are gods, sons of the Most High," a verse to which Jesus refers to assert that all those to whom the word of God came are "gods" (Jn 10:35); there are, as Paul states, many gods (1 Cor 8:5).[8] From the earliest of the

---

7 Cf. K. Rahner, "Theos in the New Testament," in idem, *God, Christ, Mary and Grace*, Theological Investigations, vol. 1, trans. C. Ernst (Baltimore: Helicon, 1965), 79-148, and R. E. Brown, "Does the New Testament Call Jesus God," in idem, *Jesus, God and Man* (Milwaukee: Bruce, 1967), 1-38.

8 The distinction between the articular and anarthrous "theos" was already made by Philo, *On Dreams*, I.229, commenting on Ex 6:3: "Accordingly the Holy Word in the present in-

New Testament writings, the title "God," with an article, is applied almost exclusively to the Father, and often used to differentiate between God himself and Jesus Christ, who is designated Lord. So, for instance, in a formula typical of Paul, he refers to "the God and Father of our Lord Jesus Christ" (Rom 15:6). An important text, emphasizing the uniqueness of these respective designations is 1 Corinthians 8:6:

> For us there is one God, the Father, from whom are all things and unto whom we exist, and one Lord Jesus Christ, through whom are all things and through whom we exist.

This affirmation that there is one God, the Father, the monotheistic heart of Christianity, and one Lord Jesus Christ, who does all the things that God himself does, so demonstrating that he is as divine as the Father, is the basic pattern for all subsequent creedal affirmations: I believe in one God the Father ... and in one Lord Jesus Christ.

There are, however, several statements in Paul and the other letters, which might be read as describing Jesus as God (ὁ θεός), though in each case it is not a deliberate, unambiguous affirmation, but depends upon texts which are problematic in various ways, either in their grammar and translation or in establishing the correct text itself. Ultimately, locating such passages is not the key to understanding the New Testament's affirmation of the divinity of Christ, but it is, nevertheless, important to establish, as accurately as possible, whether it ever used the articular "theos" for Jesus Christ. The most important passage, outside the Johannine literature, is Romans 9:5:

> ἐξ ὧν ὁ Χριστὸς τὸ κατὰ σάρκα ὁ ὢν ἐπὶ πάντων θεὸς εὐλογητὸς εἰς τοὺς αἰῶνας, ἀμήν.

> ... of whom [the Israelites] is Christ according to the flesh the one being the God over all be blessed forever, Amen.

Such is the clause in its unpunctuated form; and the earliest manuscripts of the New Testament are without any systematic punctuation.

stance has indicated him who is truly God by means of the articles, saying "I am the God," while it omits the article when mentioning him who is improperly so called."

9 For further discussion on the following passages, in addition to Rahner, "Theos in the New Testament," and Brown, "Does the New Testament Call Jesus God," see B. M. Metzger, *A Textual Commentary on the Greek New Testament* (New York: UBS, 1971).

If a comma is placed after the word "flesh" (as the United Bible Society, 4th ed. and Nestle-Aland, 27th ed.), then the articular "theos" is referred back to Christ; if it is to be a period (as the RSV, giving the alternative in a note), then a distinction is introduced between the Christ and the God who is over all. The sentence, however, would have been written without punctuation, and so it is the grammar of the passage which must decide. Here there are several considerations. If the verse were to end with a separate doxology, the word "blessed" would typically come first: "Blessed be the God of all..." Moreover, doxologies in Paul tend to refer to someone who has been mentioned earlier, in this case Christ; as "the God" is not mentioned until the end of the verse, it would be awkward to read it as referring to someone other than Christ. Moreover, if the doxology is not addressed to Christ, the participle, "being" (ὢν), is redundant. Finally, the words "according to the flesh" seem to require a parallel; usually in Paul the contrast would be "according to the Spirit," though there are places where flesh is contrasted with "theos" (e.g. 1 Cor 1:29). Overall, then, it seems probable that in Romans 9:5, Paul called Christ God (ὁ θεός), though it is the only such passage.[10]

Outside the Pauline and the Johannine material, there are only three instances where it is probable that Jesus Christ is called "God" (ὁ θεός). First, in Hebrews 1:8, though in this instance it is a citation of Psalm 44:7 (LXX), "But of the Son he says, 'Thy throne, O God (ὁ θεός), is for ever and ever.'" That Christ is "God" is not touched on again in the letter, though it is suggested that Christ is worshipped (Heb 1:6; 13:21), and in this context the ascription to Christ of a verse from the Psalms, as an aspect of worship, seems most natural. The point of the passage is to demonstrate Christ's superiority over the angels, and his divinity is thus mentioned in passing, by the use of a verse from the Psalms. The two other passages in question, Titus 2:13 and 2 Peter 1:1, speak of "our [Titus: great] God and Savior Jesus Christ" (τοῦ [μεγάλου] θεοῦ ἡμῶν καὶ σωτῆρος Ἰησοῦ Χριστοῦ). The question here is whether there is an understood article before the word Savior, so that it refers to God and to the Savior. That there is only one article, and one possessive pronoun, does indicate strongly that "the God and Savior" is to be applied to Jesus Christ. Second Peter is generally reckoned to be later, perhaps

---

10   This is also the near-unanimous reading of the Fathers, cf. Metzger, *Textual Commentary*, 520.

early second century, by which time this use is no longer exceptional. In Titus, another later writing, both God and Christ have been described as "Savior" independently (cf. Titus 1:3-4), which perhaps accounts for the transference of the title "God" to Christ.[11]

There are no applications of the term "God" (ὁ θεός) to Jesus Christ in the Synoptics, while the Gospel according to John, on the other hand, both categorically affirms and explicitly denies the applicability of this term, so presenting, again, a heightened, profound, antithetical tension. The most striking use of the term "God" occurs in Christ's own statement, "this is eternal life, that they may know you, the only true God (τὸν μόνον ἀληθινὸν θεόν), and Jesus Christ, whom you have sent" (Jn 17:3). Despite associating the knowledge of Jesus Christ with the knowledge of God in the identification of eternal life, and how could it be otherwise when John repeatedly affirms that there is no way to the Father but through the Son, nevertheless only the Father truly merits the title "God" (ὁ θεός). The description of this only true God as "Father" is frequent in John. Jesus repeatedly speaks of God as being his "Father," and although in a dispute with Jesus the Jews claimed "we have one Father, God" (Jn 8:41), Jesus himself only once described God as being "your Father," when he warns Mary Magdalene not to touch him: "... go to my brethren and say to them, I am ascending to my Father and your Father, to my God and your God" (Jn 20:17). Again the title "God" applies to the Father in a manner which makes it appropriate for Jesus to refer to him as such, distinct from himself. It is also possible that a further distinction is here being made between the way that God is a Father to Jesus and a Father to Christians, a point which is emphasized by John's use of the title "only-begotten" when speaking of Jesus as the Son.

Yet, on the other hand, John also attributes the title "God" both at the beginning and end of the Gospel to the one who is with God. In the opening verses of the Prologue, the Word is said to be God (καὶ θεὸς ἦν ὁ λόγος, Jn 1:1c). Though the article is missing from this

11   There are three other passages (2 Thess 1:12; Col 2:2; Jas 1:1) where it might be possible to read the text as ascribing the title "God" to Christ, though the RSV seems correct in its translation, and two passages where a variant reading suggests that Jesus Christ is called God (Gal 2:20; 1 Tim 3:16).

clause, it should probably be assumed, giving "theos" its full weight: the word "theos" is placed at the beginning of the clause for emphasis, where, as a predicate noun preceding the verb, it would not be expected to have an article. At the end of the Prologue, there is a problem of variant readings. According to a number of early manuscripts (such as the early third century **p**[75]), the corrected version of the Codex Sinaiticus, and the majority of early Fathers, v. 18 is, "The only-begotten God (ὁ μονογενὴς θεός), who is in the bosom of the Father, he has declared him." The other witnesses have "The only-begotten Son," or either "God" or "Son" without the article, or simply "only begotten." If Jn 1:1c should be read as implying an articular "theos," then it could be argued that v.18 should also be read as "The only-begotten God," as a more satisfactory inclusion. An inclusion is further created by the fact that only at the end of the Gospel is Jesus again called "God," when Thomas answers Christ, "My Lord and my God" (ὁ κύριός μου καὶ ὁ θεός μου, Jn 20:28). This is the most categorical and explicit affirmation of Jesus Christ as God, in the fullest (articular) sense, in the pages of the New Testament. Yet it must be held inseparably together with the affirmation that it is the Father of Jesus who alone is the one true God; on this basis, it is possible to affirm that Jesus is as divine as his Father is, and as such can be addressed as himself God. However, what is more characteristic of the New Testament, and what is more important, is what precedes "God" in Thomas' confession, the title "Lord." It is this title which, when used in its fullest sense, facilitates the application of the title "God," also in its fullest sense, to Jesus Christ.

The title "Lord" (κύριος) is an extremely flexible term, capable of sustaining various meanings: a possessive sense (the lord of a house); a polite expression of respect, but not subservience ("sir"); it could be applied in a royal manner to princes and kings; and, in a religious sense, it was used throughout the Near East, as the term with which to address the gods.[12] Some scholars, such as Bousset,[13] have argued that

12 For a full examination of the different uses, see the entries by Quell and Foerster on κύριος in G. Kittel, *Theological Dictionary of the New Testament*, trans. and ed. G. Bromiley (Grand Rapids, Mich.: Eerdmans, 1966), vol. 3, 1039-1095.

13 W. Bousset, *Kyrios Christos: A History of Belief in Christ from the Beginnings of Christianity to Irenaeus*, trans. J. E. Steely from the 2nd German edn. (1921) (New York and Nashville, Tenn.: Abingdon Press, 1970).

Jesus Christ was first called Lord (χύριος) at Antioch, under the influence of Hellenistic culture or oriental mystery religions; and that the title was not used by Jesus himself, nor by the primitive Palestinian church. They point to the fact that the first recorded instance of someone praying *to* Christ, and calling him Lord in so doing, was the Gentile Stephen at his martyrdom:

> And as they were stoning Stephen, he prayed, "Lord Jesus, receive my spirit." And he knelt down and cried with a loud voice, "Lord, do not hold this sin against them." (Acts 7.59-60)

This presents itself as the first recorded occurrence of someone praying to Christ, and, quite naturally, at the same time calling upon Christ as Lord, which, therefore, in this instance, must imply the full scope of God, rather than simply a polite expression for a teacher or leader. The importance of this otherwise isolated passage is hard to overstate, but it would be seriously misleading to use it as historical evidence of a Gentile convert bringing his own religious practices into Christianity.

The term "Lord" was certainly prevalent all around the Mediterranean, but the crucial significance it has for the writings of the New Testament, and its connection with the One God of Israel, can only be understood properly in terms of its use in Scripture.[14] The term "God" has long been used as a proper name, although originally it was a common or generic noun. For it to be used as a proper name requires monotheism, the conviction that there *is* only one being to whom this generic term can apply. While such exclusive monotheism seems to have been a fairly late development, Israel had long been committed (in principle at least) to the faithful service of only one god, the God of Israel. And from early on, they had distinguished this God of Israel from all alien gods by the proper name *YHWH*, the name which their God himself revealed to Moses, and which the story of the burning bush etymologized to the verb "to be": "I am who I am" or simply "I AM" (Ex 3:14). The Israelite catchphrase thus became, *YHWH* is our God (cf. 1 Kgs 18:39), where "*YHWH*" is the proper name, and

---

14 The following paragraph is indebted to the "history of implicit linguistic logic" given by E. Hill in the introduction to his translation of Augustine's *The Trinity* (Brooklyn: New City Press, 1991), 31-2.

"God," the predicate. The same applies in the classic statement of monotheism, the shema of Deuteronomy 6:4: "Hear O Israel, *YHWH* (is) our God, *YHWH* (is) one/alone." This, as indicated, can be rendered in various fashions, but perhaps the only way in which, strictly speaking, it should not be translated is the way in which it is done in the LXX (κύριος ὁ θεός ἡμῶν κύριος εἷς ἐστιν), and following it, the Vulgate, and, more recently, the AV, RV, RSV, NRSV etc., "The Lord our God is one Lord." Given that *YHWH* is a proper name, such a translation makes no sense.[15] What makes sense of the translation, however, is the fact that the proper name *YHWH* was replaced in speech, as being too sacred to pronounce, but not in writing, by the common noun "lord," *'adônây*/κύριος.[16] This substitution probably became customary around the time of the exile, and seems to be well established by the end of the third century B.C. It reflects a general tendency of this period to stress increasingly the transcendence of God and to introduce real or poetic intermediaries. In this way the double name for God used frequently in the Hebrew Scriptures, *YHWH Elohim*, is read as *'adônây Elohim*, and thus translated in the LXX as κύριος θεός, "the Lord God." Yet there is an important distinction between the terms: *YHWH* is still a proper name, while *'adônây*/κύριος are descriptive nouns. However, when exclusive monotheism finally becomes established, so it is held that there *is* only one God, the term "God" comes to function as a proper name, while "Lord," the spoken substitution for the proper name, can be used as a descriptive noun applicable in an incomparable fashion to the one being who alone is God. So, besides being used in a possessive, polite, courtly or religious sense, as described earlier, the term "Lord" can now be used in an absolute manner, as applying exclusively to God alone. When Jesus Christ is described as "Lord" in the New Testament, it is thus possible for this term to carry the full weight of the Divine Name.

15 Hill suggests that it would be as if one were to say, "Elizabeth our queen is one Elizabeth." Ibid.
16 This oral tradition was later indicated by means of the vowel signs introduced by the Masoretes; the combination of the vowel signs for *'adônây* and the consonants of *YHWH* produce the word "Jehovah," a misreading which dates from the sixteenth century. For the oral and written dimension of the Hebrew text, see J. Barton, *Holy Writings, Sacred Text*, 123-30.

The number of times that Paul calls the crucified and risen Jesus "Lord" needs no documenting. Nor is there any question that in using the term Lord, Paul intended the full significance of the Divine Name, *YHWH*. This is shown, for instance, by application of Joel 3:5 to Christ in Romans 10:13, "Whosoever shall call upon the name of the Lord shall be saved"—Christ is the Lord who will save those who turn to him. The most important instance of appealing to the Divine Name is of course in Philippians:

> Have this mind among yourselves which is yours in Christ Jesus, who, be-ing in the form of God, did not count equality with God a thing to be grasped, but emptied himself, taking the form of a servant, being born in the likeness of men. And being found in human form he humbled himself and became obedient unto death, even death on a cross. Therefore God has highly exalted him and bestowed on him the name which is above every name, that at the name of Jesus every knee should bow, in heaven and on earth and under the earth, and every tongue confess that Jesus Christ is Lord, to the glory of God the Father. (Phil 2:5-11)

The name above every name, the Divine Name, is bestowed upon the crucified, risen and exalted one, emphasizing, again, the centrality of the Passion. However, it is also necessary to remember that even if Paul consistently applies the title "Lord" to Jesus Christ, transferring to Christ ideas and quotations which originally belong to *YHWH* alone, this is not a direct identification of *YHWH* and Jesus Christ: Jesus is all that *YHWH* himself is, that is, fully divine, yet without actually being *YHWH* himself, for *YHWH* is his Father: "We have one God the Father... and one Lord Jesus Christ" (1 Cor 8:6). The double barreled name of God in the Scriptures ("the Lord God") is separated: the Lord, as a proper name, is reserved for the Son, while God (ὁ θεός), as a proper name, usually stands for the Father; while as common nouns, rather than names, both are applied to the Father and Son.

Compared with the writings of Paul the Synoptics only apply the term Lord to Christ on a few occasion. There are, moreover, still a few instances in the Synoptics where the title Lord is applied to God the Father (e.g., Mk 5:19). Although the title is used frequently, especially by Luke in the narrative sections of his Gospel, there are only two say-ings of Jesus which indicate that he was called Lord by his disciples:

Matthew 7:21, "Not every one who says to me, 'Lord, Lord,' shall enter the Kingdom of heaven…," and Luke 6:46, "Why do you call me 'Lord, Lord' and not do what I tell you?" However, Jesus is not described as attaching any particular significance to the term, so it is probably to be understood simply as a term of respect, similar to Teacher or Master. The most important use is Jesus' quotation of Psalm 109:1 (LXX), one of the key scriptural texts for the New Testament:

> "How can the scribes say that the Christ is the son of David? David himself, inspired by the Holy Spirit, declared, 'The Lord said to my Lord sit at my right hand, until I put thy enemies under thy feet.' David himself calls him Lord; so how is he his son?" (Mk 12:35-7; cf. Matt 22:41-6; Lk 20:41-4)

The title "Son of David" is not an adequate description of the Christ, for he is also David's Lord; not only is he a descendant of David, but he is greater than him, indeed, he is his Lord. "Lord" here would seem to imply a greater authority than simply Teacher or Master. The narrative of the Synoptics seems to suggest that although the disciples had initially addressed Christ with the title "Lord," in a polite or respectful manner, it became clear that there was more involved in the title than just respect.

More interesting is the description in Acts (whether historical or not) of how this reflection continued in the light of the Passion. It is noteworthy that the application of the term "Lord" to Jesus does not occur in the speeches of Acts 3, 4, 5 or 6. It is used, however, in Peter's speech in Acts 2, though not initially with the full sense of the Divine Name. Peter begins by citing Joel 3:1-5, which ends with the verse already considered, "And it shall be that whoever calls on the name of the Lord shall be saved" (Acts 2:21). The point of the quotation here is to justify their speaking in tongues by referring to the gift of the Spirit, rather than verse 21 itself, calling Jesus "Lord." However, at the end of the speech Peter returns to the description of Jesus as Lord, again by citing Psalm 109:1 (LXX):

> This Jesus God raised up, and of that we are all witnesses. Being therefore exalted at the right hand of God, and having received from the Father the promise of the Holy Spirit, he has poured out this which you see and hear. For David did not ascend into the heavens; but he himself says, "The Lord said to my Lord, sit at my right hand, till I make thy enemies a stool for thy

feet." Let all the house of Israel therefore know assuredly that God has made him both Lord and Christ, this Jesus whom you crucified. (Acts 2:32-6)

Here the term "Lord" signifies more than simple, or even royal, respect. It indicates the exaltation of Jesus to a supreme Lordship, yet in so doing makes Jesus the object of the action of God. The passage also refers to Jesus being appointed as the Christ through the crucifixion, just as Paul speaks of Jesus being "designated (ὁρισθέντος) Son of God in power according to the Spirit of holiness by his resurrection from the dead" (Rom 1:4). In Peter's speech, Jesus is a man witnessed to by God (Acts 2:22); when crucified, he was not abandoned to Hades, but raised up in exaltation as Christ and Lord, in the Spirit. That it is on the basis of the Passion that the disciples recognized him as Lord and Christ is clear throughout the New Testament; it is this crucified Jesus that the house of Israel is to acknowledge as Lord and Christ, the designated Son of God. The question which was to plague Christianity thereafter, whether, if he was "made" such by God, he was Lord and Christ before, is misleading in its application of temporal categories to the eternal Jesus Christ. It is the crucified and risen Jesus Christ that the Gospel proclaims as the eternal Son of God, interpreting Scripture through the prism of the word of the Cross.

The Lordship of Christ is made in a very distinctive manner in John, by an allusive play upon the etymology of the name *YHWH* offered in Exodus 3:14, "I AM who I AM," in the "I am" sayings of Jesus. The most striking occasion is when Christ asserts, "Before Abraham was, I Am" (Jn 8:58). The affirmation here is clearly not temporal, or as John Chrysostom points out, Christ should have said, "I was."[17] Similarly, when Jesus approaches his frightened disciples on the water, he reassures them by saying "I am (ἐγώ εἰμι), do not be afraid" (Jn 6:20); the RSV translates his statement as "It is I," though there is certainly an allusion to the divine name here.[18] This statement of Christ appears in the chiastic center of the Gospel, the new Exodus, when Christ declares "I AM" and leads the new Israel to the other shore of

17 "Why did he not say, 'Before Abraham came into being, I was,' instead of 'I AM'? As the Father uses this expression, 'I AM,' so also does he; for it signifies continuous existence, irrespective of all time." John Chrysostom, *Homilies On John*, 55 (on Jn 8:58-9).

18 For other nonabsolute uses of "I am" see Jn 6:35, 51; 10:7, 9, 11, 14; 11:25; 14:6; 15:1, 5.

the sea.[19] Again, John contains the most developed affirmations of the divinity of Jesus Christ.

Finally, it is in John that Jesus Christ is called for the first time by the title "Word," the term which, in abstract theological reflection, often comes to replace the name Jesus, and it is also here that the explanation of Christ's work of revelation and redemption in terms of a model of descent and ascent is sketched most clearly. In John, Christ's activity of revelation and redemption is represented as a dramatic descent and ascent, although the moments of descent and ascent are never described, but are always presumed as a means of heightening the superiority of Christ over all others.[20] Or more accurately, it is not that these moments are never described, but that they are not separated: the moment of humiliation is the moment of exaltation, and both occur on the Cross. It is when Jesus speaks of his coming glorification that we also hear that this will be a return to his eternal existence with the Father (Jn 17). The very identity of Jesus Christ has become so united with the *kerygma* about Christ, the Word of God which Paul preaches (Col 1:25-6), that Jesus Christ, according to John, is himself the Word of God incarnate. In the term "Word" (λόγος) there are at least two interconnected ideas, that of revelation and that of the revealer, and these should not be separated too hastily. Christ is the Word of God, who, as such, exists before the world, with God, and is, to use later imagery, spoken out into the world; he is God's own expression in the world. The function of revealer is so closely bound up with the person of Jesus, that he is, in fact, the embodiment of the revelation: he is the Word made flesh. Not only are his words revelatory, but he is revelatory in himself, coming into the world from above, a divine self-revelation. The identification of the crucified one as the Word of God is continued in the book of Revelation, attributed to John, where it is the rider who comes on the white horse, "clad in a robe dipped in blood," who is called by the name "the Word of God" (Rev 19:11-13).

19 Cf. P. F. Ellis, "Inclusion, Chiasm, and the Division of the Fourth Gospel," *St Vladimir's Theological Quarterly*, 43.3-4 (1999), 269-338; and his *The Genius of John: A Composition-Critical Commentary on the Fourth Gospel* (Collegeville: Liturgical Press, 1984).
20 Cf. W. A. Meeks, "The Man from Heaven in Johannine Sectarianism," *JBL* 91 (1972), 44-72.

"Unique" = "beloved" cf. Baptism & Transfiguration [handwritten annotation]

This understanding of Christ as the "Word of God" is deepened by John with the affirmation that Jesus is himself God (ὁ θεός, Jn 20:28), and by emphasizing his uniqueness as the "only-begotten" Son of God. In the New Testament, the title "only-begotten" (μονογενής) does not, strictly speaking, carry the connotation of "begetting," but refers rather to the uniqueness of the one so described, who is "one-of-a-kind."[21] It was translated in the Old Latin as *unicus*, and only later, in the context of the Arian controversy, did Jerome change it to *unigenitus*, which thereafter became the standard translation.[22] The background for this term is clearly the description of Isaac as *yahid*; this was translated in the LXX by "beloved" (ἀγαπητός, Gen 22:2, 12, 16), though Isaac is described as the *monogenes* of Abraham in Hebrews 11:17. Thus the term does not refer to the act of begetting, for Abraham had another son, Ishmael (cf. Gen 21:12-13), but refers instead to a special quality that makes a son unique to (or as the LXX puts it, "beloved" by) his father. The titles Son, Word and God, when applied to Jesus Christ, do not have the same meaning, but they are applied to one and the same subject, who is, in this way, understood to be pre-existent, beyond time and the world, who is God in God, the mediator of God in creation and the revealer of God in the world by His appearance in the flesh—the Word of God Incarnate.

The sources for this distinctive Johannine theology have been sought in all sorts of places, often furthest afield from the most obvious, that of Scripture and earlier New Testament writings. The theme of the Word of God is of course a recurrent one in Scripture: it functions to reveal God, as well as to manifest his power and his wisdom. Parallels to John can also be found in the wisdom literature of Scripture: the Wisdom of

---

21 John never ascribes a beginning/begetting to the Word and Son, Jesus Christ: the Word *was* with God (Jn 1:1), and Jesus simply *is*, he is "I AM." The only certain use of γεννᾶν for Jesus is Jn 18:37, where it is paralleled by the phrase, "for this I have come into the Word," that is, it is not a clear or purposeful reference to his birth, but applies rather to his mission. It is not certain that 1 Jn 5:18 applies to Jesus; R. E. Brown (*The Epistles of John*, The Anchor Bible [New York: Doubleday, 1982], 619-22), and R. Schnackenburg (*The Johannine Epistles: Introduction and Commentary*, trans. R. and I. Fuller [New York: Crossroad, 1992], 252-4), argue convincingly that "the one begotten by God" (a description John never uses for Jesus elsewhere) is the Christian, who is protected by God, giving a grammatical structure similar to Jn 17:2.

22 Cf. D. Moody, "God's Only Son," *JBL* 72.4 (1953), 213-19.

God exists from the beginning, dwelling with God (e.g., Prov 8:22-5); Wisdom also comes to men (Sirach [Ecclesiasticus] 24:7-22; Prov 8:31), and "tabernacles" with them (Sir 24:8); Wisdom, "the book of the commandments of God," is also said to have "appeared on earth and dwelt with men" (Bar 3:37-4:1). Other writings from the New Testament also draw upon the imagery found in the Wisdom literature, such as "image," "effulgence," and "wisdom" itself, for their interpretation of Christ (cf. Col 1:15; 2 Cor 4:4; Heb 1:3; Wisdom 7:26). It is possible that the term "Word" came to predominate in christological reflection as a reaction to the increasing use of "wisdom" in Gnostic speculation, or as an apologetic approach to Greek culture. More likely, though, is the already traditional use of the phrase "word of God" to refer to the Gospel of Jesus Christ, which he himself is: the identity between revealer and revelation.[23]

If the adoption of the term was indeed an apologetic outreach to the Greeks, this is simultaneously undermined by John. Just as significant as the introduction of the term "Word" for Christ, is the combination of this description with that of the Word "becoming flesh," diametrical opposites for any Greek philosopher. While the term "Word" appears to apply almost exclusively to Christ as divine, it is nevertheless held inseparably together with a term which stands at the opposite extreme from divinity, that of flesh. The Word becomes flesh; the Word of God is flesh, this man, Jesus Christ, crucified and risen. John heightens this contrast beyond that of any other writing of the New Testament. The Word may well be eternally divine in His eternal abode with God, but he is no less equally really flesh. With these antithetical descriptions held in such a stark unity, it is not surprising that there were continual attempts to loosen the unity of flesh and Word, or to deny the fleshly element, through some kind of docetism. It is this which makes the

23 A similar suggestion was made by E. Hoskyns, that the choice of the term "Word" in the Prologue was determined by the fact that by that time "the Word" had become synonymous with the Gospel itself, so that in using the term "the Word" the Prologue already contains a reference to the death and resurrection of Jesus; the Gospel, as the apostolic word, has become identified with the content of the Gospel, Jesus Christ (E. C. Hoskyns, *The Fourth Gospel*, 2nd rev. edn., ed. F. N. Davey [London: Faber and Faber, 1947], 159-63). A similar point is made by B. Lindars (*The Gospel of John*, New Century Bible Commentary [Grand Rapids, Mich.: Eerdmans, 1972], 83).

Alexandria imitates this paradoxical language in its theological polemics

Johannine legacy at once the most stimulating for future reflection, and also the most dangerous. F. C. Conybeare, at the beginning of this century, observed that, "If Athanasius had not had the Fourth Gospel to draw texts from, Arius would never have been confuted." To which Pollard later added, "If Arius had not had the Fourth Gospel to draw texts from, he would not have needed confuting."[24]

N.T. sets the trajectory for creedal confession of Jesus as Word Incarnate, God-Man.

Liturgy... baptismal formula, benedictions, songs/hymns... already do this prior to creedal formula.

Lex Orandi, Lex Credendi

p. 37, footnote

---

24 T. E. Pollard, *Johannine Christology and the Early Church* (Cambridge: Cambridge University Press, 1970), 3; citing Conybeare's review of A. Loisy, *Le quatrième évangile,* in the *Hibbert Journal,* 7 (1903), 620.

PART TWO

The Word of God

T he issues discussed in Part One are intrinsically bound up with reflections to be traced here. The concern there was to examine the basis and framework within which Christ's question, "Who do you say I am?" is asked and can be answered, the particular constellation of the tradition and canon of the Gospel according to Scripture, which was coherently articulated by the end of the second century yet on the basis of what was delivered by the apostles from the beginning. On this basis it was then possible to describe, albeit briefly, the interpretation of Jesus Christ given in those texts claiming apostolicity and recognized, within orthodox, catholic or normative Christianity, as the canonical New Testament. We must now retrace some of the steps taken in Part One, to look again at those figures who belong within that tradition, the Fathers, whose writings will later also be called "canonical,"[1] though not Scripture, and to consider how they also spoke of Christ. Given the extent to which the debates of this era were concerned with the nature and scope of Scripture, it is not surprising that they should reflect profoundly on how and why Jesus Christ is called "the Word of God." This designation simultaneously denotes who he is, the word which he speaks and the word which speaks of him—the revealer of God and the revelation of God, medium and message; the separation of these only impoverishes both. Although thereafter attention was increasingly focused on Christ himself, as true God and true man, yet one, this was always within the continued proclamation of the Gospel, which itself is also twofold yet one, the Word of God in the words of man (cf. 1 Thess 2:13).

The apostolic writings, in their presentation of Christ through the medium of Scripture read through the prism of the *kerygma*, had sifted

[1] The Council of Chalcedon, for instance, referred to the "canonical letters and expositions of the holy Fathers." *ACO* 2.1.1 p.195.38.

73

whatever oral reports they had and recontextualized them in the light of the Passion. In the resulting mosaic, Jesus Christ is described in a plethora of images: the Prophet, the King, the Messiah, the High Priest, the Lamb and the Suffering Servant, to name a few. Each of these images, and the many others, contain a vital insight into the person and work of Jesus Christ, who is himself more than any one of these particular elements. Subsequent theological reflection continued the interpretative task demanded by Christ. All the various aspects of the tapestry of Christ are certainly preserved and continue to stimulate reflection. When commenting on the work of salvation, reference will continue to be made, for instance, to the sacrificial nature of Christ's death, reconciling us to God by his blood, or to the didactic dimensions of his work, teaching us the saving knowledge of God. The whole of Scripture is read, and the whole picture of Christ it presents, and each element contributing to it, continues to elicit response. However, to ensure that the correct picture of Christ is being described, according to the tradition and canon of the Gospel according to Scripture, the hypothesis of Scripture and the canon of truth need to be articulated, and indeed there is no "canonical New Testament" until this is done. Intrinsic to the task of preaching Christ (Phil 1:18), learning Christ (Eph 4:20), and forming Christ in the believer (Gal 4:19), is the need to reflect specifically on the relation of Jesus Christ to the one God, his Father, and to the Holy Spirit, who spoke of him through the prophets, and of course on the one Lord Jesus Christ himself—is he both God and man, and if both, then how is he one? In this developing reflection ever greater attention was paid to particularly important or disputed passages of Scripture, cited in the manner of proof-texts, for the point was not to exegete Scripture itself, but to clarify its hypothesis and the canon by which it speaks of Jesus Christ. The increasingly abstract theological discourse which ensued was not simply the result of the transposition of the Gospel from its native Semitic soil to the supposedly alien environment of Hellenism, a contrast as specious as it is anachronistic.[2] Nor was it an attempt to

---

2   This was, of course, the premise of Adolph von Harnack in his influential *History of Dogma* (trans. of 3rd German edn. [1894], 7 vols. [London: Williams and Norgate, 1894-9]) and the so-called Biblical Theology popular in the middle of the twentieth century, though its influence remains. For a devastating critique see especially J. Barr, "Athens or Jerusalem?—The Question of Distinctiveness," chapter two in his *Old and New in Interpretation:*

"God became man so that man could become godlike."

describe the ultimate structures of "reality," to elaborate a fundamental ontology, whether of "Being" or "communion," which then comes to constitute the content of revelation itself, so substituting the explanation for that which it attempts to explain. Rather, the aim of the theological project responding to Christ's question is to articulate, in the face of perceived aberrations, the canon of truth as precisely as possible, constantly returning, as Polycarp urged his readers in the early second century, to "the Word delivered in the beginning."[3]

The most important soteriological model which nourished this increasingly focused theological reflection was that of healing and salvation through sharing, solidarity and exchange. The basic pattern can be found in many passages from Scripture, and is exemplified in Paul's words: "For you know the grace of our Lord Jesus Christ, that though he was rich, yet for your sake he became poor, so that by his poverty you might become rich" (2 Cor 8:9). This soteriological paradigm takes Christ's humiliation and exaltation on the Cross and extends it to embrace the whole course traversed by Christ, from his entry into human existence to his return, in our human nature, to the Father. There are two basic axioms that determine this model and the theological reflection of the centuries covered in this series. The first is that only God can save. It is God who is at work in Christ; Christ himself is the very Word of God, just as the Gospel is of God not of man (Gal 1:11; Rom 1:1). The second axiom is that only as a human being can God save human beings. While forgiveness could be bestowed from afar, the last enemy, death, was not overcome except by Christ voluntarily dying on behalf of all, so demonstrating his divinity (Rom 5:6-8), ensuring his victory over death, and transforming death itself, for all those who die with Christ, into a life-giving death. Unless the very divinity of God itself is revealed in the flesh, in this manner, it remains incomprehensible to created human nature, and therefore intangible and inaccessible. Christ, by sharing in the poverty of the human condition, enables human beings to share in the riches of his divine life, to become "partakers of the divine nature" (2 Pet 1:4). The interplay between these two axioms can be seen in many of the familiar patristic dicta,

A Study of the Two Testaments (New York: Harper and Row, 1966), 34-64.
3 Polycarp, *Letter to the Philippians*, 7.2.

such as Athanasius' statement, "He became man, so that we might become god,"[4] and Gregory of Nazianzus' rejoinder to Apollinarius, "What is not assumed, is not healed."[5] Like is healed and saved by like.

Following through the logic of these two axioms leads inexorably to Chalcedon. Along the way, various attempts to interpret the person and work of Christ, based on other soteriological paradigms fall by the wayside, occasionally aided, from the fourth century onwards, by political might. It is important to recognize that the figures that did so fall outside the bounds of what was recognized as Orthodox were nevertheless usually intent on preserving other elements which were also part of the total scriptural picture of Christ. For instance, those early Christian thinkers who were criticized and condemned for teaching that Jesus was a "mere man" adopted at his baptism as the Christ, could refer to passages in the New Testament, such as the opening of the Gospel according to Mark where Jesus simply appears and is baptized while a voice from heaven declares, "You are my beloved Son, with you I am well pleased" (Mk 1:11), or other passages where Jesus is described as being "made" the Christ (e.g., Acts 2:36) or appointed to sonship (e.g., Rom 1:4). Yet such individual passages are already marginal within the overall witness of Scripture, in the abundance of imagery with which it describes Christ, in and through which a particular figure is revealed. As greater attention was devoted to articulating the hypothesis of Scripture itself in the canon of truth, such passages were increasingly left to one side or even, in the earliest period, altered in the light of the canon.[6]

During the second and third century, the period under review in Part Two and Part Three, there was an immense variety of different patterns of reflection concerning Jesus Christ. As they will not themselves be the subject of study in Part Two, it is worth noting here a few general but salient points. Apart from those who were alleged to teach that Christ was a "mere man" adopted as the Son of God,[7] there were

4 Athanasius, *On the Incarnation* 54.
5 Gregory Nazianzus, *Ep.* 101.32.
6 For detailed discussion of such alterations, see B. Ehrman, *The Orthodox Corruption of Scripture.*
7 Often associated with these are the so-called "Ebionites" ("the poor ones"), Jewish Christians who also regarded Christ as a "mere man," the son of Joseph and Mary, who, at his baptism, was designated by God as his Son on account of his exceptional righ-

77

also those who sought to loosen the antithetical tension of confessing Jesus Christ to be both God and man by denying the human element. The First Epistle of John and the letters of Ignatius of Antioch are directed at opponents who seem to have claimed that Christ was not really "in the flesh," but only appeared to be so, a position thus described as "docetism" (from the Greek δοχεῖν, "to appear" or "to seem"). Marcion is also alleged to have taught that Christ was not really a flesh and blood being, but a "salutary spirit" who descended from heaven, in the fifteenth year of Tiberius Caesar, fully grown.[8] And Basilides is claimed to have taught a form of docetism, in which the divine aeon Nous, also called Christ, was sent by the Father to those on earth to deliver them from the creator of the world. This aeon only appeared as a man, and so was able to exchange his form, before the crucifixion, with that of Simon of Cyrene, so that Simon was crucified in his stead, while Jesus stood by laughing; anyone who continues to confess the crucified one thus declares that he is still enslaved.[9] Such an account probably plays on the ambiguity of the Markan account, where following the mention of Simon of Cyrene, the name "Jesus" is not used until after the one referred to only by a pronoun is hanging on the Cross (Mk 15:21-34). A third general tendency retained both the divinity and the humanity, but separated, as two distinct beings, the divine Christ from the human Jesus. According to their opponents, some Gnostics taught that Christ was a divine being who descended from the Pleroma, the divine realm, dwelling temporarily in the man Jesus to instruct the spiritual elect in saving knowledge, and then departed again before the crucifixion, though sending a power to raise up Jesus in a spiritual body, in which he remained for eighteen months instructing the spiritual elect who alone were capable of bearing the knowledge of the truth.[10]

As diverse as these approaches are, they share certain important features. The first is that they all attempt to circumvent the involvement of God with the Cross. Instead of the *kerygma* proclaiming that the

death, suffering

teousness. For the texts of their opponents, and discussion, see A. F. L. Klijn and G. J. Reinink, *Patristic Evidence for Jewish-Christian Sects* (Leiden: Brill, 1973).

8 Tertullian, *Against Marcion*, 1.19.

9 Such is the account of Basilides' teaching given by Irenaeus (*AH* 1.24.4); a similar account can be found in the Nag Hammadi text, *The Second Treatise of the Great Seth*, 56.

10 Cf. Irenaeus, *AH* 1.30.12-14.

crucified and risen one is Lord, God and Savior, they take refuge in a
secret teaching, for which they account by refashioning the narrative of
the scriptural Christ, in the case of the Gnostics into larger cosmic
dramas. The strength and wisdom of God are found elsewhere, rather
than in the weakness and folly of the Cross. The second point is that in
none of these approaches is God really "with us" (cf. Matt 1:23). As
Irenaeus pointed out, in none of these systems does the Word of God
actually become flesh (cf. *AH* 3.11.3). Here soteriology is understood
primarily as the revelation of secret knowledge, or in terms of exemplary righteousness, and so there is no requirement for the exchange of
properties between God and man, for Christ to share in our poverty so
that we may partake in his riches. Finally, a third common element is
that they share a rather crude, somewhat materialistic approach to
understanding the identity of Christ, thinking to explain his identity
by an analysis of his being, as if the divinity and humanity of Christ are
locatable "parts" of a composite being. So, it will later be argued, those
who hold that Christ is fully human, a "complete" or "perfect man"
(τέλειος ἄνθρωπος), such that there is no "remainder part" of his
being which can be divine, must also teach that he is merely human, a
"mere man" (ψιλός ἄνθρωπος). The docetists seem to have taken the
alternative route, and denied any genuine humanity in Christ at all; in
this case Christ is fully, but only, divine. The third tendency tries to
maintain both elements, but does so by denying the unity of Christ. As
Irenaeus points out, they "divide the Lord … saying that he was
formed of two different substances" (*AH* 3.16.5); it is not Christ who
suffers in the flesh (1 Pet 4:1), but the human Jesus who suffers, while
the divine Christ remains aloof. This compositional approach to
Christology, and the problems it raises, appears at various points in the
theological debates of the early centuries, for instance at the Council of
Antioch in 268/9 and its condemnation of Paul of Samosata, and most
dramatically, a century later, with Apollinarius of Laodicea.

In various ways, then, the reflection on and interpretation of Christ
selectively focused on one particular explanation. Just as the apostles
and evangelists had selectively utilized the oral reports about Christ in
their presentation of Christ according to the Scriptures, read in the
light of the Passion, so also the ever-increasing number of works

claiming apostolicity were narrowed down to a canonical collection of Scripture,[11] the hypothesis of which, as articulated in the canon of truth, is that one and the same Jesus Christ is both what it is to be God and what it is to be man. Before looking more closely at the development of this pattern of theology, a further issue must be briefly addressed. The combined effect of applying diverse scriptural titles to Christ, in the light of the Passion, was the reinterpretation of the meaning and content of these titles, resulting in a distinctive figure, the scriptural Christ. If the process of selection continued in patristic reflection, then did the process of reinterpretation and transformation also continue? And if so, did the theological endeavor end up with a different Christ than that presented in the New Testament?

There is certainly a development, in the sense that the *kerygma* becomes crystallized in the canon of truth, which is the very presupposition for a "canonical New Testament." Though tempted otherwise, patristic reflection ultimately had nothing else to work with apart from what was presented in the *kerygma*, as it is contained in Scripture, both Old and New Testament, and as it is also expressed, for instance, in the Eucharist, especially the anaphora, which, in its classic forms, is a rehearsal of Scripture culminating in the partaking in Christ's body and blood, and in baptism, performed in the name of the Father, Son and Holy Spirit, the three articles of the canon of truth. While this *kerygma* may be expressed in the eucharist, and although the significance of the eucharist for Christology was at times an issue,[12] the primary source for this *kerygma* was of course Scripture. As Irenaeus comments, "since therefore the tradition from the apostles does exist in the Church, and is permanent among us, let us revert to the exposition from the Scriptures of the apostles who wrote the Gospel, in which they recorded the doctrine regarding God, pointing out that our Lord Jesus Christ is the truth" (*AH* 3.5.1). Theology developed by reflecting upon Scripture, but, as discussed earlier, it did so selectively. As theology attempted to remain true to the *kerygma*, it found itself focusing ever more restrictively on

---

11   The general tendency of the "apocryphal" material is to expand the details of the earthly life of Jesus rather than elaborating on the proclamation of the crucified and risen Christ.

12   See the classic study of H. Chadwick, "Eucharist and Christology in the Nestorian Controversy," *JTS* ns 2.2 (1951), 145-64.

particularly important and disputed texts of Scripture, which were
cited in the manner of proof-texts rather than exegeted. In this transition from *kerygma* to dogma, a certain reinterpretation of the material
handed down did take place, though this does not necessarily entail
any distortion. Just as the Septuagint and the writers of the New Testament had themselves done, the Fathers utilized the language and con-
cepts of their environment to pursue their reflection. The language
used was philosophical, and became increasingly so, as christological
reflection focused ever more precisely upon the issues it was dealing
with. In this, there was the danger that the philosophical language used
might overshadow the theological *kerygma* it was attempting to articulate or that the reflection might dissolve into mythology. But the
danger is more often our own; in concentrating on the details of ever
more abstract theology, it is easy to lose sight of just what is being written about. One must keep in mind that just as the apostolic *kerygma*
about Lord Christ refers to none other than the earthly Jesus, so also,
patristic theology, even at its most abstract, always refers back to the
kerygma, as its defense and confirmation, which it was always intended
to be.

꙳

He asked to let the lion's teeth grind him like fine flour as Eucharistic bread.

3

Ignatius of Antioch

Ignatius was taken under guard from Antioch to Rome, to be martyred there in the early years of the second century. Along the way he was received by Polycarp, in Smyrna, where he was visited by Christians from the neighboring areas and also wrote letters to the churches in Ephesus, Magnesia, and Tralles, encouraging and exhorting them to keep steadfast in the unity of the faith and in unity with their bishop, and a fourth letter to the church in Rome, asking them not to interfere with his impending trial. After Smyrna, Ignatius was taken to Troas, where he wrote further letters to the churches of Philadelphia, Smyrna, and a personal letter to Polycarp. The letters of Ignatius are one of the most important early witnesses, outside the New Testament, to the development of both church structure and theological reflection.[1] Ignatius emphasizes very strongly the importance and centrality of the bishop, flanked by his presbyters and deacons, for the constitution of the Church; without these three orders, the community cannot be called a "church" (*Trall.* 3.1). He urges the Smyrneans, for example, to follow the bishop as Christ follows the Father, and to do nothing pertaining to the church without the bishop; without him, they are neither to baptize nor hold an *agape*, and only that eucharist which he, or his delegate, celebrates is to be considered certain (βεβαία); in sum, "whenever the bishop appears, let the congregation be present, just as wherever Christ is, there is the

---

[1] For discussion concerning the authenticity of the collection of seven Ignatian letters, the middle recension, used in this chapter, see the R. Hübner, "Thesen zur Echtheit und Datierung der sieben Briefe des Ignatius von Antiochen," *ZAC* 1 (1997), 44-72; and the replies by A. Lindemann, "Antworf auf die 'Thesen zum Echtheit und Datierung der sieben Briefe des Ignatius von Antiochen," *ZAC* 1 (1997), 185-94; G. Schöllgen, "Die Ignatian als pseudepigraphisches Brief-corpus. Anmerkung zu den Thesen von Reinhard M. Hübner," *ZAC* 2 (1998), 16-25; and M. Edwards, "Ignatius and the Second Century. An Answer to R. Hübner," *ZAC* 2 (1998), 214-26.

catholic church" (*Smyrn.* 8). That there is only one Christ means that there can only be one eucharist, one altar, one bishop (*Phld.* 4). However, this emphasis on the role of the bishop, monepiscopacy, should be neither overstated nor construed in terms of the later "monarchical" bishop.[2] The obedience that the Smyrneans owe to their bishop, for instance, is also due to the presbyters (*Smyrn.* 8.1). Ignatius likewise urges the Magnesians and the Ephesians to do nothing without the bishop and the presbyters; they are to obey both, and also be subject to one another (*Magn.* 7.1, 13.2; *Eph.* 2.2, 20.2). More importantly, the bishop is not, for Ignatius, the successor of the apostles, nor are the apostles reckoned as the first bishops. Rather, in the typological parallels that Ignatius draws between, on the one hand, the Father, Christ and the apostles, and on the other, the bishop, deacon and presbyters (*Trall.* 3.1; *Magn.* 6.1), the apostles are always placed on the eternal, universal level of the Church, along with Christ and His Father, while the ranks of clergy are historically and geographically specific. Ignatius repeatedly states that as a bishop himself, he is not in a position to give orders as did the apostles (διατάσσομαι, *Rom.* 4.3; *Eph.* 3.1; *Trall.* 3.3); it is the apostles who have laid the ordinances (διαταγμάτων, e.g. *Trall.* 7.1). As Christ was subject to the Father, and the apostles to Christ and the Father, Ignatius will even speak of the precepts or teachings (δόγμα) as coming from the Lord and the apostles together (*Magn.* 13.1),[3] and when, in reverse, Christians refresh or encourage (ἀναψύχειν) the bishop, it is to the honor of the Father of Jesus Christ *and the apostles* (*Trall.* 12.2). For Ignatius, the position of the apostles in the work of God in Christ (cf. *Magn.* 7.1) is foundational for the Church at all times and in all places, in contrast to the circumscribed role of the bishop.[4]

2　Cf. A. Brent, "The Relations between Ignatius and the *Didaskalia*," *Second Century*, 8.3 (1991), 129-56.

3　Clement of Rome, a decade earlier, makes a similar point: "The apostles received the Gospel for us from the Lord Jesus Christ, Jesus the Christ was sent from God. The Christ therefore is from God, and the apostles from the Christ. In both ways, then, they were in accordance with the appointed order of God's will." *First Epistle of Clement*, 42.1-2.

4　The same disjunction is made in the *First Epistle of Clement*, 44. This heavenly authority of the apostles is rejected by W. R. Schoedel, *Ignatius of Antioch*, Hermenia (Philadelphia: Fortress Press, 1985), 112-3; but upheld by C. E. Hill, "Ignatius and the Apostolate: The Witness of Ignatius to the Emergence of Christian Scripture," forthcoming in *St. Patr.*

As such, the unity of Christians with their one bishop, in the one eucharist celebrated on the one altar, is dependent upon a prior unity in the apostolic faith. So, in his letters, which with the exception of the letter to Polycarp are addressed to the churches at large, Ignatius urges all his recipients to remain steadfast in the unity of the true faith. He exhorts them all to "be deaf when anyone speaks apart from Jesus Christ" (*Trall.* 9.1), and "not even listen to anyone unless they speak concerning Christ in truth" (*Eph.* 6.2). There are many "specious wolves" out there, Ignatius warns, so "the children of the light of truth [must] flee from division and evil teaching," and, as sheep, follow the shepherd (*Phld.* 2). However, to be able to discriminate in this manner requires a knowledge of the true teaching about Jesus Christ, and so Ignatius fulfills his pastoral duty by repeatedly stating what he holds to be the true faith. So, for example, after his opening greeting to the Smyrneans, he immediately turns to state the key elements of this faith:

> I glorify Jesus Christ, the God who has thus made you wise, for I observed that you are established in an immovable faith, as if nailed to the Cross of the Lord Jesus Christ, both in flesh and spirit, and firmly established in love by the blood of Christ, fully persuaded with regard to our Lord that he is truly of the family of David according to the flesh, Son of God with respect to the will and power of God, truly born of a virgin, baptized by John, that all righteousness might be fulfilled by him, truly nailed [to the tree] for us in the flesh under Pontius Pilate and Herod the Tetrarch—from the fruit of which are we, from his divinely blessed Passion—that he might raise an ensign to the ages, through his Resurrection, for his saints and faithful, either among the Jews or the Gentiles, in the one body of his Church. (*Smyrn.* 1)

Recounting the various events proclaimed in the Gospel, culminating in the Passion and Resurrection, this passage contains all the essential elements of faith in Jesus Christ that will later be cast into creedal form. Echoing both Isaiah (5:26; 49:22; 62:10) and Ephesians (2:16), it is the Cross of Christ, raised as an ensign or banner, that unites all the faithful, who are established in their faith by being, as it were, nailed to his Cross, making them, as the fruit of his Passion, into the one body of his Church. This passage also echoes the idea of Christ's double lineage, from David and from God, found already in Paul (e.g., Rom 1:3-4). The emphasis that Christ has "truly" undergone all these things, is most probably a reaction to docetist teaching, which Ignatius mentions elsewhere (*Trall.* 10; *Smyrn.* 2-4). Thus aspects of the *kerygma* which might previously have been taken for granted, that Jesus Christ was indeed a man, now have to be stated explicitly. It is also noteworthy how Ignatius emphatically describes Christ as God, using the articular "God" (ὁ θεός) in a quite dramatic fashion. This is characteristic of Ignatius, and could well indicate his familiarity with the Gospel according to John. Yet, as with John, this use of the articular "God" for Jesus is predicated upon the recognition that he is the Son of (the one true) God, his Father.

Crystallized statements of faith, such as this passage, are also found in the writings of the New Testament (e.g., Rom 1:3-4; 1 Cor 8:6; 1 Tim 2:5-6; 1 Pet 3:18-22).[5] However, with Ignatius these statements of faith are used not only to expound the content of the Gospel, in kerygmatic fashion, but also to act as a test or criterion of true belief (cf. *Trall.* 9-10), just as the First Epistle of John discerned false spirits by the confession that Christ has indeed come in the flesh (1 Jn 4:2-3). Ignatius' statements of faith are more developed, reacting against errors which have since arisen. This faith is, according to Ignatius, what his readers must adhere to if they are to remain within the bounds of correct belief; they are meant both as a safeguard against specific threats, and also as a norm for Christian belief. Ignatius makes these statements in a similar fashion to the way in which Irenaeus later appeals to the canon of truth. Ignatius also follows the New Testament pattern of combining doctrinal norms with ethical norms (e.g., Jn 13:35; 1 Jn 2:7-10); statements of faith are to be confirmed by actual deeds. According to Ignatius, those who have strange opinions (ἑτεροδοξοῦντας) concerning the grace of Christ and are contrary to the mind (τῇ γνώμῃ) of God, have no love, neither for the widow, nor the orphans, the distressed, afflicted, prisoners, the hungry nor the thirsty (*Smyrn.* 6.2).

Rarely, however, does Ignatius intimate the source for his proclamation. He knows the letters of Paul, and refers to them in the plural (*Eph.* 12.2), perhaps even as a collection,[6] and his writings are certainly

---

5 Cf. J. N. D. Kelly, *Early Christian Creeds*, 3rd edn. (London: Longman, 1972), 1-29.
6 Gamble, *Books and Readers*, 58-65.

imbued with the thought and vocabulary of both Paul and John, though this is only to be expected, given that they are dealing with the same proclamation. However, Ignatius never appeals to their writings to substantiate his own theological affirmations. For Ignatius the content of this proclamation, Jesus Christ, is also the locus of revelation, "the mouth which cannot lie by which the Father has spoken truly" (*Rom.* 8.2). Ignatius is focused upon the revealer and the revelation, not the instruments by which that revelation has been mediated to him. Ignatius is certainly unambiguous about the role of the apostles in establishing the Church, and their work alongside Christ in the delivery of precepts or teachings (cf. *Magn.* 13.1), but he does not actually defer to the apostles, let alone their literary remains, to substantiate what he himself writes. While it was almost certainly not even possible for him to refer to Scripture or the apostolic writings while escorted to Rome under guard, Ignatius gives no indication that he feels any need to validate his statements of faith in this way.[7] Ignatius simply continues proclaiming the Gospel, preaching and teaching, just as Timothy was exhorted to do (1 Tim 4:13). And the various statements of faith he gives for his readers, to enable them to discern true teaching, function as "the pattern of sound words" (ὑποτύπωσιν ὑγιαινόντων λόγων) which Timothy had heard and was exhorted to follow (2 Tim 1:13), a reference point which would later be supplied by the canon of truth. Ignatius also has to bring out particular aspects of this pattern, facets that had previously been unstated, to address his current situation. In this context, it is also noteworthy that despite his emphasis on the centrality and importance of the bishop, Ignatius nowhere explicitly connects the role of the bishop with teaching. Rather, as with Clement of Rome, the focus of the role of the bishop is primarily cultic and sacramental.[8] Nor does Ignatius derive this role of the bishop from any apostolic institution, but rather legitimizes it himself by speaking

7 Ignatius does occasionally refer to Scripture, though not in the context of giving statements of faith: two quotations from Scripture are introduced by "it is written" (γέγραπται, *Eph.* 5.3, *Magn.* 12); an allusion to Is 52:5 is introduced by "for" (γὰρ, *Trall.* 8.2); only on one occasion does he give the words of Jesus (*Smyrn.* 3.2), the nearest parallel being Lk 24:39, though it cannot be a quotation; and despite the numerous allusions to the writings of Paul and John, none are given as quotations.

8 Cf. *First Epistle of Clement*, 40-1.

prophetically, "I cried out while I was with you, I spoke with a great voice—with God's own voice— "Give heed to the bishop and to the presbytery and deacons."[9]

However, while Ignatius may not appeal to Scripture to any great extent in his expositions of Christian teaching, the Christ he writes about is, nevertheless, intimately related to the Scriptures and the Gospel preached by the apostles. In the writings which would later be grouped together as the New Testament, the relationship between Christ, the Gospel and Scripture, though ever present in the background and, indeed, intrinsic to the proclamation of Christ "according to the Scripture," was not itself directly addressed (though it is intimated in 2 Cor 3:12-4:6). It was, however, a direct point of contention between Ignatius and some Christians from Philadelphia. The theme is introduced in chapter five of the letter to the Philadelphians, where Ignatius speaks of the "bonds" of Christ which he bears, entreating the Philadelphians for their prayers that he may be made perfect for God, so that he can attain the lot wherein he has found mercy,

> taking refuge in the Gospel as in the flesh of Jesus, and the apostles as the presbytery of the Church. And the prophets also do we love, because they also have announced the Gospel, and are hoping in him and waiting for him, by faith in whom they also obtain salvation, being united with Jesus Christ for they are worthy of love and saints worthy of admiration, approved by Jesus Christ, and numbered together in the Gospel of common hope. (*Phld.* 5.1-2)

The prophets have announced the Gospel, which is related to the flesh of Christ as the apostles are the archetype of the college of presbyters (*Trall.* 3.1; *Magn.* 6.1). The prophets were waiting for him, for it is in him that they obtain salvation, in the Gospel of common hope. Therefore, both the prophets and the apostles preached Christ, and as such both have the same authority. Moreover, there is thus only one revelation of God, in and through Jesus Christ, a revelation already anticipated in Scripture.

9 *Phld.* 7.1. Cf. D. E. Aune, *Prophecy in Early Christianity and the Ancient Mediterranean World* (Grand Rapids, Mich.: Eerdmans, 1983), 291-3. Clement of Rome could also claim to compose his letter "through the Holy Spirit," *First Epistle of Clement*, 63.2; cf. 59.1.

Later in the same letter, Ignatius reports a discussion he had had with the Philadelphians. After exhorting his listeners to do nothing apart from that which is "according to the teaching of Christ" (κατὰ χριστομαθίαν), he says that he heard some saying:

> 'If I do not find it in the charters (ἐν τοῖς ἀρχείοις),[10] I do not believe it in the Gospel.'
> And when I said to them, 'It is written' (γέγραπται), they answered me, 'that is exactly the question' (ἀπεκρίθησάν μοι ὅτι πρόκειται). (*Phld.* 8.2)

That Ignatius speaks of the Gospel in the singular, and the way in which he uses the term in other parts of this letter (*Phld.* 5.1, 2; 9.2), as well as elsewhere (*Smyrn.* 5.1; 7.2), suggests that he is referring to a proclamation rather than a written work.[11] Those whom Ignatius was addressing were clearly only prepared to accept the Christian message insofar as it was in accord with what was already written, Scripture. When Ignatius replied, "it is written," again he is not referring to an apostolic writing, but to his conviction that "the charters," Scripture (the "Old Testament"), does indeed contain the revelation of Christ. His interlocutors would not accept this; Ignatius' christological interpretation of Scripture answered none of their problems. Realizing on reflection where the issue lay, Ignatius stated his opinion much more clearly in the letter, which continues:

> But to me the charters are Jesus Christ (ἐμοὶ δὲ ἀρχεῖά ἐστιν Ἰησοῦς Χριστός), the inviolable charter is his Cross, and Death, and Resurrection, and the faith which is through him—in these I desire to be justified by your prayers. The priests are noble, but the High Priest who has been entrusted with the Holy of Holies is greater and he alone has been entrusted with the secret things of God; he is the door of the Father, through which enter Abraham and Isaac and Jacob and the Prophets and the Apostles and the Church. All these things are joined in the unity of God. But the Gospel has somewhat of pre-eminence (ἐξαίρετον δὲ τι ἔχει), the advent (τὴν παρουσίαν) of the Savior, our Lord Jesus Christ, his Passion and the Resurrection. For the beloved

10 The term τὸ ἀρχεῖον, was used for "public records," "archives." Cf. H. G. Liddell and R. Scott (*A Greek-English Lexicon*, rev. ed. H. S. Jones [Oxford: Clarendon Press, 1996] s.v.). That here it refers to "Scripture," see Schoedel, *Ignatius*, 208.

11 Schoedel, *Ignatius*, 208, n.6; C. T. Brown, *The Gospel and Ignatius of Antioch*, Studies in Biblical Literature, 12 (New York: Peter Lang, 2000).

prophets had a message pointing to him, but the Gospel is the perfection of incorruption. (*Phld.* 8.2-9.2)

Ignatius's opening statement here is somewhat ambiguous: is it the charters which are Jesus Christ for him or Jesus Christ who is his charters?[12] Given that Ignatius has been trying to persuade his disputants that Scripture does indeed speak of Christ, that it is indeed "written" thus, as he has just affirmed, it does not seem plausible that he should now make an about turn to state that he was speaking of something else all along, that his own charters are in fact "Jesus Christ" in distinction to "the charters" of his Judaizing disputants, Scripture.[13] Certainly Jesus Christ alone, his Passion and Resurrection, is the sole locus of the revelation of God; it is only through this door, Jesus Christ, that the prophets, apostles and all those who have harkened to their call, the Church, enter to the Father. But for Ignatius, the prophets were already speaking about Jesus Christ. So, when Ignatius states that "to me the charters are Jesus Christ," he is not implying that Jesus Christ is a higher authority than Scripture (the "Old Testament"). Instead, for Ignatius, the archives when understood correctly speak of Jesus Christ, more, they *are* Jesus Christ, in the sense that he is the embodiment of Scripture, the Word made flesh. Everything that it has ever said, pertaining to the revelation of God, all Scripture, is identical with the revelation given in Christ.

All that the Gospel proclaims, in turn, has already been written down; the Gospel contains no new word or revelation. Its distinctiveness lies in the fact that it contains, and so re-presents, what had only been announced (cf. *Phld.* 5.2): the advent of Christ, his Passion and Resurrection. This does not detract, however, from the value of the

---

12 The assertion is taken in the second sense, that it is Jesus Christ alone, in distinction to the Scriptures, that is the norm for Christian faith, by J. B. Lightfoot (*The Apostolic Fathers,* part 2, vol. 2, 273) and D. van den Eynde (*Les normes de l'enseignement Chrétien dans la littérature patristique des trois premiers siècles* [Paris: Gabalda, 1933], 37); similarly Schoedel, who claims that Ignatius here appeals to a "higher authority" than Scripture (*Ignatius,* 209), and F. Young, who argues that he seems "to 'demote' the ancient scriptures in comparison with Christ" (*Bibilical Exegesis,* 59, cf. 15-16). E. Flesseman-van Leer, on the other hand, argues otherwise (*Tradition and Scripture in the Early Church* [Assen: Van Gorcum, 1954], 34-5).

13 In his debate with Judaizing Christians, Ignatius goes so far as to assert, "Christianity did not base its faith on Judaism, but Judaism on Christianity" (*Magn.* 10.3).

revelation of Christ himself: as Ignatius puts it, the Gospel has something preeminent, for it *has* the advent (παρουσία) of Christ, his Passion and Resurrection, while the prophets were only pointing towards it. As such, all the prophets looked to him and spoke of him, as Ignatius put it elsewhere, for "they lived according to Jesus Christ" and "were inspired by his grace" to proclaim "that there is only one God, who has manifested himself through Jesus Christ his Son, who is his Word proceeding from silence" (*Mag.* 8:2). On the connection between Christ and the Gospel, it is also worth noting how Ignatius exhorts his readers to pay heed to the prophets and especially to the Gospel, "in which the Passion has been revealed to us and the Resurrection has been accomplished."[14] The inseparability, for Ignatius, of Christ and the Gospel is further shown in his comment that "Jesus Christ, being now in the Father, is more plainly visible" (*Rom.* 3.2): it is in the apostolic preaching of the crucified and risen Christ, embodying Scripture ("according to the Scriptures," though this formula is not found in Ignatius), that we see and understand Jesus Christ, rather than through a merely "earthly" contact with him or traditions purporting to derive from him. It is in the *kerygma*, the preaching about the crucified and risen Christ, that we can see and understand who Jesus Christ is.

Despite not appealing to Scripture or the writings of the apostles in his presentation of the Christian faith, Ignatius is nevertheless thoroughly within the perspective of seeing Christ in terms of the apostolic interpretation of Scripture: Jesus Christ, whose flesh is seen in Gospel proclaimed by the apostles, is the embodiment of Scripture. Given this matrix of his theology, and his evident familiarity with the Johannine theology if not literature, it is somewhat surprising that Ignatius rarely describes Jesus Christ as the Word of God. One passage where he does this has already been noted, but deserves closer attention. According to Ignatius, the prophets lived according to Jesus Christ and tried to persuade the disobedient people that "there is one God who manifested

---

14 *Smyrn.* 7.2: ἐν ᾧ τὸ πάθος ἡμῖν δεδήλωται καὶ ἡ ἀνάστασις τετελείωται. On the significance of the term τετελείωται, Lightfoot simply comments that "the word cannot signify… 'is demonstrated, assured, attested.'" (*The Apostolic Fathers*, part 2, vol. 2, 308).

himself through Jesus Christ, his Son, who is his Word proceeding from silence, who in all respects was well-pleasing to him that sent him" (*Magn.* 8.2). Ignatius is emphatic that there is only one God, and that it is this God whom the Son reveals, implying further that the Son is as divine as the Father. The image of the Son proceeding from silence has been taken by some to be an echo of a Gnostic view of Christ, revealing an unknown God,[15] or to refer to the decline and absence of prophets in the period prior to Christ, so that God appeared to have stopped speaking through the prophets resulting in a silence from which the Word appears. A more immediate explanation is simply that if Jesus Christ is, for Ignatius, the sole locus of the revelation of God, "the mouth which cannot lie by which the Father has spoken truly" (*Rom.* 8.2), the "door of the Father" (*Phld.* 9.1) already announced by the prophets, then all else apart from him is silence. This again emphasizes the identity between revealer and revelation: the one by whom the Father speaks, the one who delivers to us the Word of God, is himself the Word of God.

Alongside this deepening reflection on the matrix within which Jesus Christ is to be understood, Ignatius also reflects on the double lineage of Christ, found in Paul, and does so by considering further the two aspects of Christ himself, again perhaps influenced by the Johannine predilection for holding opposites, divinity and flesh, together in unity without mitigating their tension. One of the most striking examples from Ignatius comes from his letter to the Ephesians (7.2):

> There is one Physician,
> both fleshly   and spiritual,
> born (γεννητὸς)   and yet eternal (ἀγέννητος),
> in flesh,   God,
> in death,   true life,
> both from Mary   and from God,
> first passible   and then impassible,
> Jesus Christ our Lord.

The first contrast probably comes from Romans 1:3-4, as does the fifth, from Mary (i.e. descended from David), yet from God (cf. *Smyrn.* 1,

---

15 For comments and discussion see Schoedel, *Ignatius*, 120-1, and Edwards, "Ignatius and the Second Century," 222-6.

cited above). The second contrast would be the cause of much confusion several centuries later. In the way in which the terms were later employed, "begotten" (γεννητός) was used as the particular characteristic of the Son distinguishing him from the Father, who alone is "unbegotten" (ἀγέννητος), and so one could no longer use this latter term to refer to the eternity of Christ. Accordingly Theodoret changed the text to "and from the unbegotten" (καὶ ἐξ ἀγεννήτου), so destroying the balance of Ignatius' words. Ignatius is not, however, using these terms in their later technical trinitarian sense, but to specify that Christ belongs both to the temporal world, as having been born, and to the divine, eternal realm. Likewise, the third contrast, "in flesh, God" (ἐν σαρκὶ γενόμενος θεός), should not be taken in a fourth-century, Apollinarian, perspective, where the divine Word inhabits flesh, taking the place of the soul. Rather, Ignatius is simply reaffirming the point that in the one physician, Jesus Christ, God has indeed become flesh. Finally, although Jesus Christ was passible (παθητός), subject to all the things which belong to created being, such as change and death, nevertheless *through* his death he has manifested true life and impassibility. This passage is as close as Ignatius gets to a "two-nature" Christology. It is clear that Ignatius affirms all the key points which will later be made: one Lord Jesus Christ, who is both divine and human, with all the properties pertaining to both, and does so in a manner which remains true to the Gospel itself. Ignatius does not mitigate either the divine or the human, by separating different elements in the composition of Jesus Christ: for Ignatius, the one who suffered is impassible, demonstrating life in death.

In other passages Ignatius explores the significance of the suffering of God by connecting it to his own impending suffering. For instance:

> Be deaf, therefore, when anyone speaks to you apart from Jesus Christ, who was of the family of David, and of Mary, who was truly born, both ate and drank, was truly persecuted under Pontius Pilate, was truly crucified and died in the sight of those in heaven and on earth and under the earth; who was also truly raised up from the dead, when his Father raised him up, as in the same manner his Father shall raise up in Christ Jesus us who believe in him, without whom we have no true life. But if, as some affirm who are without God—that is, are unbelievers—his suffering was a pretence (τὸ δοκεῖν)—although they are a pretence—why am I a prisoner, and why do I

pray to fight with the beasts? In that case, I am dying in vain. Then indeed I
am lying concerning the Lord. (*Trall.* 9-10)

Ignatius again emphasizes the central aspects of the Christian proclamation concerning Christ, though this time, without describing his
double lineage. What is particularly interesting is the way that this confession of faith is intrinsically connected, for Ignatius, to witness, and
for Ignatius himself this is realized in a very personal way, in his impending death as a martyr. As the faith which is confessed is that of the
death and resurrection of Christ, so also our acceptance of this faith is
also our death and resurrection with him. And our belief in him is our
life, again pointing to a Johannine influence. Undergoing death in witness to Christ, the "perfect man" (*Smyrn.* 4.2) or the "new man" (*Eph.*
20.1), is a birth into a new life, to emerge as Christ himself, a full
human being:

> It is better for me to die in Christ Jesus than to be king over the ends of the
> earth. I seek him who died for our sake. I desire him who rose for us. The pains
> of birth are upon me. Suffer me, my brethren; hinder me not from living, do
> not wish me to die. Do not give to the world one who desires to belong to God,
> nor deceive him with material things. Suffer me to receive the pure light; when
> I shall have arrived there, I shall become a man. Suffer me to follow the exam-
> ple of the Passion of my God (τοῦ πάθους τοῦ θεοῦ μου). (*Rom.* 6)

This is one of the strongest affirmations, from the early centuries, of
the real involvement of one who is God in the affairs of this world, to
the point of suffering and death, the "theopaschite" affirmation that
the one who underwent the Passion is indeed God. Yet the one so confessed is at the same time a human being, of a stature that can only be
attained by following the example of Christ (cf. Eph 4:13). For
Ignatius, moreover, the connection between the Passion of Christ and
the title "Word of God," is also shared by one who confesses Christ in
martyrdom. Ignatius beseeches the Romans not to interfere with his
martyrdom, but rather to keep silence, "For if you are silent concerning me, I am a word of God (ἐγὼ λόγος θεοῦ); but if you love my flesh,
I shall be only a cry" (*Rom.* 2.1). By undergoing the same martyr's
death as Christ, the suffering God, he hopes to attain to the true light,
to true manhood after the stature of Christ, and so, to be a word of
God, rather than only an inarticulate cry.

4

Justin Martyr

With Justin Martyr we begin to enter a very different world to that of the New Testament and Apostolic Fathers such as Ignatius. While they wrote to Christian communities, the extant writings of Justin are directed outwards, ostensibly at least, towards pagans in his *Apology* and its "postscript" (the so-called *Second Apology*), probably written in the middle of the reign of the Emperor Antoninus Pius (c. 150-5), and towards the Jews in his *Dialogue with Trypho the Jew*, written a few years later. In the opening chapters of the *Dialogue*, Justin describes his search for truth, through the various philosophical schools, and how he was converted to Christianity by being directed, by an anonymous old man, to the Scriptures. Justin eventually ended up in Rome, as had Marcion and Valentinus, where he gathered a group of disciples around himself, one of whom, according to Irenaeus, was Tatian.[1] The *Martyrdom of Justin* describes how he met with his disciples "above the baths of Martin," where he "imparted the words of truth" to those who wished to come.[2] This community was not a place of catechetical instruction alongside an otherwise constituted church; Justin's companions were not converted by him, but claimed instead to have received "the good confession" from their parents.[3] Rather, such Christian communities, of which there were many in Rome, embraced all the dimensions of ecclesial life, including the liturgical.[4] Justin himself provides a precious description of how his community celebrated baptism and the eucharist, and gathered together weekly, on Sundays, for the reading of Scripture, instruction and exhortation by the president (ὁ προεστώς) of the

---

1   Irenaeus, *AH* 1.28.1.
2   *The Martyrdom of Justin*, A 3 and B 3.
3   Ibid., A 4 and B 4.
4   On the organization of the Church in Rome during the second century, see P. Lampe, *Die stadtrömischen Christen*, and A. Brent, *Hippolytus and the Roman Church*.

community, the offering of prayer and the eucharist, and the gathering and distribution of charity (*Ap.* 61, 65-7).

The writings of Justin are much more sophisticated than those of Ignatius, both in their mode of demonstration and in their content. Justin continues to reflect on the *kerygma*, but now tries to relate almost everything he states to the Scriptures, and occasionally makes reference to the writings of the apostles. His interest in Scripture is primarily in terms of its prophetic character, referring to Christ: Moses is the first of the prophets (*Ap.* 32.1), and the whole of Scripture can be referred to simply as "the prophets." Justin frequently refers to "the prophetic Spirit" as speaking through the passages of Scripture, though, as all these prophecies refer to Christ, the inspired prophets do not speak from themselves but "by the divine Word who moves them" (*Ap.* 36.1). It is probable that, when writing his *Apology*, Justin knew some form of Christian testimony-book, a handbook of passages from Scripture, each accompanied by an exegesis referring it to Christ, and perhaps even having these passages arranged according to the basic structure of the *kerygma*.[5] When composing the *Dialogue*, on the other hand, Justin seems to have had recourse to the complete text of Scripture, for, although he refers to the same scriptural passages, he gives them at greater length and in the Septuagint version. Occasionally his inherited exegesis does not always fit with the longer text, which may indeed have been of a hebraizing recension as Justin frequently complains.[6]

Justin also uses Scripture differently in his two works. As the *Apology* is written for pagans, he does not appeal in it to the Scriptures as an authoritative source of truth. Rather he appeals to them to provide evidence that the Gospel believed in by Christians is not simply the latest claims, but ancient prophecies, written in publicly available books, which have now been fulfilled in Christ:

> But lest anyone should argue against us, what prohibits [the claim that] the
> one we call Christ, being a man born of men, performed what we call his

---

5   For full discussion, see O. Skarsaune, *The Proof from Prophecy: A Study in Justin Martyr's Proof-Text Tradition: Text-Type, Provenance, Theological Profile* (Leiden: Brill, 1987), esp. 228-34.

6   Skarsaune, *Proof*, 43-6.

mighty deeds by magical art, and by this appeared to be the Son of God?—we will now offer proof, not trusting in mere assertions, but being of necessity persuaded by those who prophesied [these things] before they came to pass, for with our own eyes we see things that have happened and are happening, just as they were predicted; and this will, we think, appear even to you as the strongest and truest evidence. (*Ap.* 30)

This method of using the Scriptures is often referred to as the "proof from prophecy"—the attempt by Christians to relate what they claim about Christ to these ancient texts, so answering the charge of novelty by assuming the mantle of antiquity, and appropriating (illegitimately) this body of literature in a supersessionary "cultural take-over bid."[7] Justin himself, however, did not consider his use of Scripture to be an *ad hoc* attempt to establish points of contact between Scripture and the events of Christ's life, because, for him, Scripture itself is the primary source for our knowledge of these events. Thus, after explaining who these prophets were, and how their works came to be translated into Greek, Justin continues by specifying what it is that these prophets foretold:

In these books, then, of the prophets, we found foretold as coming, born of a virgin, and growing to adulthood, and healing every disease and every sickness, and raising the dead, and being hated and unrecognized, and crucified, Jesus our Christ, and dying, and rising again and ascending into heaven, and being and being-called the Son of God, and certain persons being sent by him to every race of men proclaiming these things, and [that] from the Gentiles, rather, people would believe in him. (*Ap.* 31.7)

The claim that all these things are found in Scripture might seem far-fetched, and the proof from prophecy therefore no more than an *ad hoc* measure. As an interpretation of the text of Scripture it is implausible, according to the canons of modern hermeneutics. But the interpretation here is *of Christ*, accomplished by exegeting Scripture from the perspective of the *kerygma*. It is the *kerygma* itself that gives the basic structure to the sequence of events, centered upon the crucified Jesus Christ (following the Greek word order), as outlined by Justin.[8] Yet it is Scripture, read in this manner, which supplies the fabric of this

---

7 Cf. Young, *Biblical Exegesis*, 49-54; the phrase is found on p. 51.
8 It also is the order of sections of Justin's works, cf. Skarsaune, *Proof*, 139-64.

proclamation. This means that, on the one hand, the apostolic preaching is both the key to understanding the prophetic character of Scripture and simultaneously the confirmation of its fulfillment, while, on the other hand, it is Scripture itself that is the matrix within which the Christian revelation takes form. What Justin claims to find in Scripture is the account of Christ already presented within the terms of Scripture. There is unquestionably a certain circularity involved here, but it is one which turns, as it were, upon the Scriptural Christ himself, who is presented as "according to the Scriptures" and, within this account, as himself revealing the way in which Scripture refers to himself.[9] The meaning and content of Scripture here is not a human construction, but is Christ himself, the Word of God, latent in what is written, Scripture, but clearly proclaimed in and as the Gospel of God.

The weakness of this approach is evident in the *Dialogue with Trypho*. Here, in the form of a dialogue with a Jew, Justin does not need to argue for the legitimacy of the appeal to Scripture, but instead needs to demonstrate that the correct reference of Scripture is indeed Christ, that Isaiah 7:10-17, for instance, refers to Christ not Hezekiah (*Dial.* 77). As they are using Scripture in two different ways—Justin to attain, through the Scriptures, the "knowledge of the Christ of God" (*Dial.* 8.2); Trypho to establish the original, or at least what was by then the traditional meaning, and so confirm the ancestral religion[10]—a resolution of the debate is not possible. What is at issue here is the presupposition, or hypothesis, by which one finds meaning from these texts, and ultimately, as with all first principles, this is based on faith. Although Justin does not articulate this principle with the philosophical sophistication of Clement of Alexandria,[11] he makes the same point by appealing to "the grace of understanding." Just as Paul had claimed that it is only by the Holy Spirit that one can say "Jesus is Lord" (1 Cor 12:3), that is, understand Jesus in terms of the Divine Name of God revealed in Scripture, so Justin also points out that "the grace of understanding"

9   For full discussion, see Chapter One.
10   For the importance, for those who returned from exile, of establishing from the Scriptures the patterns of life of their ancestors, see J. L. Kugel, "Early Interpretation: The Common Background of Late Forms in Biblical Exegesis," in J. L. Kugel and R. A. Greer, *Early Biblical Interpretation* (Philadelphia: Westminster Press, 1986), 31-51.
11   See the discussion in Chapter One, 33-4.

the Scriptures is required if they are to be interpreted as speaking of Christ (cf. *Dial.* 92.1; 119.1).[12] The Scriptures only became clear when, after the Resurrection, Christ taught his apostles to consult the prophecies (*Ap.* 50.12) and removed their "obscurity" by persuading the apostles that the prophets did indeed explicitly announce his suffering and Lordship (*Dial.* 76.6). It is thus Christ himself who has "revealed to us all that we have understood from the Scriptures by his grace," that he is the firstborn Son of God and son of the patriarchs, born of the virgin, a man without comeliness or honor and subject to suffering (*Dial.* 100.2). This "grace of understanding," in other words, is nothing other than the apostolic demonstration from Scripture. It was revealed by the scriptural Christ and proclaimed by the apostles. However, once revealed, Justin seems to hold that this demonstration is clear and cogent, and that it is therefore possible to teach it to others: "God's grace alone was given to me to understand his Scriptures, of which grace I exhort everyone to share freely and abundantly"—by following this exposition (*Dial.* 58.1). If Trypho refuses to accept the validity of this apostolic demonstration, it is because of his hardness of heart (e.g., *Dial.* 53.2) or his fear for the penalty of death inflicted upon Christians (*Dial.* 44.1). Moreover, if Trypho persists in refusing to understand this interpretation of Scripture, he has, according to Justin, forfeited his right to them: these things, Justin tells Trypho, "are contained in your Scriptures, or rather not in yours but ours, for we believe them, but you, though you read them, you do not catch the spirit (τὸν νοῦν) in them" (*Dial.* 29.2). A further corollary of the position which Justin takes with regard to the interpretation of Scripture is that, for him, Scripture is thought of as one whole, homogenous work. Given the uniqueness of the revelation of God in Christ, to which the whole of Scripture testifies, it is impossible, moreover, that there could be any contradiction in Scripture or that any part of it does not have significance. If Trypho presents him with an apparent contradiction, Justin simply admits his inability to understand the passage fully.[13]

12 My comments on this topic follow Skarsaune, *Proof,* 11-13.

13 Cf. *Dial.* 65.2. According to H. von Campenhausen, Justin was the first to have a "doctrine of holy scripture" (*The Formation of the Christian Bible*, trans. J. A. Baker [Philadelphia: Fortress Press, 1972], 88).

As well as speaking of Christ, Scripture, according to Justin, also foretold the apostles who would proclaim the Gospel about Christ (cf. *Ap.* 31.7 cited above); the authority of the apostles is thus grounded in that of Scripture, and they are also, therefore, scriptural characters. According to Justin, Isaiah 2:3-4, "Out of Zion shall go forth the Law and the Word of the Lord from Jerusalem," refers to the twelve illiterate men who "by the power of God proclaimed to every race of men that they were sent by Christ to teach all the Word of God" (*Ap.* 39.3). The Word of God spreads out from Jerusalem through the apostles. After Christ, and on his command, the apostles are the source and vehicle of the Christian faith in the world; it is through them that the voice of God's glory and grace has filled the earth. More importantly, the apostles are not just representatives or delegates of Christ, for it is Christ himself who speaks through them:

> Our Jesus Christ, being crucified and dead, rose again, and having ascended to heaven, reigned; and by those things which were preached by him through the apostles among all the nations (καὶ ἐπὶ τοῖς παρ' αὐτοῦ διὰ τῶν ἀποστόλων ἐν τοῖς πᾶσιν ἔθνεσι κηρυχθεῖσιν) there is joy afforded to those who expect the incorruption promised by him. (*Ap.* 42.4)

Just as it is the Word of God or the Spirit of God who spoke through Moses and the prophets in Scripture, so now it is Christ who preached through the apostles. This parallel is brought out by Justin in the *Dialogue:*

> For as he [Abraham] believed the voice of God, and it was imputed to him for righteousness, in like manner we, having believed God's voice spoken again through the apostles of Christ and preached to us through the prophets, have renounced even to death all the things of the world.[14]

The apostles can be put alongside the prophets, as mouthpieces of God, because they have conveyed the same message, confirming what had previously been announced.

Not only does Justin reflect more deeply on the role of the apostles, but he also utilizes much more frequently and concretely the writings of the apostles, in particular the Synoptics.[15] He refers to their writings

---

14 *Dial.* 119.6: καὶ ἡμεῖς τῇ φωνῇ τοῦ θεοῦ, τῇ διά τε τῶν ἀποστόλων τοῦ Χριστοῦ λαληθείσῃ πάλιν καὶ τῇ διὰ τῶν προφητῶν κηρυχθείσῃ ἡμῖν...

15 Justin's knowledge and use of Paul and John remains a subject of debate. For a trenchant statement to the effect that Justin deliberately refrained from making any reference to

as "memoirs" (τὰ ἀπομνημονεύματα), a word which was used by Xenophon for his work, the *Memorabilia* (of Socrates, cited by Justin in *App.* 11), and which would be used soon after by Philostratus to describe his collection of material for the lives of the Sophists, collections which consisted principally of their sayings. Justin also has Trypho refer to "the so-called Gospel" which contains the Christian precepts (*Dial.* 10.2), and himself refers to "the Gospel" in which the words of Christ have been written (γέγραπται, *Dial.* 100.1), and, moreover, notes that the memoirs composed by the apostles are also called "Gospels," using the word for the first time in the plural (*Ap.* 66.3). Justin also mentions that "the memoirs of the apostles or the writings of the prophets" were read during the Sunday services of his community,[16] and that it is in these memoirs that the apostles delivered what had been enjoined upon them concerning the celebration of the eucharist (*Ap.* 66.3). Given the associations of his preferred word, "memoirs," it is sometimes argued that the value of these works for Justin is primarily as historical documentation, recording the factuality of the events reported about Jesus Christ.[17] Justin's argument, however, works in the opposite direction: he offers proof from the prophetic writings specifically so that we do not have to put our trust in mere assertions.[18] Justin's concern is *not* with the historicity of the apostolic accounts of Christ, but rather with the continuity of their preaching

them, see C. H. Cosgrove, "Justin Martyr and the Emerging Christian Canon: Observations on the Purpose and Destination of the *Dialogue with Trypho*," *VC* 36 (1982), 209-32; and, for a critique of this position, see C. E. Hill, "Justin and the New Testament," *St. Patr.* 30 (Leuven: Peeters, 1997), 42-8. The only quotation of John (Jn 3:3-5 at *Ap.* 61.4) noted by B. Metzger seems in fact to have more in common with Matt 18:3 (*The Canon of the New Testament: Its Origin, Development, and Significance* [Oxford: Clarendon Press, 1989], 147). There are also sayings attributed to Jesus (*Dial.* 47.5: "In whatsoever things I shall take you, in them I shall judge you"), and pieces of information about him (*Dial.* 88.8, that he was a carpenter), which are not found in the canonical New Testament.

16 *Ap.* 67.3. Too much weight should not be given to the fact that the apostolic writings were read in the context of worship; Eusebius preserves a letter written in the middle of the second century from Dionysius of Corinth to Soter in Rome, which mentions how, on the holy day of the Lord, they had read out the letter written to them by Clement of Rome and the letter of Soter himself (*EH* 4.23.11).

17 As argued by H. Koester, *Ancient Christian Gospels: Their History and Development* (London: SCM Press; Philadelphia, Trinity Press, 1990), 42.

18 Cf. *Ap.* 30, cited above, and *Dial.* 48.4: "we were enjoined by Christ himself to put no faith in human doctrines, but in those proclaimed by the blessed prophets and taught by himself."

with that of Scripture. Yet, although the apostolic preaching is now sometimes derived from their literary remains, this remains a corpus distinct from Scripture itself, though intrinsically related to it: to demonstrate that their content is the same, Justin refers to the words of Christ written in the apostolic memoirs and correlates it to what the grace of Christ has enabled us to understand from the Scriptures (*Dial.* 100.1-2). Justin recognizes that not all of these memoirs are actually apostolic, but asserts that those which were not written by the apostles themselves were drawn up by those who followed them (*Dial.* 103.8). The locus of authority is the apostles, and so everything to do with the Christian revelation must be capable of being traced back to the apostles.[19]

While the greatest concern of Justin, at least in the *Dialogue*, is the relationship between Scripture and the apostolic preaching, he also turns his attention to the proclamation about Christ, and attempts to determine the essential elements of the Christian faith. For instance, in *Dialogue* 46-7, Trypho asks Justin whether a man will be saved who wants to fulfill the prescriptions given by Moses and yet who believes in this Jesus who was crucified, recognizing him as the Christ of God, who has received the judgement over all men and whose kingdom will be everlasting. After trying to convince Trypho of the futility of the Mosaic prescriptions, Justin does concede that someone who believes these things about Jesus will be saved, as long as he does not insist that others also fulfill the Mosaic prescriptions. It would seem, then, that the items of belief mentioned constitute, as it were, the essence of the Christian faith, at least for that specific context. A similar issue arises later in the *Dialogue*, where, against some "so-called Christians," Justin takes the faith in the God of Abraham, Isaac and Jacob, and the affirmation of the resurrection of the dead (rather than the soul being taken to heaven at death), as the key affirmations of the Christian faith. But he also admits the existence of some Christians who, as he puts it, "belong to the pure and pious faith," that is, who accept the items of faith just mentioned, yet who do not accept the teaching concerning the millennial kingdom held by those who are "right-minded

---

19 Papias had already recorded the tradition that Mark had acted as Peter's interpreter in writing out his Gospel (Eusebius, *EH* 3.39.15); Irenaeus will later make the connection between Luke and Paul (*AH* 3.1.1).

Christians on all points" (ὀρθογνώμονες κατὰ πάντα Χριστιανοί, *Dial.* 80). Justin therefore does seem to have some kind of standard or canon in mind for the Christian faith, which he believes it is necessary to hold, even if there are permissible variations within it. He makes no attempt, however, to articulate it expressly, nor to explain how it relates to Scripture or the Gospel.[20]

Given the concern that Justin has for Scriptural demonstration, it is not surprising that Christ appears, in the writings of Justin, primarily as the teacher (διδάσκαλος),[21] the one who opens up Scripture so that it can be read with understanding as referring to himself. Jesus Christ is "our teacher and interpreter (ἐξηγητής) of the prophecies which were not understood" prior to his appearance (*Ap.* 32.2). This teaching of Christ, as in the New Testament and the Apostolic Fathers, includes both theological aspects and moral implications: "let those who are not found living as [Christ] taught (ὡς ἐδίδαξε) be understood to be no Christians, even if they profess with their lips the precepts (διδάγματα) of Christ" (*Ap.* 16.8). The teaching of Christ, as with Christ himself, is made known through the apostles; people from all races have been "persuaded by his teaching through the apostles," and have abandoned their former ways, turning to Christ (*Ap.* 53.3).

Besides this didactic dimension, there are also many passages in Justin which reflect more specifically on the relation of Christ to the Father, and his role within the overall plan of God. As with Ignatius, these often take the form of summary statements of faith.[22] For instance:

> We say that the Word, who is the first offspring (γέννημα) of God, was begotten without carnal intercourse, Jesus Christ our teacher, and that He was crucified, and died, and rose again, and ascended to heaven. (*Ap.* 21.1)

The subject of this sentence is still Jesus Christ, the Word of God, and it is he who is the first offspring of God, begotten without sexual

---

20 A. Grillmeier suggests that "what the *regula fidei* means for Irenaeus and Tertullian, the christological intention is for Justin—mutatis mutandis—in his exposition of scripture." (*Christ in Christian Tradition*, vol. 1, 90). The weight of Justin's work is certainly concerned with the Christocentric reading of Scripture, and, as explored in Chapter One, this is the basic dynamic of the canon of truth, but Justin does not really attempt to use this interpretative method as a canon.

21 Cf. *Ap.* 4.7; 12.9; 13.3; 15.5; 19.6; 21.1; 32.2; *App.* 8.5.

22 For a list of such statements see Kelly, *Early Christian Creeds*, 70-6.

union, and who was crucified, died, rose again and ascended. However, in the way that Justin phrases the sentence, the first point of reference is the Word, who thus appears as the offspring of God. This subtle shift in focus intimates a deeper change which needs to be addressed later. Although Justin is known for his "Logos-theology," he uses many of the other scriptural terms to describe Christ, often bringing them together:

> It is wrong, therefore, to understand the Spirit and the Power of God as anything other than the Word, who is also the First-born of God, as the prophet Moses declared; and it was this which, when it came down upon the virgin and overshadowed her, caused her to conceive, not by intercourse, but by power. (*Ap.* 33.6)

It is the Word himself, who is also the Spirit and the Power of God, who forms for himself a body in the virgin's womb by power.[23] With Justin the term "Word" is certainly becoming the central term for describing Jesus Christ, but it is by no means exclusive; Justin can use it alongside other terms which soon drop out of theological use, such as "Angel" and "Apostle" (*Ap.* 63.5). Moreover, it is also still possible for Justin to make a distinction between Christ and the Word of God. For instance, in his description of the liturgical celebrations of his community, Justin explains why the eucharist is not open to all:

> For not as common bread and common drink do we receive these; but in like manner as Jesus Christ our Saviour, having been made flesh by the Word of God (διὰ λόγου θεοῦ σαρκοποιηθεὶς Ἰησοῦς Χριστὸς), had both flesh and blood for our salvation, so likewise have we been taught that the food which is blessed by the prayer of his word (τὴν δι᾽ εὐχῆς λόγου τοῦ παρ᾽ αὐτοῦ εὐχαριστηθεῖσαν τροφήν), and from which our blood and flesh, by transformation, are nourished, is the flesh and blood of that Jesus who was made flesh. (*Ap.* 66.2)

Christ is made flesh and blood *by* the Word of God, and by his word we also make the bread and wine into his flesh and blood. The fluidity with which these terms can still be used by Justin is also shown by his description of the precepts taught by Christ: "Brief and concise

---

23   When Justin refers to the Word as the "Spirit" of God, it is unlikely that he intends this in the sense of a "binary" theology (as perhaps is indicated in *The Shepherd* of Hermas, *Similitude,* 5.6.5-6), but simply as a reference to the "pre-Incarnate" state of the Word, on which, more later.

utterances (βραχεῖς δὲ καὶ σύντομοι λογοί) come from him, for he was no sophist, but his word (ὁ λόγος αὐτοῦ) was the Power of God" (*Ap.* 14.5). The concise words uttered by Christ, the word of him who is himself the Word and Power of God, is also the Power of God: the identity between revealer and revelation, the scriptural Christ and his interpretation of the Scriptures, cannot be divorced into separate categories by restricting the designation "Word of God" to either the medium or the message exclusively.

This increasing use of the term "Word" was no doubt due to Justin's apologetic aim of dialoguing with pagan philosophers. But this dialogue reciprocally influenced Justin's theology in various ways. The first modification is the result of the "middle-platonic" framework within which Justin attempts to articulate the relation between Christ and the Father.[24] Although Justin speaks in the traditional manner of Jesus Christ, as the Word, revealing God, he shares the common philosophical presupposition of his day that as God is so totally transcendent to created reality he needs an intermediary, his Word, to act for him and to mediate between himself and creation. Commenting on the theophany in Exodus 3, Justin states:

> ...the God who said to Moses that he is "the God of Abraham and the God of Isaac and the God of Jacob," [is] not the Creator of all things, but the one who has been proved to you to have appeared to Abraham and Jacob, ministering to the will of the Creator of all... For no-one, who has but the smallest intelligence, will dare to say that the Maker and Father of all things, having left everything beyond the heavens, became visible on a tiny portion of earth. (*Dial.* 60.2)

Similarly, when Scripture says that "The Lord spoke with Moses" or that "God shut Noah into the ark," Justin asserts:

> You must not imagine that the unbegotten God himself came down or went up from any place. For the ineffable Father and Lord of all has no place... but remains in his own place, wherever it may be... he is not moved or confined to a spot, even the whole world, for he existed before the world was made. (*Dial.* 127.1-2)

24 For Justin's philosophical background, see C. Andresen, "Justin und der mittlere Platonismus," *ZNTW* 44 (1952/3), 157-95; M. J. Edwards, "On the Platonic Schooling of Justin Martyr," *JTS* ns 42.1 (1991), 17-34; C. Nahm, "The Debate on the 'Platonism' of Justin Martyr," *Second Century,* 9.3 (1992), 129-51.

As it was not God himself who thus appeared and spoke with man, the Word of God who did all of these things is, for Justin, "another God and Lord besides (ἕτερος παρὰ) the Maker of all," who is also called his "Angel," as he brings messages from the Maker of all, "above whom there is no other God" (*Dial.* 56.4). The one who appeared to Abraham, Jacob and Moses, and who is also called God, is thus distinct from the Maker of all things, "in number but not in will," for he has done only what the Creator of the world wished (*Dial.* 56.11). Justin is clearly trying to find a way to explain how it is that Jesus Christ is God, yet distinct from the God and Creator of all, his Father. However, his manner of explanation, in terms of the divinity of the ineffable Father being transcendent in a manner which prohibits him from being seen on earth, in fact undermines the very revelation of God in Christ. The divinity of Jesus Christ, an "other God," is no longer that of the Father himself, but is subordinate to it, a lesser divinity, and so it would no longer be true for the agent of such a theophany to claim, as Christ does, "he who has seen me has seen the Father" (Jn 14:9). This position would later be criticized by Irenaeus, though without mentioning any names. For Irenaeus, such subordination would destroy the whole economy: if God himself has not become visible in his Son, Jesus Christ, then no real communion between God and man has been established. This same debate would be played out a couple of centuries later, between the Arians, for whom the transcendence of God was preserved by the mediating activity of the Son as a lower divinity, and Athanasius, for whom the Son, consubstantial with the Father, "true God from true God," was the guarantee that God had indeed come into the closest possible contact with the world.[25]

Irenaeus' explanation of this subordinationist tendency points to a second modification, a corollary to the first, made by Justin. According to Irenaeus, what was said by the prophets, about God being seen on earth, was said prophetically, and does not mean "as some allege, that, the Father of all being invisible, the one seen by the prophets was another [God]. Yet this is what those declare who are altogether ignorant of prophecy."[26] For both Ignatius and Justin, it is the Word who

25 Cf. Hanson, *The Search for the Christian Doctrine of God*, 422-6.
26 Irenaeus, *AH* 4.20.5.

reveals God. However, for Ignatius, the prophets looked forward to Christ as the sole locus of revelation, while for Justin, the revelation of God in the Incarnate Word is the last, even if the most important, in a series of discrete revelations. Commenting again on Exodus 3, with the help of Matthew 11:27, Justin addresses the Emperor in this way:

> Now, the Word of God is his Son... And he is called Angel and Apostle: for he declares whatever we ought to know, and is sent forth to declare whatever is revealed... But these words are for the sake of proving that Jesus the Christ is the Son of God and His Apostle, being formerly the Logos (πρότερον λόγος ὢν) and appearing sometimes in the form of fire and sometimes in the likeness of angels; but now (νῦν δὲ), by the will of God, having become man for the human race, he endured all the sufferings which the devils instigated the senseless Jews to inflict upon him... The Jews, being throughout of the opinion that the Father of the universe had spoken to Moses, though he who spoke to him was the Son of God, who is called both Angel and Apostle, are rightly censured... [they do not know] that the Father of the universe has a Son, who, being the Word and the First-begotten, is even God. And formerly (πρότερον) he appeared in the shape of fire and in the image of a bodiless [angel], but now (νῦν δὲ), in the time of your rule, having become man by a virgin according to the will of the Father for the salvation of those who believe in him, he endured both to be set at nought and to suffer, that dying and rising again he might conquer death. (*Ap.* 63.4-16)

Justin here describes a series of revelatory events in which the Word has appeared in different forms. The last event in this sequence is, nevertheless, somewhat different, as the Word does not simply appear as man, but *becomes* man. Although Justin specifies that the Word has become man so that he can conquer death by his own death, this dimension of the work of Christ does not seem to have been as central for Justin, as it is was for Ignatius and Irenaeus; for Justin, Christ is primarily the teacher. The sequence of events outlined by Justin is not yet completed: some of the scriptural prophecies refer to the "first advent" of Christ, in which he is *preached* as inglorious, obscure and mortal, while others refer to the "second advent" (a term coined by Justin), when Christ will *appear* in glory (cf. *Dial.* 14.8). Through the Word's continuous work of revelation, Scripture is seen as describing a carefully-planned economy, with a beginning, purpose and an end. However, the change of perspective involved in portraying such a biography of the Word ultimately, and ironically, given the stated rationale of

Justin's subordinationism, makes this second God an inhabitant of the universe, sharing in its time and subject to change, temporalizing God.[27] Justin himself, in his extant works, does not give a continuous description of this history. This was first done by Irenaeus, in his *Demonstration of the Apostolic Preaching;* but Irenaeus does so having returned to the position of the New Testament and Ignatius, focused on the centrality and uniqueness of the revelation of God in Christ, the one to whom the prophets looked forward and about whom the Scriptures were written.

The third and equally pregnant area in which the influence of contemporary philosophy can be felt in Justin's further reflections on the Word of God is in his deployment of the idea of the "sowing Word" (λόγος σπερματικός) and the "seed of the Word" (σπέρμα τοῦ λόγου) implanted through this activity.[28] The background for this aspect of Justin's Logos theology is usually traced to an eclectic mixture of Stoicism, Middle-Platonism and Philo. The way that this idea is generally presented is to say that the Son of God, as the *Logos spermatikos,* implants in human beings a seed, a *sperma,* which enables them to think and live in accordance with the Logos. Such a seed of the Word gives them a dim perception of "the whole Word," the Son, so that some, like Plato and Socrates, were enabled, through their natural constitution (possessing a seed of the Logos), to live and think, or at least attempt to do so, according to the Word. So Justin can claim that Christ "was partially known even by Socrates, for he was and is the Word who is in every person" (*App.* 10:8), and that "whatever things were rightly said among all people, are the property of us Christians...

27 Just as Nicaea corrected subordinationism with its emphasis that the Son is true God of true God, by its denial of a temporal generation of the Logos it corrects any attempt to temporalize God. As R. Williams comments, "Rather paradoxically, the denial of the 'history' of transactions in God focuses attention on the history of God with us in the world: God has no *story* but that of Jesus of Nazareth and the covenant of which he is the seal. It is a matter of historical fact that the Nicene *verus Deus* was stimulus to a clarification of the *verus homo* in the century and a half after the council: the Word of God is the condition of there being a human identity which is the ministering, crucified and risen saviour, Jesus Christ; but the existence of Jesus is not an episode in the biography of the Word. It remains absolutely—and crucially—a fact of our world and our world's limits." (*Arius: Heresy and Tradition* [London: Darton, Longman and Todd, 1987], 244).

28 Cf. R. Holte, "Logos Spermatikos: Christianity and Ancient Philosophy according to St Justin's *Apologies,*" *Studia Theologica,* 12 (1958), 109-68.

For all the writers were able to see realities darkly through the presence in them of an implanted seed of the Word" (*App.* 13:4-5).

As Christians began to turn outwards to address the wider world, such a position would clearly have tremendous apologetic value. This idea has often been appealed to, either by those who want to maintain a place for a purely "natural theology," or by those who want to show how early Christian thinkers corrupted the pure evangelical message, incorporating elements of pagan thought. But this is not the last word of Justin on the matter. For in his *First Apology* (59-60), Justin also maintained that the Greek philosophers had read, and indeed plagiarized, Moses. Yet, despite this clue, little effort has been given to integrate Justin's "Logos theology" with the position found in his *Dialogue with Trypho the Jew*, where he devotes himself almost exclusively to scriptural interpretation. So there seem to be, as it were, two Justins: the Justin of the *Apologies*, who addressed the Greek world and was prepared to see in Greek philosophy a means of partially knowing God, and the Justin of the *Dialogue*, who engaged with Jewish thought, demonstrating on the basis of Scripture that Christ is indeed the Son of God.[29]

But nowhere does Justin indicate that he is aware of holding two unrelated theories concerning the knowledge of God, one through a natural kinship with the Word and the other through Scripture. In fact, Justin specifically rejects the possibility of there being a natural affinity between God and man permitting some kind of intuitive knowledge of God. In the prologue to the *Dialogue*, in the person of the old man who converts the young philosopher Justin to the ancient scriptural truths of Christianity, Justin renounces his earlier Platonism, and confesses that the mind has no innate natural communion or kinship with God by which it comes to a knowledge of God (*Dial.* 4).[30] Justin, however, does indicate an alternative framework for understanding his assertion that all men possess a seed of the truth or of the Word, in a passage from the *First Apology* where he integrates the two supposedly unrelated epistemologies:

29 The exception to this standard presentation is M. J. Edwards, "Justin's Logos and the Word of God," *JECS* 3.3 (1995), 261-80, to which the following paragraphs are indebted.
30 On the question of whether τὸ συγγενὲς, in *Second Apology* 13.3, refers to the Logos or the seer, see Edwards, *ibid.* 270-3.

> And whatever both philosophers and poets said about the immortality of
> the soul or punishments after death or of the contemplation of the heav-
> ens or other such doctrines, they have been able to know and have ex-
> pounded by beginning from the prophets (παρὰ τῶν προφητῶν τὰς
> ἀφορμὰς λαβόντες); hence there appear to be seeds of truth among all.
> (*Ap.* 44.9-10)

If seeds of truth are present in human beings, it is as the result of their
acquaintance with Scripture. Whatever one thinks of the possibility of
the Greek philosophers or poets actually having read the Hebrew
Scriptures (a point used by the apologists to demonstrate that Moses
was older, and so more authoritative, than them all),[31] it is a point of
importance for Justin: it is the principle by which he explains whatever
truths may be found in their writings. Discussing this passage, Edwards
comments:

> Here at least the theory of dissemination is also a theory of plagiarism; we
> have to do, not with two competing theories, but with complementary
> statements of the same one. Not nature, but the written text, is the vehicle
> of enlightenment, and the point of the metaphor lies not so much in any la-
> tent properties of the seed, as in the fact that it is sown.[32]

Edwards is referring to the characteristic employment of this metaphor
in Platonic and Stoic philosophy, for which the importance of a seed
lies in its potential for maturity; as an anticipation of the plant, the seed
already contains latent within itself that which it will be.[33] But the etymology of the word *sperma* (a cognate of the verb *speiro*, to sow), connects it, not so much to the growth of that which is already there, but
to the activity of sowing, the imparting of that which was not previously there, and this is the point which Justin makes.

For Justin, then, if human beings possess a "seed of the Word," it is
not as a natural property implanted in them. It is rather, as he specifies,
through encountering the words conveying the *Logos spermatikos*,
Christ, that some have received these seeds. Thus, in his scriptural
demonstration that Christ is the Son of God, the Word Justin appeals

---

31 On the "potential cultural take-over bid," implied by this claim, see A. J. Droge, *Homer or
   Moses? Early Christian Interpretation of the History of Culture* (Tübingen: Mohr, 1989) and
   Young, *Biblical Exegesis*, esp. 49-75.
32 Edwards, "Justin's Logos," 275.
33 *Ibid.* 274-8.

to, the Word which is often the subject of a verb, speaking to or through a prophet, implying an authorial responsibility for the words uttered thereby, nevertheless refers concretely to a text.[34] The Word is the ultimate author of that which is written as well as the meaning of that which is written when interpreted correctly. To do justice to Justin's simultaneous deployment of different meanings of the term *logos*, we must, as Edwards notes, "unify the original, divine *communication* with its material *expression* and the *sense* read into this by a discerning commentary."[35] This inherence of the divine Word in the words of Scripture and its meaning, is no mere sophistic play upon an accidental ambiguity, but is of the essence of divine revelation, as we have repeatedly seen: the inseparable unity of revealer and revelation.

One final instance of Justin's use of the terminology of "Word" should be noted. In the *Second Apology* Justin argues that the superiority of Christianity lies in the fact that Christians now know the Word in its entirety, rather than only partially, as had the philosophers. In the course of his argument, Justin comments on Christ himself:

> Our position is clearly more sublime than any teaching of man for this reason, that the logos-principle in its totality became the Christ who appeared for our sake, body, reason and soul (διὰ τὸ τὸ λογικὸν τὸ ὅλον τὸν φανέντα δι' ἡμᾶς Χριστὸν γεγονέναι, καὶ σῶμα καὶ λόγον καὶ ψυχήν). For all that the philosophers and legislators at any time declared or discovered aright, they accomplished by investigation and perception in accordance with that portion of the Word which fell to their lot. But because they did not know the whole of the Word, who is Christ, they often contradicted each other. (*App.* 10.1-3)

The subject of the sentence is the neuter, "the logos-principle," perhaps to be understood as some kind of inherent cosmological rationality as the Stoics, or the world-soul as for Plato, though, in view of what we have seen of the overall theology of Justin, it could also refer to Scripture, that which speaks about the Word of God, and which Jesus Christ, as preached by the apostles, embodies. For both the Stoics and for Plato, this rationality or world-soul is what sustains and orders the

---

34 E.g. [Justin asks] "Does not the Word through Zechariah say that 'Elijah shall come before that great and terrible day of the Lord'?" (*Dial.* 49:2; Mal 3:23 [4:5]); a structure repeated throughout the *Dialogue*.
35 Edwards, "Justin's Logos," 268.

cosmos; for Justin, this is identified with the Christ who has appeared for our sake, "body, reason (λόγος) and soul." This phrase, which echoes traditional tripartite anthropological formulae, emphasizes the completeness of Christ's being, rather than attempting to analyze the relationship in which the Word stands to the body, reason and soul that he has taken upon himself or become. With Justin we are not yet in a position of analyzing the being of Christ; however, by his extended use of the Word-terminology, his reflection on Scripture, and the beginnings of a sense of the history of revelation it contains, we have moved one step further.

5

Irenaeus of Lyons

The tangle of roads, represented by such diverse figures as Ignatius, Marcion, Valentinus, Justin, and numerous others, which met in Rome during the first half of the second century, found their resolution not in Rome, but further West, in Lyons. It is from here, shortly after the violent persecutions in Lyons and Vienne in 177 A.D., that Irenaeus was sent to Rome as an ambassador of peace between the churches, bearing letters from the martyrs to Eleutherius urging him to be reconciled with the Asian and Phrygian Christians.[1] Irenaeus was also from the East; in his youth he had seen and heard Polycarp of Smyrna, a man who had received the things concerning the Lord from the "eyewitness of the Word of Life" and had "reported all things in agreement with Scripture."[2] It is on this basis, the Gospel "according to the Scriptures" as delivered in the beginning by the apostles, that Irenaeus sought unity amongst the bewildering varieties of primitive Christianity, a basis which became the accepted framework for normative Christianity thereafter, or at least in the period considered in this series. This was the most significant transition in early Christianity. Thereafter Christians were committed to a common body of Scripture, including the apostolic writings (though the extent of the list would long be debated), the canon of truth, apostolic tradition and succession—a complex of themes examined in detail in Chapter One—in a unity of faith which marked out the "Great Church" from the various

---

1   The letter to Eleutherius introduces Irenaeus as a "presbyter" (*EH* 5.4.2), a word which at the time was used interchangeably with "bishop." P. Nautin suggests that Irenaeus was the head of the Christian community in Vienne, and that he is the author of the Letter from the Christians of Vienne and Lyons (given in that order) to the brethren in Asia and Phrygia (Eusebius, *EH* 5.1.3-3.3), and that when Pothinus of Lyons died during the persecution, Irenaeus received episcopal responsibility for both cities (*EH* 5.5.8; cf. P. Nautin, *Lettres et écrivains chrétiens des IIe et IIIe siècles* [Paris: Cerf, 1961], 54-61, 93-5).

2   Irenaeus, Letter to Florinus, in Eusebius, *EH* 5.20.5-6; cf. *AH* 3.3.4.

sects. Yet the unity of faith constituting the "Great Church" not only tolerated a variety of practices, but found in it a cause for celebration. When Irenaeus intervened in the dispute between Victor (189-98) and the Asian Christians of Rome concerning the keeping of the Christian Pascha, he pointed out to Victor that "the disagreement in the fast confirms our agreement in the faith."[3]

Only two writings of Irenaeus survive, the *Demonstration of the Apostolic Preaching* and the five books of *Against the Heresies*,[4] the third of which was written while Eleutherius was presiding in Rome (174-89). Despite a reference to *Against the Heresies* in the concluding chapters of the *Demonstration*, it seems, on account of its more primitive use of Scripture, that the *Demonstration* is the earlier work.[5] In it, Irenaeus gives a clear, coherent and concise exposition of the apostolic preaching, without, however, making extensive use of their writings. Rather, Irenaeus demonstrates that their preaching is "according to the Scriptures" by deriving the whole content of the apostolic preaching from Scripture, the medium through which the apostles had understood and proclaimed Christ. After outlining the faith handed down by the elders who had known the apostles, epitomized in the three articles of the "canon of faith"—the one God and Father; the one Lord, the crucified and risen Jesus Christ; and the one Holy Spirit—through which the baptismal regeneration is wrought (*Dem.* 3-7), Irenaeus turns to the two interrelated projects of this work: first, recounting, in the manner of the great apostolic speeches in Acts, the scriptural history of God's work of salvation culminating in Christ (*Dem.* 8-42a); second, demonstrating that what the apostles proclaimed as fulfilled in Christ, shaped as it is by Scripture, was indeed foretold in Scripture (*Dem.* 42b-97). At the beginning of the second part, Irenaeus observes that while, for God, the Son is in the beginning before the creation, he has only been revealed to us now (in the apostolic preaching) and so "before this he was not for us who did not know him" (*Dem.* 43). As such, it is only after having described the scriptural history which

---

3   Eusebius, *EH* 5.24.13.
4   This is the "title" as given by Eusebius (*EH* 3.23.3); Irenaeus refers to the work as *The Refutation and Overthrowal of Knowledge falsely so-called* (*AH* 4.Pref.1).
5   *Dem.* 99; this is also indicated by certain stylistic points of the Armenian used in the last two chapters. Cf. *St Irenaeus of Lyons: On the Apostolic Preaching*, trans. J. Behr, 118, note 229.

culminates in the apostolic preaching of Christ, a preaching which is articulated through the medium of that Scripture, that Irenaeus, in the second part of the *Demonstration*, is able to describe, retrospectively, how Jesus Christ was present throughout, being seen, in anticipation, by the patriarchs (cf. esp. *Dem.* 44-5) and being spoken of, in anticipation, by the prophets. The apostolic preaching, the presentation of Christ according to the Scriptures, is the key to understanding Scripture fully. In doing this, Irenaeus was following in well established tracks, and indeed many of the texts he uses, and the interpretation he gives them, can already be found in Justin. However, unlike Justin, whose exposition of Scripture in the *Dialogue with Trypho* takes place without any obvious order or structure, Irenaeus provides a complete, if brief, coherently arranged presentation in the *Demonstration*.

If Irenaeus does not make any great use of the apostolic writing in the *Demonstration*, the same cannot be said for *Against the Heresies*. Here the continuity between Scripture and the apostolic preaching is not only affirmed, but the apostolic writings are abundantly used as Scripture. Irenaeus directly addresses the challenges presented by Marcion and the Gnostics, and does so by appealing to the very texts of Paul and John upon which they claimed to stand and which other writers in the mid-second century, such as Justin, seemed reluctant to handle. Irenaeus knows and uses practically the full range of apostolic writings that are regarded today as canonical (with the exception of Philemon and 3 John). More importantly, Irenaeus insists that there can only be four Gospels, or rather, one Gospel in four forms (τὸ εὐαγγέλιον τετράμορφον, *AH* 3.11.8). The reasons given for this by Irenaeus—that there are only four winds and four corners of the earth—are hardly likely to persuade anyone who does not already accept the fact, but this is itself important: Irenaeus is musing on what is already a given fact, the fixed number of Gospels, rather than himself imposing the limit. In his debate with the Gnostics in *Against the Heresies* (especially in *AH* 1.8-10 and 3.1-5), Irenaeus examines the relationship between the *hypothesis* of Scripture and the canon of truth, the role of tradition and apostolic succession, before turning, in books three to five, to the exposition of the apostolic demonstrations from Scripture. On the basis of these interrelated canons, treated in detail in

Chapter One above, Irenaeus outlines the contours of what became the classical form of theological reflection.

Irenaeus departs from Justin's position, where the Word is a second God able to manifest *himself*, to reiterate the earlier position, that the Son reveals the Father. His characteristic position is that "the Father is the invisible of the Son, but the Son the visible of the Father" (*AH* 4.6.6). To suppose, as Justin had done, that the Son was distinct from the Father as "another God," one who, unlike the God of all, is able to come into contact with created reality, would simply undermine Irenaeus' theology—Christ would no longer be manifesting the Father, we would no longer be looking upon the one true God, and so would not be brought into communion with him. The Father of all is certainly invisible and infinitely beyond human comprehension, and so, Irenaeus argues, if human beings are to see him and thus enter into communion with him, rather than simply hear reports about him, a "measure" of the "immeasurable Father" (*AH* 4.4.2) is needed, and this is the Son, *in* whose human nature, rather than behind it, we can see the invisible Father.[6] Yet at the same time, the Son preserves the invisibility of the Father, so that human beings might never think they comprehend all there is to know, despising the Father and turning away from their source of life and thus become subject to death, but rather that there might always be something towards which they might advance, in order that the glory of God might continue to be demonstrated for, as Irenaeus concludes, "the glory of God is a living man, and the life of man consists in beholding God" (*AH* 4.20.7).

Similarly, against those who have misunderstood the workings of prophecy, Irenaeus returns to Ignatius' position that it is *only* in Jesus Christ that God is revealed. For Irenaeus all scriptural theophanies and visions are prophetic, pointing forward to Christ: "So Abraham was a prophet and saw things of the future, which were to come to pass, the Son of God in human form—that he was to speak with men and eat food with them... All such visions signify the Son of God speaking with mankind and being amongst them."[7] In such passages

6 Cf. Minns, *Irenaeus*, 38-43; R. Tremblay, *La Manifestation et la vision de Dieu selon saint Irénée de Lyon* (Münster: Aschendorff, 1978).

7 *Dem.* 44-45. For the continuation of this passage, and its relationship to Justin, see *St Irenaeus of Lyons: On the Apostolic Preaching*, trans. J. Behr, 110-11, note 127.

Irenaeus is not straightforwardly asserting that Jesus of Nazareth was visible before his Incarnation, that his human nature somehow pre-existed his birth in this world. Such visions are described as prophetic precisely because they announce what will happen. As Irenaeus puts it, in a long section (*AH* 4.20.1-22.2)[8] devoted to the subject of prophecy:

> In this manner, therefore, they did also see the Son of God as a man conversing with men; they prophesied what was to happen, saying that he who was not come as yet is present (*eum qui nondum aderat adesse*) and proclaiming the impassible as passible, and declaring that the One in the heavens had descended into the "dust of death" [Ps 21:16 LXX]. (*AH* 4.20.8)

Christ is not yet present, but his saving Passion, proclaimed in the Gospel, is already the subject of the prophets' words and visions. Similarly, having the Gospel pre-preached to him by Scripture, that in him all nations will be blessed (cf. Gal 3:8), "the prophet Abraham saw in the Spirit the day of the Lord's coming and the dispensation of his suffering," that those who follow his example, trusting in God and taking up the Cross as Isaac did the wood, might be saved (*AH* 4.5.4-5).

Not only is the subject of Scripture, from beginning to end, Jesus Christ, but he also is its ultimate author. Jesus Christ is, for example, the author of the covenants with Abraham and with Moses:

> One and the same Householder produced both covenants, the Word of God, our Lord Jesus Christ, who spoke with both Abraham and Moses, and who has restored us anew to liberty, and has multiplied that grace which is from himself. (*AH* 4.9.1)

Christ's claim, that "Moses wrote of me" (Jn 5:46), is taken by Irenaeus to mean that "the writings of Moses are his [Christ's] words," and extended to include "the words of the other prophets" (*AH* 4.2.3). This prophetic element is clearly important for Irenaeus, and it gives a very dynamic quality to his presentation of the economy of God unfolded in the scriptural history of salvation.[9]

---

8   For this division see P. Bacq, *De l'ancienne à la nouvelle Alliance selon S. Irénée: Unité du livre IV de l'Adversus Haereses* (Paris: Éditions Lethielleux, Presses Universitaires de Namur, 1978), 163-87.

9   For a presentation of Irenaeus' understanding of "the economy of God," see J. Behr, *Asceticism and Anthropology in Irenaeus and Clement* (Oxford: Oxford University Press, 2000), 34-85.

The key to Irenaeus' understanding of the mechanism of prophecy is to be found in the manner in which he relates the Gospel to Scripture. Irenaeus' focus is not on a continuous history of the Word of God, from the "Old Testament" to the "New Testament," in the sense of a continuity of personal subject acting throughout time in different ways and revealing God in a variety of forms, but rather on the unchanging and eternal identity of the Word of God as the crucified and risen Jesus Christ. Although the identity of the Word of God, the crucified and risen Jesus Christ, is revealed first in the Gospel, which is, as we will see, an epitome of Scripture, the same one is nonetheless the author of the Abrahamic and Mosaic covenant, as indicated in *AH* 4.9.1 cited above, and is indeed the author of the whole of Scripture and its subject throughout. Given this identity, Irenaeus exhorts Marcion:

> …read with earnest care that Gospel which has been given to us by the apostles, and read with earnest care the prophets, and you will find that the whole conduct, and all the doctrine and all the sufferings of our Lord, were predicted through them. (*AH* 4.34.1)

To those who, presented with such a claim, ask, "what new thing then did the Lord bring by his advent?" Irenaeus simply answers, "Christ himself!" Irenaeus compares this to the announcement of the arrival of a king and his actual arrival: the king's arrival is heralded beforehand, so that those who will entertain the king can prepare; the king's arrival brings nothing new apart from himself, though the joyful fulfillment of what had previously only been announced is itself a novelty—"Know that he brought all novelty by bringing himself who had been announced" (*AH* 4.34.1). As the prophets foretold all that would happen to and through Christ, the Law itself is therefore our pedagogue to Christ in the sense that it directs us to believe in him:

> For the Law never hindered them from believing in the Son of God; but it even exhorted them to do so, saying that men can be saved in no other way from the old wound of the serpent than by believing in him who, in the likeness of sinful flesh, is lifted up from the earth upon the tree of martyrdom and draws all things to himself and vivifies the dead. (*AH* 4.2.7)

It is by being lifted up on the tree, the Passion, that Christ draws all things to himself. When read from the perspective of the Cross, the

Law already points to the Gospel of Christ, which is thus seen to be the true meaning of Scripture.

In doing this, Irenaeus has simply taken further what had already been partially carried out by Ignatius and Justin. But Irenaeus also considered the reverse implications of this, giving us a further insight into his understanding of the mechanism of prophecy: if the apostolic preaching is drawn from Scripture, then those who wrote Scripture implanted the seeds of the Gospel. To elaborate this idea, Irenaeus modifies Justin's imagery of the seeds of the Word being inseminated in all men through their reading of Scripture. For Irenaeus, the one who is sown is Christ, and he is inseminated in Scripture. Irenaeus develops this idea in two important passages, *AH* 4.10 and 4.23-26, where it continues his discussion of the nature of prophecy. In *AH* 4.10, Irenaeus comments on the words of Christ in John 5:46, that "Moses wrote of me":

> [He said this] no doubt because the Son of God is implanted everywhere throughout his writings: at one time, indeed, speaking with Abraham; at another time with Noah, giving him the dimensions [of the Ark]; at another inquiring after Adam; at another time, bringing down judgement upon the Sodomites; and again, when he becomes visible, and directs Jacob on his journey, and speaks with Moses from the bush. The occasions are innumerable in which the Son of God is shown forth by Moses. (*AH* 4.10.1)

Here the witness of Moses to the presence of the Son of God is described in terms of the Son of God being inseminated throughout Scripture: *inseminatus est ubique in Scripturis ejus Filius Dei.* That is, the preexistence of Christ, the Word of God, is inextricably connected with his seminal presence in Scripture, the word of God. [10]

The discussion beginning in *AH* 4.23 is more extensive and penetrating. Irenaeus begins by citing the words of Christ in John 4:35-8, that the fields are ready for harvest and the disciples are sent to reap

---

10 *Dem.* 32 similarly indicates the scriptural preexistence of Jesus Christ, the Word of God: Christ was born from a virgin, that he might "demonstrate the likeness of embodiment (σάρκωσις) to Adam and might become the man, written in the beginning (καὶ γένηται ὁ γεγραμμένος ἐν ἀρχῇ ἄνθρωπος), 'according to the image and likeness of God.'" The Greek retroversion is by A. Rousseau (*Irénée de Lyon: Démonstration de la Prédication Apostolique*, trans. and annotations by A. Rousseau, SC 406 [Paris: Cerf, 1995], 268).

what others have sown. Irenaeus begins by identifying the sowers as those who have "helped forward the economies of God":

> It is clear that they are the patriarchs and prophets, who even prefigured our faith and disseminated throughout the earth the advent of the Son of God, who and what he should be: so that the posterity, possessing the fear of God, might easily accept the advent of Christ, having been instructed by the Scriptures. (*AH* 4:23:1)

It is for this reason that those who are familiar with the word of God (Irenaeus gives as examples Joseph and the Ethiopian eunuch) are ready to be instructed in the advent of the Son of God, the true interpretation of the text (*AH* 4:23:1-2). Those who do not know the word of God, the Gentiles, present a harder task, and for this reason, Irenaeus explains, Paul can justly say "I laboured more than the rest" (1 Cor 15:10). So, Irenaeus concludes:

> The patriarchs and prophets sowed the Word concerning Christ, but the Church reaped, that is, received the fruit. For this reason also, do these very men pray to having a dwelling-place in it, as Jeremiah says, "Who will give me in the desert the final dwelling-place" [Jer 9:1], "in order that both the sower and the reaper may rejoice together" [Jn 4:36] in the kingdom of Christ, who is present to all those to whom, from the beginning, God was pleased to make present the Word. (*AH* 4.25.3)

Christ is present with all those who disseminated the Word in Scripture, preparing in this way for the advent of Christ himself.

Irenaeus then continues, by linking his exposition of John 4 with an exegesis of Matthew 13, in a lengthy passage which deserves to be quoted in full:

> If anyone, therefore, reads the Scriptures this way, he will find in them the Word concerning Christ and a foreshadowing of the new calling. For Christ[11] is the "treasure which was hidden in the field" [Matt 13:44], that is, in this world—for "the field is the world" [Matt 13:38]—[a treasure] hidden in the Scriptures, for he was indicated by means of types and parables which could not be understood by men prior to the consummation of those things which had been predicted, that is, the advent of the Lord. And

---

11 Following the Greek preserved in the *Catena in Matt.* (*Irénée de Lyon: Contre les hérésies. Livre IV*, ed. A. Rousseau et al., SC 100 [Paris: Cerf, 1965], 712), the Latin simply has "Hic", and similarly the Armenian, indicating the unity between the word about Christ and Christ himself.

therefore it was said to Daniel the prophet, "Shut up the words and seal the book until the time of the consummation, until many learn and knowledge abounds. For when the dispersion shall be accomplished they shall know all these things" [Dan 12:4, 7]. And Jeremiah also says, "In the last days they shall understand these things" [Jer 23:20]. For every prophecy, before its fulfilment, is nothing but an enigma and ambiguity to men; but when the time has arrived and the prediction has come to pass then it has an exact exposition (ἐξήγησις). And for this reason, when at this present time the Law is read by the Jews, it is like a myth, for they do not possess the explanation (ἐξήγησις) of all things which pertain to the human advent of the Son of God; but when it is read by Christians, it is a treasure, hid in a field but brought to light by the Cross of Christ, and explained, both enriching the understanding of men and showing forth the wisdom of God and making known his dispensations with regard to man and prefiguring the kingdom of Christ and preaching in anticipation the good news of the inheritance of the holy Jerusalem and proclaiming beforehand that the man who loves God shall advance so far as even to see God and hear his Word and be glorified from hearing his speech to such an extent that others will not be able to behold his glorious countenance [cf. 2 Cor 3:7], as was said by Daniel, "Those who understand shall shine as the brightness of the firmament, and many of the righteous as the stars for ever and ever" [Dan 12:3]. In this manner, then, I have shown it to be, if anyone read the Scriptures. (*AH* 4.26.1)

The image given by Christ, of treasure hidden in the field, or the world, is used by Irenaeus to refer to Christ himself: prior to the Incarnation, or more exactly, prior to the Cross, Christ is hidden as a treasure in Scripture. Christ is hidden in Scripture in prophecies and types, in the words and events of the patriarchs and prophets, which prefigure what was to happen in and through Christ in his human advent as preached by the apostles. The patriarchs and prophets disseminated these prophecies and types throughout the world in the writings of Scripture, preparing those who read Scripture for the advent of Christ himself. However, they are only prophecies and types; what they indicate is not yet known. And so, for those who read Scripture without the explanation of what it is that they foreshadow, the Word they contain and the Gospel they anticipate, Scripture remains only myths and fables. It is through the Cross, the Passion of Christ, that light is shed on these writings, revealing what they in fact mean and how they are thus the Word of God. So, for Irenaeus, the crucified Jesus Christ, the Gospel of the apostles, was present prior to the Passion as the veiled content of Scripture, the Word of God hidden in the words of Scripture.

With regard to Christ being disseminated in Scripture, and, in reverse, being foreseen by the patriarchs and the prophets, it is particularly important to note that the mechanism turns upon the Cross: it is by the Cross that the types and prophecies are brought to light, given their proper exegesis. Irenaeus continues in the passage cited above by noting how this manner of reading the Scriptures was revealed only after the Passion, when the risen Christ demonstrated to his disciples from the Scriptures that "the Christ must suffer and enter into his glory" (*AH* 4.26.1; Lk 24:26, 47). Similarly, when the prophets say that "he who was not come as yet is present," they are "proclaiming the impassible as passible, and declaring that the one in the heavens had descended into the dust of death" (*AH* 4.20.8). In *AH* 5.17.4 Irenaeus again specifies that it is by the Cross that the Word is revealed. Discussing Elisha's actions in 2 Kings 6:1-7, and interpreting the axe by means of the words of John the Baptist (Matt 3:10), Irenaeus comments:

> By this action the prophet pointed out that the sure Word of God, which we, having negligently lost by means of a tree, did not discover, we should receive anew by the dispensation of a tree... This Word, then, which was hidden from us, did the dispensation of the tree make manifest, as we have said. For as we lost it by means of a tree, by means of a tree again was it made manifest to all, showing the height, the length, and the breadth, in itself; and, as one of our predecessors observed, "Through the extension of the hands, gathering together the two peoples to one God."[12]

This emphasis, that it is through the Cross that the Word is revealed, means that the Word of God is always related to the Cross, is always, as it were, cruciform. Just as the written Word of God is permeated by the figure of the Cross, Irenaeus also points out, following Justin, that

---

12 *AH* 5.17.4. It is important to note the explanation given for the significance of the Cross: the inclusion of the Gentiles. Cf. *AH* 4.2.7, cited above. R. Hays similarly notes that Paul's interpretive strategies are more ecclesiocentric, concerned with the inclusion of the Gentiles, rather than Christocentric, and that, when seen from this perspective, "[h]is typological reading strategy extends a typological trajectory begun already in the texts themselves," referring to the typological reading of Yahweh's dealings with Israel in Deut. 32 and Isaiah (*Echoes of Scripture*, 164, cf. 84-7).

the Word of God which adorned and arranged the heavens and earth is likewise cruciform.[13]

The claim that the crucified Christ, the Gospel preached by the apostles, unlocks the treasury of Scripture is simply the reverse side of the fact that the apostolic preaching of the Gospel is, from the beginning, "according to the Scriptures," exegeting Scripture to interpret Christ. In doing this, as indicated in Chapter One, the apostles and evangelists, and those writers who followed them, were doing what Israel had always done, employing Scripture to understand and explain the present by means of the past, so elaborating a typological relationship between past and present. What is unique about the Gospel, for Irenaeus, is precisely its claim to apocalyptic uniqueness: only through this act of God in Christ, as preached by the apostles, is Scripture seen to be types and prophecies referring to the one and only Word of God, rather than mere myths and fables.[14] Irenaeus appeals directly to this apocalyptic imagery in *AH* 4.20.2, where he points out that, as he has been given all things by his Father (Matt 11:27), Christ alone, as the judge of the living and the dead, has the key of David, and so he alone opens and shuts (Rev 3:7). Using the imagery of Revelation 5, Irenaeus continues:

> "No one, either in heaven or on earth, or under the earth, was able to open the book" of the Father, "nor to look into it," with the exception of "the Lamb who was slain and who redeemed us with his own blood," receiving from the same God, who made all things by the Word and adorned them by [his] Wisdom, power over all things when "the Word became flesh" [Jn 1:14]. (*AH* 4.20.2)

Only the slain Lamb has received all power, wealth, wisdom and might (Rev 5:12), and so he alone is able to open the book, and this, Irenaeus

---

13   Cf. *Dem.* 34, and Justin, *First Apology*, 60. This tradition is echoed, a couple of centuries later, by Gregory of Nyssa (*On the Three Day Period*, GNO 9.303; trans S. G. Hall, 48). Similarly, in the seventh century, Isaac of Syria (*The Second Part*, Chapter 11.3) comments, "We do not speak of a power in the Cross that is any different from that (power) through which the worlds came into being, (a power) which is eternal and without beginning, and which guides creation all the time, without any break, in a divine way and beyond the understanding of all, in accordance with the will of his divinity."

14   In *AH* 3.1.1, Irenaeus specifically notes that "we have learned from none other the plan of our salvation than from those through whom the Gospel has come down to us." For the pivotal role of the apostles in providing the christological key to Scripture, see Chapter One.

specifies, is the book of the Father. The revelation of the content, the Word, of the paternal book by the slain Lamb, is associated by Irenaeus, with the Word becoming flesh, for it is the enfleshed, revealed, Word who alone makes known or exegetes (ἐξηγήσατο) the Father, as the Prologue of John concludes (Jn 1:18). Just as the Gospel alone unlocks the treasures of Scripture, so also it is only in the Son, as preached in the Gospel, that the invisible and immeasurable God becomes visible and comprehensible, as Irenaeus repeatedly insists. The Cross is *the* definitive event in the revelation of God, occurring within our history yet with a significance that is eternal; the only perspective from which one can speak of the Word of God is that of the Cross. It is this retrospect opened up by the "eschatological *apokalypsis* of the Cross"[15] that facilitates the evangelical rereading of Scripture and the proclamation of Christ which, as we have seen, is the unique locus of the revelation of God.

For Irenaeus the subject is clearly always the crucified and risen Jesus Christ as preached by the apostles, and it is to him that all the various divine titles are attributed, just as in the book of Revelation it is to the one "clad in a robe dipped in blood" that the title "Word of God" is ascribed (Rev 19:13). Countering the Valentinian Ptolemy's interpretation of the Prologue of John, Irenaeus insists that the identity of the subject of predication, Jesus Christ, must be maintained:

> To be sure, John preached one God Almighty, and one Only-begotten Christ Jesus, through whom, he says, "all things were made"—this is the Word of God, this is the Only-begotten, this the Maker of all things, this "the true light who enlightens every man," this the Maker of the world, this the one who "came into his own," this the one who "became flesh and dwelt among us" ... [while the Gnostics maintain that the Only-begotten, Logos, Christ, etc. are all different aeons] But that the apostle did not speak concerning their conjunctions, but concerning our Lord Jesus Christ, whom he knows to be the Word of God, he himself has made evident. For, recapitulating what had previously been said by him about the Word in the beginning, he specifies, "the Word became flesh and dwelt among us." (*AH* 1.9.2)

All the divine titles are applied to Christ Jesus, and the recapitulation of everything that has previously been said is how Irenaeus interprets

15   The phrase is that of Hays, *Echoes of Scripture*, 169.

the statement that "the Word became flesh."[16] The Gospel of the crucified One is, as we have seen, the prism by which Scripture is seen as speaking of Christ, recapitulating what had previously been written in the proclamation of the earthly sojourn of the Word of God.

For Irenaeus, this relationship between Scripture and the Gospel, established by the preaching of the Cross, is precisely that described by the term "recapitulation" (ἀνακεφαλαίωσις). The background for this term, as many other key terms used by Irenaeus, such as *hypothesis* and *economia*, is literary or rhetorical theory.[17] According to the Roman Rhetorician Quintilian (40-90AD):

> The repetition and grouping of the facts, which the Greeks call ἀνακεφαλαίωσις [recapitulation] and some of our own writers call enumeration, serves both to refresh the memory of the judge and to place the whole case before his eyes, and, even although the facts may have made little impression on him in detail, their cumulative effect is considerable.[18]

In other words, recapitulation summarizes the whole case, presenting a restatement of the case or story in epitome, bringing together the whole argument in one conspectus, so that, while the particular details made little impact, the picture as a whole might be more forceful. Recapitulation provides a résumé which, because shorter, is clearer and therefore more effective. This idea of recapitulation as a literary summary is also used by Paul, when he comments that the various commandments of Scripture have been "summed up in this word (ἐν τῷ λόγῳ τούτῳ ἀνακεφαλαιοῦται), 'You shall love your neighbour as yourself'" (Rom 13:9).[19] And it is precisely in this way, and in reference to this passage, that Irenaeus explains how God has provided us with an epitome or résumé of the Law in the Gospel:

16 R. M. Grant commenting on this passage, suggests that "[h]is context is strictly literary when he asserts that the evangelist John 'sums up' the account in his prologue (John 1:1-13) by saying that the Word became flesh (1:14)." (*Irenaeus of Lyons* [New York: Routledge, 1997], 50).

17 Cf. E. Osborn, "Reason and the Rule of Faith in the Second Century AD"; R. A. Norris, "Theology and Language in Irenaeus of Lyons," *Anglican Theological Review*, 76.3 (1994), 285-95; P. Blowers, "The *Regula Fidei* and the Narrative Character of Early Christian Faith"; Grant, *Irenaeus*, esp. 46-53, "Rhetoric in Theology."

18 Quintilian, *Institutio Oratoria*, 6.1.1.

19 Most commentators on Irenaeus use Eph 1:10 as the basis of their interpretation, and so overlook the literary background of the term.

And that, not by the prolixity of the Law, but according to the brevity of faith and love, men were going to be saved, Isaiah, in this fashion, says, "he will complete and cut short [his] Word in righteousness; for God will make a concise Word in all the world" [Is 10.22-3; Rom 9.28]. And therefore the Apostle Paul says, "Love is the fulfilment of the Law" [Rom 13:10], for he who loves God has fulfilled the Law. Moreover, the Lord also, when he was asked, which is the first commandment, said, "You shall love the Lord your God with [your] whole heart and [your] whole strength; and the second is like it, you shall love your neighbour as yourself. On these two commandments," he says, "depend all the Law and the Prophets" [Matt 22:37-40]. So he has increased, by means of our faith in him, our love towards God and towards the neighbour, rendering us godly, righteous and good. And therefore he made "a concise word <...> in the world." (*Dem.* 87)

The prolixity of the Law, which only serves to render the Word of God obscure, invisible and incomprehensible, has been "cut short," resulting in a "concise word," which as an epitome or résumé is clearer and therefore more effective, increasing our faith in God, our love for him and our neighbour, and so providing salvation. Yet, while being "cut short," the Word of God remains identical; the Gospel, as the recapitulation of Scripture, is its fulfilment.

The recapitulation of Scripture in the Gospel provides Irenaeus with the key to understanding the person and work of Jesus Christ. This is dealt with most fully in *AH* 3.16-18, a section in which he counters the divisive tendencies of Gnostic Christologies and sets forth what he considers to be "the entire mind of the apostles regarding our Lord Jesus Christ" (*AH* 3.16.1). In an earlier chapter Irenaeus argued that his opponents keep the Word separate from the flesh, for according to none of them did the Savior really become flesh or suffer (*AH* 3.11.3). But, as Irenaeus points out, the apostles taught otherwise. John "knew one and the same Word of God, the only-begotten, incarnate for our salvation, Jesus Christ our Lord" (*AH* 3.16.2). This formula, "one and the same" (εἷς καὶ ὁ αὐτός) is used frequently by Irenaeus and thereafter became one of the basic assertions of the unity of the one Jesus Christ; it is, for instance, repeated many times within the Chalcedonian definition. Irenaeus continues by pointing out that Matthew, also "recognized one and the same Jesus Christ," when he recounted "his human birth from the Virgin": Matthew did not write that the "birth of Jesus took place in this way," but that "the birth of Christ took place in this way," who was called Emmanuel, so demonstrating that "the Son of God was born from a Virgin," in order that "we should not imagine that Jesus was one, and Christ another, but should know them to be one and the same" (*AH* 3.16.2). Irenaeus then points out that Paul also knew only one God and one Son, Jesus Christ, bringing together his statements concerning the appointing of Christ as the Son of God at the resurrection (Rom 1:1-4), his descent according to the flesh (Rom 9:5) and his birth at the fullness of time (Gal 4:4-5). Irenaeus indicates a similar position in Mark and Luke. And then concludes, apropos of Luke:

> The Gospel, therefore, knew of no other Son of man but him who was of Mary, who also suffered, and no Christ who flew away from Jesus before the Passion; but him who was born it knew as Jesus Christ, the Son of God, and that this same suffered and rose again, as John the disciple of the Lord verifies, saying, "These things are written so that you might believe that Jesus is the Christ, the Son of God, and believing you might have eternal life in his name" [Jn 20:31]—foreseeing these blasphemous systems (*regulas*) which divide the Lord, as far as lies in their power, saying that he was formed of two different substances (*ex altera et altera substantia dicentes eum factum*). (3.16.5)

There is one Jesus Christ, the one Son of God; he it is who was born, suffered and rose again. There are not two "parts," as it were, to Jesus Christ, one of which was passible and visible, the other impassible and invisible. For Irenaeus the distinction between God and created reality is not to be conceptualized in terms of an opposition between two distinct substances, existing in parallel and therefore commensurate with each other.[20] Rather, for Irenaeus the distinction is primarily thought of in terms of their relationship to each other: "In this God differs from man, that God creates and man is made" (*AH* 4.11.2). For Irenaeus,

---

20 An essential truth of theology, reiterated explicitly by Gregory Palamas, over a millennium later: "Every nature is utterly remote and absolutely foreign to the divine nature. For if God is nature (φύσις), other things are not nature; but if each of the other things is nature, he is not nature: just as he is not a being (ὄν), if others are beings; and if he is a being (ὤν), the others are not beings (ὄντα)." (*The One Hundred and Fifty Chapters*, 78). It is for this reason that, especially after Dionysius the Areopagite, it became customary to refer to the οὐσία of God as ὑπερούσιος.

Jesus Christ is, without question, everything it is to be God, and every-thing it is to be man. On the one hand, he is the one who *creates*, fash-ioning us into the image and likeness of God; on the other, he does this by himself being obedient to God, fulfilling and exemplifying, because being, the Word of God—he is *made* man. Jesus Christ, as God, fash-ions us into the image and likeness, by himself being made man and undergoing the Passion.[21] Irenaeus clearly anticipates the key point which emerged centuries later in the christological controversies sur-rounding Chalcedon: the one and the same Jesus Christ is what it is to be both God and man. In the Chalcedon definition this is, of course, affirmed in the language of two natures, but these two natures, and their natural properties, are predicated upon the same subject, the one and the same Jesus Christ who died on the Cross and by his death de-stroyed death, so granting life to all. That is, the language of two na-tures is Chalcedon's way of attributing both divinity and humanity to one and the same Jesus Christ, not, as with the Gnostics, a means of di-viding the passible from the impassible, keeping the Word separate from the flesh.

Irenaeus, as already noted, applies the dyad invisible-visible to the relationship between Father and Son, the Son being the visible of the invisible Father, not to two aspects of one and the same Jesus Christ. However, Irenaeus also uses this dyad to speak of the two states or modes of being of one and the same Word, Jesus Christ, who, as we have seen, was hidden under the types and prophecies but revealed in the Gospel. To further explain this, Irenaeus continues his exposition by appealing to the "recapitulation" effected by Christ. Against the Gnostics who divide not only the Father of Christ from the Creator of the world, but also the passible Jesus from the impassible Christ, Irenaeus reaffirms one God and one Lord:

> [the Gnostics] wander from the truth, because their thought departs from him who is truly God, not knowing that his only-begotten Word, who is always present with the human race, united to and mingled with his own handiwork, according to the Father's pleasure, and who became flesh, is himself Jesus Christ our Lord, who did also suffer for us, and was raised

---

21 For a full analysis of this aspect of Irenaeus' theology, see J. Behr, *Asceticism and Anthropol-ogy*, 23-127.

again on our behalf, and who is again coming in the glory of his Father, to raise up all flesh, and for the manifestation of salvation, and to apply the rule of just judgement to all who were made by him. There is, therefore, as I have pointed out, one God the Father and one Christ Jesus, who is coming throughout the whole economy, recapitulating all things in himself (*veniens per universam dispositionem et omnia in semetipsum recapitulans*). But in this "all" is man, the handiwork of God; and thus he recapitulated man in himself, the invisible becoming visible, the incomprehensible becoming comprehensible, the impassible becoming passible, and the Word man, thus recapitulating all things in himself, so that as in the super-celestial, spiritual and invisible things, the Word of God is supreme, so also in the things visible and corporeal he might possess the supremacy, and, taking to himself the pre-eminence, as well as constituting himself the head of the Church, he might draw all things to himself at the proper time. (*AH* 3.16.6)

The affirmation of one Jesus Christ coincides with the affirmation of one God the Father. Just as the Gnostic theological dualism leads to a Christological dualism, so Irenaeus' insistence on the unity of God entails an affirmation of the unity of the Son. A further consequence of the Gnostics' distinction between two beings in Jesus Christ, is that they forget that he is always present to the human race: there is, for Irenaeus, a total identity between the Word of God in Scripture (the "Old Testament") and the one spoken of in the Gospel: it is Jesus Christ who is coming throughout the economy—the "Coming One." More particularly, by recapitulating all things in himself, including man, the invisible, incomprehensible, impassible Word becomes visible, comprehensible and passible—becomes man. The recapitulation of the whole economy unfolded in Scripture, the subject throughout which is the Gospel of Christ, in a concise epitome makes visible and comprehensible what had previously been hidden in the prolixity of the Law. The points seen earlier, that Christ draws "all things to himself at the proper time" by ascending the Cross,[22] and the way in which the Passion acts as a lens by which Scripture is focused into an epitome, are picked up in the following section when Irenaeus interprets the exchange between Mary and Christ at Cana (Jn 2:3-4) as Mary urging Christ to perform the miracle because she "desired before the

22 Cf. *AH* 4.2.7; 5.17.4, both cited above.

appointed time to partake of the cup of concision" (*compendii poculo*, *AH* 3.16.7): the cup which results from Christ's Passion is the epitome in which salvation is granted.

Irenaeus picks up the theme of recapitulation in *AH* 3.18. The description of the Word being "united to his own handiwork" given in *AH* 3.16.6 to emphasize the continual presence of the Word to the human race, is made again in *AH* 3.18.1: the Word who was with the Father in the beginning, and always present to the human race, "in the last times, according to the will of the Father, was united to his own handiwork and became man."[23] After voicing a possible objection, Irenaeus continues:

> For we have shown that the Son of God did not then begin to exist, being eternally with the Father; but when he became incarnate, and was made man, he recapitulated in himself the long narration (*expositionem*) of human beings, furnishing us, in résumé (*in compendio*), with salvation, so that what we lost in Adam—to be according to the image and likeness of God—that we might recover in Christ Jesus. (*AH* 3.18.1)

The Word becoming flesh, an eschatological event in the "last times," is not, therefore, a new episode in a biography of the Word, but a recapitulation, providing a résumé, of the continual presence and identity of the same Word: it is Christ Jesus who, according to *AH* 3.16.6, comes throughout the whole economy, or, who, in *AH* 3.18.1, recapitulates the long narrative recorded in Scripture.[24] Recapitulating in himself the exposition of the economy, Jesus Christ furnishes us with salvation through a résumé, an epitome, which condenses or concentrates, and so makes visible and comprehensible, what had previously been invisible and incomprehensible.

23 The specification that Christ became man "in the last times" is significant: "Incarnation" and the "Passion" cannot be separated, either as "events" or in terms of their effects, but both are embraced by the term "parousia." Cf. *AH* 3.16.6; 4.10.2; 5.17.3. R. Noorman, *Irenäus als Paulusinterpret* (Tübingen: Mohr, 1994), 451.

24 The specification that the "narrative" recapitulated by Christ is that recorded in Scripture is based upon the allusion to the genealogy given in Luke 3:23-38, a connection which is made more explicit a few chapters later, when Irenaeus takes Luke's genealogy of the seventy-two generations from Christ back to Adam as demonstrating that Christ has joined the end to the beginning, recapitulating all nations, languages and generations in himself (*AH* 3.22.3)—the "all" in question is certainly universal in its scope, but it is so by virtue of the scriptural framework within which the claim is made.

For Irenaeus, the Word becoming flesh and the recapitulation effected in this way by Jesus Christ— "the one coming throughout the whole economy" recapitulating the whole economy, the "long narration of human beings" unfolded in Scripture—cannot be separated from the literary recapitulation made by God through the apostles and their "concise word." What the apostles proclaimed about Christ is, as we have seen, made up of the texture of Scripture, no longer proclaimed in the obscurity of types and prophecies, but clearly and concisely, in a résumé: what was prolix becomes condensed, what was unseen becomes seen, the invisible become visible—the Word becomes flesh. Thus, rather than presenting, as did Justin, a biography of the Word, describing the *continuity* of the Word's activity, *from* a history recorded in Scripture (the "Old Testament") *to* a history of the Incarnate Word recorded in the Gospels, Irenaeus' emphasis is on the *identity* between the Word of God in and through Scripture *and* the Word preached concisely, as become flesh, by the apostles, For Justin, the identity of the Word is understood in terms of the continuity of a personal subject, its "subjectivity"; for Irenaeus the identity of the Word of God is revealed by the way in which the subject throughout Scripture is the Gospel of Christ and Christ himself—it is one and the same Word of God, Jesus Christ, who is spoken of by the prophets' words (the Law, the Psalms and the Prophets) and the words of the apostles. Thus Irenaeus can maintain against Marcion, on the one hand, that there is nothing new in the Gospel, that what Christ is preached as having done, in the Gospel, is what he has done in directing the economy from the beginning.[25] What is new is that Christ himself, who previously had only been announced, has arrived—the concise Word, the

---

25 This is not to deny, of course, that the encounter with the Word in Scripture takes place through a variety of figures ("the Word himself, the interpreter of the Father [cf. Jn 1:18], being rich and multiple, was beheld by those seeing him, not in one figure nor in one character, but according to the workings of his dispensations," *AH* 4.20.11), nor that these do not have an order and arrangement ("all things which had been foreknown by the Father, our Lord did accomplish in the order, season and hour known in advance and fitting; being indeed one and the same, but rich and multiple" *AH* 3.16.7), but to caution against the scriptural unfolding of the riches of God manifest in the treasury of Scripture being taken as a biography of the Word within which existence "as" Jesus Christ is but one phase; these scriptural riches all speak, in different forms and figures, of the same Word of God, Jesus Christ and his Gospel.

Gospel, is clearly proclaimed. On the other hand, with the eschatological character of the Gospel reflecting the divine perfection of Christ,
Irenaeus can also maintain, against the Gnostics, that there is nothing
more to be added to it. Recapitulating this history in himself, Jesus
Christ furnishes us with salvation through a concise word or epitome,
which, as a résumé, provides the guidelines for the correct reading of
the same Word throughout the long narrative written in Scripture.[26]
Yet the Gospel of Christ, and Christ himself, still belong to the last
times; the Gospel is the concise, enfleshed, proclamation of the one
who is coming throughout the *whole* economy, and who is himself still
the Coming One (ὁ ἐρχόμενος).

An interesting consequence of the need for Christ to recapitulate the
whole economy, is that for Christ's work of recapitulation to be complete
he must recapitulate not only Adam's formation, by becoming man, but
also all the stages pertaining to human life. So Irenaeus states that Christ
"therefore passed through every age, becoming an infant for infants, thus
sanctifying infants," a child for children, a youth for youths, and an old
man for old men, offering to each an example appropriate to their age
(*AH* 2.22.4; cf. *AH* 3.18.7). According to Irenaeus, the Gnostics taught
that Christ preached for one year and suffered in the twelfth month (*AH*
2.22.5). But, as Irenaeus notes, according to the Gospels, Jesus was thirty
years old when he was baptized and as such he was still a young man and
not yet old enough to be a teacher. Irenaeus then adds what he claims to
the tradition deriving from John:

26 T. F. Torrance's comments on the significance of the economy of Christ are perceptive,
but not sufficiently sensitive to the scriptural, or literary, fabric of the discussion: "In the
whole course of Christ's life from birth to Passion and resurrection, there is presented an
epitome of God's saving acts, so that it is to the pattern enshrined in the humanity of Jesus
Christ that Irenaeus turns for his precise undestanding of the universal economy of God.
The principle term he uses to express this is ἀναχεφαλαίωσις or *recapitulatio*, which he
applies both to what happened in the life of Jesus himself and to what God accomplished
through him and will accomplish in the final actualisation of his saving will within creation. 'Recapitulation' means that redemptive activity of God in Jesus Christ was not just a
transcendent act that touched our existence in space and time at one point, but an activity
that passed into our existence and is at work within it, penetrating back to the beginning in
the original creation retracing and re-affirming in it the divine Will, and reaching forward
to the consummation in the new creation in which all things are gathered up, thus *connecting the end with the beginning*." (*Divine Meaning: Studies in Patristic Hermeneutics* [Edin-
burgh: T. and T. Clark, 1995], 121).

Now, that the first stage of early life embraces thirty years, and that this extends onwards to the fortieth year, everyone will admit; but from the fortieth and fiftieth year a man begins to decline towards old age, which our Lord possessed while he was teaching, even as the Gospel and all the elders testify—those who were conversant in Asia with John the disciple of the Lord, [affirming] that John conveyed to them that information. (*AH* 2.22.5)

Irenaeus continues by pointing out that the Jews' question, "You are not yet fifty years old and you have seen Abraham?" (Jn 8:57), is only really applicable to one who is passed the age of forty and is not yet fifty. So, Irenaeus concludes, at least ten years must have passed between Christ's baptism and his death (*AH* 2.22.6).[27] The literary coherence of Scripture, and the rhetorical coherence derived by engaging with Scripture to interpret Christ, is the ultimate criterion for Irenaeus' reflections on the eternal Word of God.[28]

The language used by Irenaeus, describing how the invisible became visible and the impassible passible, became standard thereafter, both in theological reflection and especially in the poetry of hymnography. The rhetoric employed here also implies the basic soteriological axioms outlined at the beginning of Part Two of this work, that only God can save, and that it is only as a human being that God saves human beings. For Irenaeus, salvation is not simply a restoration to our original paradisaical state, which we have lost since Adam, but also effects our adoption as sons in the Son and our communion with God:

For it was for this that the Word [became] man, and the Son of God, Son of man, that man, joined (*commixtus*) to the Word and receiving adoption, might become a son of God. For by no other means could we participate in incorruptibility and immortality, unless we had been joined to incorruptibility and immortality. But how could we be joined to incorruptibility and immortality, unless, first, incorruptibility and immortality had become that which we also are, so that the corruptible might be swallowed up by in-

27 That Christ was an "old man" is also indicated when Irenaeus carefully specifies that Christ was crucified under Pontius Pilate, the procurator of Claudius Caesar (*Dem.* 74). As Jesus was born about the forty-first year of the reign of Augustus (*AH* 3.21.3; starting from 44 B.C.), he would have been in his forties when Claudius began his reign (41-57 A.D.). Cf. Grant, *Irenaeus*, 51.

28 Grant describes Irenaeus here as "convert[ing] grammar into theology" (*Irenaeus*, 50; cf. 52-3).

corruptibility and the mortal by immortality, "that we might receive the adoption of sons"? [cf. 1 Cor 15:53-4; 2 Cor 5:4; Gal 4:5]. (*AH* 3.19.1)

Or put more simply:

The Word of God, our Lord Jesus Christ, through his transcendent love, became what we are, that he might bring us to be even what he is himself. (*AH* 5.Pref.)

Irenaeus' theology is remarkably sophisticated, and especially sensitive to the literary dimension in which such interpretative reflection is elaborated, giving a very profound insight into why Jesus Christ is confessed as the Word of God. Irenaeus refuses to distinguish between two beings or two elements in one and the same Jesus Christ (one part human and visible, the other part divine and invisible), preferring instead to think in terms of two states of the same Word: the invisible, incomprehensible Word, becoming visible and comprehensible. Yet, in doing this, Irenaeus does not temporalize the eternal Word of God, Jesus Christ. The apostolic proclamation, the Gospel, is made up of the texture of the Scripture, no longer proclaimed in the obscurity of types and prophecies, but refracted through the Cross, and proclaimed clearly and concisely in a résumé. Thus, when Irenaeus says that the Son becoming flesh recapitulates the long narrative of the economy, this is a recapitulation made by God through the apostles and their concise word: the same Word of God, obscurely written at length in Scripture, is preached concisely and clearly, enfleshed, by the apostles in their Gospel proclaiming the human sojourn of the Word of God. The unique revelation of God in Jesus Christ, the Word become flesh, is located specifically in the apostolic preaching of him, the Gospel which refracts Scripture through the Cross, and in which the Word hidden in Scripture becomes visible and comprehensible—becomes flesh. The Word of God becomes flesh as the Jesus Christ, the unique Son of God, preached by the apostles, the Gospel, which itself is the concise, clear, embodied, revelation of the one and the same Word of God contained in Scripture. The affirmation that Jesus Christ is the Word of God become flesh is thus not based upon a historicizing conflation of John 1:14, which does not speak of a birth, with the infancy narratives, which do not speak of an incarnation of a heavenly being. Rather, the confession that Jesus Christ is the Word of God is based in the literary dynamics of this relationship between Scripture and the Gospel, how it is that the apostles and those following them reflect upon Christ "according to the Scriptures," and thus directs attention back to Scripture, to reflect yet further on the identity of Christ.

PART THREE

The Son of the Father

In the closing years of the second century and during the course of the third, a number of debates were sparked off by various attempts to explain the place of Jesus Christ, long since worshipped as God, in a monotheistic religion. That there is only one God and one Jesus Christ had been reaffirmed in the earlier debates with Marcion and the Gnostics, but the relationship between Jesus Christ and God required further clarification. Some of the issues involved in this were already intimated in the differences, examined in Part Two, between Justin Martyr, for whom the Logos is another God who, unlike the totally transcendent Father, is able to reveal himself and in due course became incarnate as Jesus Christ, and Irenaeus of Lyons, according to whom Jesus Christ, as preached by the apostles in the Gospel recapitulating Scripture, is the eternal Word of God, the Son who reveals or makes known (ἐξηγήσατο, Jn 1:18) the Father.

In subsequent decades, in a series of debates between the Christian communities in Rome (though the errors are usually traced back to heretics from the East), the issues at stake became more explicit, and, as a result of polemic not infrequently deriving from other motives, often caricatured. Victor (189-98) excommunicated Theodotus the Cobbler for teaching that Jesus was merely a man, a belief that resurfaced a few decades later with the shadowy figure of Artemon (or Artemas). Zephyrinus (198-217) and Callistus (217-22) raised the ire of the author of the *Refutation of all Heresies*, mistakenly attributed to Hippolytus, for their apparent laxity in admitting to their community those who had been expelled from his community for serious moral lapses, and also by their accusation that he was a "ditheist" who had undermined the oneness of God through his teaching about the Logos; he in turn associated Zephyrinus and Callistus with Noetus and

Sabellius, accusing them all of teaching that the Father himself had become the Son in the Incarnation and that the Father himself died on the Cross.[1] Finally a rapprochement seems to have been effected by Hippolytus, perhaps the successor of the author of the *Refutation*, both through the articulation of trinitarian theology in more Irenaean lines (in the *Contra Noetum* and other, undisputed, works of Hippolytus) and by subordinating his community to the current leader of Callistus' community, Pontian (230-5).[2]

Origen (c. 185-c. 254) had visited Rome during these debates and, back in Alexandria, he began to assert more emphatically the real and eternal distinct subsistence of the Son and the Spirit alongside the one God, who therefore begins to be understood primarily as the Father. This affirmation does not stand alone, but emerged from Origen's extensive engagement with Scripture and his profound reflection on how Christ, both God and man, is the Word of God. His vast theological vision is matched only by his massive literary output, and is

---

1   I have avoided Harnack's categories of "dynamic monarchianism" or "adoptionism" for those who asserted that Christ was a "mere man," and "modalistic monarchianism" for those who identified the Father and Son (*History of Dogma*, vol. 3, 1-118). The author of the *Refutation* only alludes once to a concern for the "monarchy" of God on behalf of his opponents (*Ref.* 9.10.11); and, although it occurs more concretely in Tertullian's *Against Praxeas* (3, 9), the relation between Tertullian's rhetorical arguments and the situation in Rome is far from clear. That both of these positions were alternative responses stemming from the same concern for the singularity of the one God is suggested by Origen (*ComJn.* 2.16) and Novatian (*On the Trinity*, 30), though only Origen (elsewhere) refers to "the illusory notion of monarchy" (*Dialogue with Heraclides*, 4). To classify both positions as "monarchian" is inappropriate (at least for the "Dynamistic Monarchians," as Harnack himself admits, *History of Dogma*, vol. 3, 10, ftn. 1), and more importantly overlooks the charge of "ditheism" raised against the author of the *Refutation*, preferring instead to use this newly discovered work (the full text was found in 1841) to discredit Zephyrinus and Callistus, who in the early Church were never otherwise maligned; the decree on papal infallibility issued in 1870 probably lurks in the background of this taxonomy. In the early Church, genealogy was more important than taxonomy—it was the names of Artemon and Paul of Samosata, Noetus and Sabellius that haunted later theologians.
2   This reconstruction is that elaborated at great length and in minute detail by A. Brent in his weighty tome, *Hippolytus and the Roman Church in the Third Century*. With regard to the issue of "monarchy," Brent takes the record (in the Liberian *Depositio*) of "bishop" Pontian and "presbyter" Hippolytus having been buried on the same day, the 13th of August, the feast of Diana that commemorated the incorporation of the allied cities into the Roman federation, as a symbolic cipher marking the establishment of monarchical episcopacy in Rome. The picture drawn by Brent is very persuasive, though I have serious reservations regarding his depiction of the theology of the *Contra Noetum*.

reflected only palely in the lengthier treatment, compared to others, that he receives here. His work was fundamental for later theological reflection, but also ambiguous, containing tensions that he was able to hold together but which would eventually, in different contexts, fragment into opposing positions. An indication of how the affirmation of the distinct subsistence of the Son and the Spirit was perceived elsewhere is given a couple of decades later when Dionysius of Alexandria (d. c. 264) set out to counter Sabellian teaching in a nearby region and found himself accused of tritheism, of teaching three separate gods, by Dionysius of Rome (259-68), though the Alexandrian's explanation satisfied his Roman namesake.

Dionysius of Alexandria was also invited to Antioch to examine the case of Paul of Samosata. The affair concerning Paul, embroiled in politics as much as theological divergences, is extremely difficult to reconstruct. The theological charges raised against Paul revolve around the accusation that he taught that Christ was a mere man, so reviving the heresy of Artemon. It seemed to his critics that Paul separated Jesus from the Word as two distinct entities, the eternal Word and the newly revealed Jesus. They, on the other hand, seem to suggest that the Word should be understood as taking the place of the soul in the composite being that is Jesus Christ, introducing an analogy which was to reappear frequently, and often dubiously, in subsequent theological reflection.

Common to all these third-century debates is the issue of the identity of Christ as the Son and Word of God. As Son, Christ is distinct from the Father, rather than being a new form or manifestation of the one God, though it is the Father that the Son reveals, not simply himself and his own divinity. That granted, the problem then is how to conceive the divinity and identity of Christ, the Son of God: is he divine because "part" of his being is divine, the Word which animates a soulless flesh, and does this "part" then constitute his identity, in the sense of the continuity of subject understood by analogy with a soul? Or, alternatively, should the identity of Christ be understood in terms of his defining characteristics, as articulated in the *kerygma*, the proclamation of the crucified and risen Son of God, which, recapitulating Scripture, provides the context for contemplating how the Son Jesus

Christ is confessed precisely as the *Word* of God. The contrast raised here goes to the very heart of the theological endeavor, whether it understands its task to be that of analyzing the composition of the being of Christ and then elaborating an account of how it came to be, or of reflecting on the *kerygma* within the canon and tradition of the Gospel according to Scripture. Put provocatively, in terms that are certainly modern but nonetheless apt: mythology or proclamation and confession?

The third century by no means saw a resolution to these issues. If anything, it brought them to a crisis point, ready to explode in the following centuries. Certain aspects, however, were now ensured, if only by charting out forbidden territory. The specters of Sabellius and Paul of Samosata loomed heavily over later Trinitarian and Christological reflection, capable of damning by association anyone who ventured to confuse Father and Son or to claim that the Son was merely a man who had been adopted and deified. Christ, unambiguously, was not a man become God, but God become man, "from above" as it were, just as the Gospel of Jesus Christ is not the Gospel of men but the Gospel of God (cf. Gal 1:11-12; Rom 1:1, etc.). A more positive contribution was provided by the Alexandrians and developed by their later heirs, especially the affirmation of the eternal subsistence of the Son, and the corollary that the one God *is* Father, and the manner, sensitive to the scriptural fabric of theology, in which they understood the identity of the Son and acknowledged him as the Word of God.

⁓

6

Hippolytus and the
Roman Debates

In Rome, during the last years of the second century and the opening decades of the third, a series of controversies continued to address the issue of the place of Christ in a monotheistic religion: is Jesus Christ to be thought of as divine, and if so, how is one to speak of his divinity and explain his relationship to the one God? The epicenter of these debates seems to have been the community led by Victor (189-98), Zephyrinus (198-217) and Callistus (217-22). Many notorious heretics, such as Theodotus, Noetus and Sabellius, make their first appearance during the course of these controversies, not in their own right, however, but indirectly, being brought in to blacken the opponent currently in view, though thereafter they continue to haunt later generations of theologians. Thus, that Victor expelled Theodotus from the community for teaching that Christ was merely human is known from the *Little Labyrinth*, written a few decades later against the revival of Theodotian teaching by Artemon (or Artemas). Noetus and Sabellius are brought in by the author of the *Refutation of all Heresies*, mistakenly attributed to Hippolytus, as the alleged heretical ancestors of Zephyrinus and Callistus, who had charged the author of the *Refutation* with being a "ditheist," imperiling the singularity of the one God by his Logos theology, and had also admitted to their community some who had been expelled from his community for serious moral misdemeanors, so provoking the vitriolic polemic launched against them in the ninth book of the *Refutation*. Despite the fact that this book is our primary source for determining their theology, enough is indicated to suggest that Zephyrinus and Callistus were maintaining the style of theology developed by Irenaeus, as explored above in Part Two. The final protagonist in this series of debates was Hippolytus who, in his

Contra Noetum and other undisputed works, developed a more Irenaean theology. Criticizing the supposed forbear of Zephyrinus and Callistus, and expounding a theology more akin to theirs, prepared the way for the final reconciliation which occurred, in Brent's reconstruction, when Hippolytus, as the successor of the author of the *Refutation*, subordinated his own community to the current leader of Callistus' community, Pontian (230-5). The primary protagonists of this series of events, and the points they considered to be at stake, are the subject of this chapter, together with the heretics with whom they are aligned.

Theodotus and the Little Labyrinth

The first episode in the series of debates at Rome centered upon Theodotus the Cobbler, about whom information is sparse. The earliest evidence is provided by three fragments from an anonymous treatise (σπούδασμα), preserved by Eusebius and usually identified as the *Little Labyrinth*,[1] written against the heresy of Artemon who seems to have revived the teachings of Theodotus several decades later but about whom nothing else is known. The *Refutation of all Heresies* attributed to Hippolytus also contains a few chapters devoted to Theodotus and his followers.[2] Theodotus gained his notoriety for teaching, so the *Little Labyrinth* claims, that "the Christ was a mere man" (ψιλὸς ἄνθρωπος), and for this Victor of Rome excluded him from the community.[3] According to the *Refutation*, Theodotus originated from Byzantium and taught that, after an ordinary life, Jesus demonstrated exceptional piety and at his baptism received the Spirit, who declared that Jesus was the Christ and empowered him to fulfill his divine mission.[4] Theodotus

---

1   Eusebius, *EH* 5.28. The title (ὁ σμικρὸς λαβύρινθος) comes from Theodoret's discussion of Theodotus (*Comp.* 2.5; PG 83.392b). For discussion concerning this work, the *Labyrinth* mentioned by Photius (*Bibl.* 48), and their place within the Hippolytan corpus, see Brent, *Hippolytus*, 115-203.

2   *Ref.* 7.35-6; 10.23-4.

3   *EH* 5.28.6: ἀπεκήρυξεν τῆς κοινωνίας

4   *Ref.* 7.35. This passage also suggests that Theodotus claimed that the divine Christ descended upon the man Jesus at his baptism, but, as Ehrman points out, the charge of separating Jesus Christ into two beings, divine and human, is quite distinct from the accusation leveled by the fragments in Eusebius (that Christ was a mere man), and probably results from the aim of the *Refutation* to demonstrate a common deviation, assimilating Theodotus to the various Gnostics (*The Orthodox Corruption of Scripture*, 101, n. 33).

himself denied that this meant that Jesus became God, though apparently some of his followers held that he did become God, either at the baptism or the Resurrection (*Ref.* 7.35). The *Little Labyrinth* further reports how under Zephyrinus, Theodotus the Banker and Asclepiodotus, both disciples of Theodotus the Cobbler, persuaded a certain Natalius to be their bishop. Despite his salary of one hundred and fifty denarii a month, the first clear record of a bishop receiving an income, Natalius soon repented of his actions (*EH* 5.28.8-12). The followers of Theodotus also claimed, according to the *Little Labyrinth*, that "the truth of the preaching," that is, their position that Christ was a man, not God, was held by all, from the apostles to the time of Victor, only to be "corrupted" by his successor, Zephyrinus (*EH* 5.28.3).

In response to the appeal to history by the Theodotians, the *Little Labyrinth* mounted its own appeal to historical evidence, referring to the Scriptures and the writings of Christians prior to Victor: in the works of Justin, Miltiades, Tatian and Clement and "many others," it says, "Christ is spoken of as God" (θεολογεῖται ὁ Χριστός), and, more recently, the books of Irenaeus and Melito clearly "proclaim Christ as God and man" (*EH* 5.28.4-5). Moreover, it continues, the traditional worship of the Church also evidences the same belief: "all the psalms and hymns, which were written by the faithful from the beginning, hymn Christ as the Word of God, speaking of him as God" (θεολογοῦντες, *EH* 5.28.6). Finally, Victor's action of excommunicating Theodotus is given as a clear testimony to his stand on the matter. However, more interesting than the appeal to historical testimonies is the explanation suggested by the *Little Labyrinth* for the errors of the Theodotians: "They have not feared to corrupt divine Scriptures, they have set aside the canon of ancient faith, they have not known Christ, not inquiring what the divine Scriptures say," preferring instead to reduce the issues to syllogisms: "abandoning the Holy Scriptures of God, they pursue the study of geometry."[5] The underlying concern of

5   *EH* 5.28.13-14. The *Little Labyrinth* continues by claiming that the Theodotians study the geometry of Euclid, admire Aristotle and Theophrastus, and it even alleges that "Galen is perhaps worshipped by some." On the issue of the corruption of Scripture (a charge repeated in *EH* 5.28.15-19), both by the Theodotians and their opponents, see R. M. Grant, *Heresy and Criticism: The Search for Authenticity in Early Christian Literature* (Louisville, KY: Westminster-John Knox Press, 1993), and Ehrman, *Orthodox Corruption*, 47-118.

the *Little Labyrinth* is that the Theodotians have devoted themselves to
the things of this world (i.e. "geometry")—"they are of the earth and
speak of the earth"—and so, it concludes, they do not know "him who
comes from above" (τὸν ἄνωθεν ἐρχόμενον, *EH* 5.28.14). The point of
this criticism is not to deny the claim that Jesus Christ was indeed a
man, nor to suggest that the Theodotians are willfully neglecting a
divine "part" in Christ alongside the human "part," but rather to point
out that they do not *understand* who this Jesus Christ is, for this is an
interpretation which can only be made on the basis of Scripture, the
Law, the Psalms and the Prophets—"they have set aside the canon,
they have not known Christ, not inquiring what the divine Scriptures
say." Origen, who visited Rome a couple of decades later during the
time of Zephyrinus (*EH* 6.14.10), made a similar point, commenting
that the majority of believers "know Christ only according to the
flesh," that they know nothing "'except Christ and him crucified' [1
Cor 2:2] and see the Word as flesh," rather than understanding the one
whom they see, the crucified Christ, as the Word that was in the beginning, was with God, and was God (cf. Jn 1:1-3).[6] Despite the apparent
denigration of Paul's avowal to know "nothing except Christ and him
crucified," Origen, and the author of the *Little Labyrinth*, are clearly
concerned with the further point made by Paul to the Corinthians,
that "though we once knew Christ according to the flesh, we no longer
know him thus" (2 Cor 5:16). That Jesus Christ died in the flesh is
indisputably important, but that he died and rose "according to the
Scriptures" is the basis of the Christian faith; it is in this way, through
the interpretative engagement with Scripture, that Jesus Christ is
"theologized" (θεολογεῖται), that is, confessed as God.

Zephyrinus and Callistus, Noetus and Sabellius

The next, more turbulent, round of debates in Rome is described in
the ninth book of the *Refutation of all Heresies* and concerns similar
issues but approached from the opposite direction. Besides all their
other points of contention, Zephyrinus and Callistus accused the
author of the *Refutation* of being a "ditheist" (*Ref.* 9.11.3, 12.16), and

6   *ComJn.* 2.21-33. The first two books of this commentary were written shortly after
    Origen's return from Rome, and seem to reflect debates current there.

he retaliated by claiming that their teaching, that the Father and the Son were the same, derived from a certain Noetus, and, though unknown to his opponents themselves, was ultimately based on Heraclitus, "the Obscure" (*Ref.* 9.8.1). In large measure, this debate turned upon the appropriateness of a theology, already outlined by Justin Martyr, which understood the Word of God as functioning in a similar manner to the second god of Middle Platonism, the assimilation of the Stoic logos and the Platonic demiurge, who bridged the gap between the completely transcendent God and the realm of creation,[7] and then identified this divine being as the one who became incarnate. The author of the *Refutation* follows this approach, in a fairly developed and sophisticated fashion. His opponents, Zephyrinus and Callistus, on the other hand, began from Jesus Christ, as had the Theodotians, though they also acknowledged Jesus Christ as God, the one who reveals the Father. Unlike Gaius, a presbyter under Zephyrinus who was alleged to have simply rejected the Gospel and Revelation of John as the work of a certain Cerinthus,[8] both sides of this debate used the Johannine writings. The opponents of the *Refutation* appealed particularly to Christ's words to Philip in John 14 (e.g., *Ref.* 9.12.17), but they were not prepared to read into the Johannine use of the term "Word" the theology which they regarded as being ditheistic. Indeed, as Harnack pointed out (using his categories), "Monarchians of all shades had a common interest in opposition to Logos Christology: *they represented the conception of the Person of Christ founded on the history of salvation, as against one based on the history of his nature.*"[9] Inasmuch as this was indeed their intention, Zephyrinus and Callistus stood within the tradition represented by Irenaeus.[10] If

---

7 Cf. J. Dillon, *The Middle Platonists: 80 B.C. to A.D. 220*, rev. edn. (Ithaca, N.Y.: Cornell University Press, 1996), 46.

8 On the various testimonies concerning Gaius see Brent, *Hippolytus*, 131-44.

9 A. von Harnack, *History of Dogma*, vol. 3, 62, his emphasis. Cf. F. Loofs, *Leitfaden zum Studium der Dogmengeschichte*, 5th edn., rev. K. Aland (Halle-Saale: Max Niemeyer Verlag, 1950-3), vol. 1, 142.

10 This is acknowledged by Harnack, in a different part of his work, where he comments that, "Whereas Tertullian and Hippolytus [in his interpretation of the *Contra Noetum*] developed their Logos doctrine without reference to the historical Jesus, the truth rather being that they simply add the incarnation to the already existing theory of the subject, there is no doubt that Irenaeus, as a rule, made Jesus Christ, who he views as God and man, the *starting point* of his speculation." (*History of Dogma*, vol. 2, 262).

they were not successful at defending their position, a rapprochement was nevertheless subsequently worked out by Hippolytus. It is important to bear this polemical context in mind, for what we know of the opponents of "Logos theology" is mediated, no doubt selectively, by its proponents.

Of Noetus himself we know very little. The author of the *Refutation* is primarily interested to establish "the genealogy" of his contemporary opponents in Rome, whose teaching derives from "the unintelligent successors of Noetus."[11] Hippolytus' *Contra Noetum*, the other primary source for Noetus, also begins by referring to "certain others, [who are] introducing a strange teaching, disciples as they are of a certain Noetus, a Smyrnaean by origin, who lived no great length of time ago."[12] Hippolytus continues by reporting the teaching of Noetus himself: "excited by a conceit of an alien spirit, he said that Christ was the Father himself, and that the Father himself was born, suffered and died" (*CN* 1.2). Presented in this way, such teaching seems to reflect an urge to maintain the oneness of God, allegedly by identifying Christ with God the Father, and to emphasize this unity by proclaiming that it was the Father himself who died on the Cross, a position that soon came to be described as "patripassian."[13] However, the report of Noetus' condemnation suggests that there were other motives involved. Noetus was condemned for his "other actions," and this, according to the *Contra Noetum*, sufficiently demonstrated that his teaching was erroneous and so justified his being "cast out of holy office." The nature of these "other actions" is perhaps intimated in Noetus' reply to the presbyters, before whom he had been brought for apparently claiming that he was Moses and his brother Aaron, that he was "not aiming at the top ranks."[14] After gathering around himself a number of followers, he was again brought before the presbyters, but

---

11 *Ref.* 9.7.1-8.1; 9.10.9: τοὺς <ἀ>νοήτους Νοητοῦ διαδόχους.
12 *CN* 1.1. On the translation of the opening phrase of *CN*, and for further discussion concerning the integrity of this work, see C. P. Bammel, "The State of Play with Regard to Hippolytus and the *Contra Noetum*," *Heythrop Journal*, 31 (1990), 195-9; Brent, *Hippolytus*, 116-27. *CN* also plays upon the name "Noetus" at *CN* 3.3; 8.3.
13 E.g., Cyprian, *Ep.* 72 (73).4; in the East, for reasons to be examined later, this position was usually designated as "Sabellianism."
14 *CN* 1.3-4, following Butterworth's translation of τὰς ἀρχὰς μὴ φρονεῖν.

this time the charges seem to have been more theological, for his response was simply, "What wrong do I do by glorifying Christ?" (*CN* 1.6). Noetus was again condemned, expelled from the Church, and founded his own "school."

That Noetus defended himself, when questioned on theological matters, by focusing on Christ suggests that his position was fundamentally christocentric, perhaps to the point of exclusivity. This christocentric emphasis is further evidenced when the *Contra Noetum* then turns to the Scriptural support given by Noetus and his disciples for their position.[15] They appealed to passages from the Law (Ex 3:6; 20:3) and the Prophets (Is 44:6), which they used "to establish a single God."[16] On this basis they argued, according to the *Contra Noetum*, that "If therefore I confess that Christ is God, then he is the Father himself if he is God" (*CN* 2.3). That there is only one God is affirmed by both these texts of Scripture, and the application of Scripture to Christ was a hermeneutic principle that was standard by this time, as was the confession that Christ is indeed God and the worship of him as such. Given these premises, the conclusion seems inescapable. This conclusion was then used as a premise for a second argument, though no further scriptural support is offered for its patripassianist thesis: "Christ, being God, suffered. Then, did not the Father suffer? For he was the Father" (*CN* 2.3). Further "testimonies" from Scripture (Bar 3:36-8; Is 45:14-15) are offered to demonstrate that "the Scriptures proclaim one God, the one visibly revealed," before an appeal is made to the Apostle (Rom 9:5) to the effect that Christ is indeed God, and finally Noetus' arguments are restated in an even more provocative fashion (*CN* 2.5-3.2). There is no doubt, from the account given in the *Contra Noetum*, that Noetus was concerned to maintain that Jesus Christ is indeed God, the one (and only one) spoken of by the Scriptures. It is debatable, however, whether the conclusion drawn from these scriptural testimonies, that the Father and Christ are to be completely identified, was ever really intended by Noetus or his disciples, or

15 *CN* 2.1-8; the verbs in this section vacillate between single and plural, thus blurring the distinction between Noetus and his disciples.

16 *CN* 2.1-3. The passage from Is 44:6 (where the LXX has "and I am after these things") has been conflated with Revelation (1:17; 2:8; 22:13) to read "and I am the last," thus emphasizing that these passages were being read in a christocentric manner.

is perhaps due to polemical rhetoric, drawing out unintended consequences in a *reductio ad absurdam*. As regards the patripassianist claim,
that it was the Father who died, as this is offered no scriptural support
at all, but is presented as a logical deduction from the conclusions of
other arguments, it is likely to be a polemical invention.[17]

According to the *Refutation*, Epigones, the "minister (διάκονος)
and disciple" of Noetus, brought his teaching to Rome and instructed a
certain Cleomenes, who then "strengthened the doctrine" during the
time of Zephyrinus (*Ref.* 9.7.1). Of Noetus and Epigones, the *Refutation* does not have much to say, though a short section (*Ref.* 9.10.9-12)
seems to be devoted to the teachings of Cleomenes and his followers,
and includes brief reports of sayings attributed to Noetus.[18] The
account of this Roman circle begins by making what seems to be an
anti-Marcionite point, that "one and the same God is the creator of all
and the Father," and then continues by affirming that it is this God
who revealed himself: "he being invisible, was pleased to appear to the
just men of old" (*Ref.* 9.10.9). Although the reference is to "the just
men of old," the subject of this manifestation of God is most probably
Jesus Christ, rather than the Logos-Son appearing in a pre-incarnate
form as these theophanies were interpreted by, for instance, Justin
Martyr. This would follow the way in which Noetus took the words of
Isaiah to refer to Christ, in a traditional christocentric reading of
Scripture, so that he could claim "the Scriptures proclaim one God, the
one visibly revealed" (*CN* 2.6-7; 4). That they are alleged, in this section of the *Refutation*, to have taught that it is the invisible God himself
who became visible, rather than a second God who is visible in distinction to the transcendent, invisible Father, probably reflects an attempt
to maintain that what is seen in Christ is indeed truly God, that he is
"the visible of the Father" as Irenaeus had put it, though reported

---

17   In Harnack's opinion, "It is very questionable, however, whether it [the formula "the Father
     suffered"] was ever roundly uttered by the theological defenders of Modalism. They probably
     merely said that 'the Son, who suffered, is the same with the Father.'" (*History of Dogma*, vol.
     3, 65). Cf. R. E. Heine, "The Christology of Callistus," *JTS* ns 49.1 (1998), 83.

18   The passage is introduced by the claim that "the unintelligent successors of Noetus …
     speak as follows" and concludes with "… thus says Cleomenes and his chorus." The two
     singular "he says" within this passage (*Ref.* 9.10.10-11) are most naturally attributed to
     Noetus, though the "he thinks" (*Ref.* 9.10.11) is clearly the author's interpretation of
     Noetus' intention. Cf. Heine, "Callistus," 85-9.

Modalistic ...

without the necessary stipulation that he is the Son revealing the Father.[19] Along with this visible manifestation of the invisible God, the circle around Cleomenes also described God as being unconfined (ἀχώρητος) when he does not wish to be confined, yet "confined when he confines himself" (χωρητὸς δὲ ὅτε χωρεῖται, *Ref.* 9.10.10). The description of the unconfined God being confined, or comprehended, also echoes a point made by Irenaeus in similar terms,[20] and so again seems to be referring to the Son, Jesus Christ, in whom the Father is "contained," enabling us also to comprehend what would otherwise be beyond our capacity.

The remainder of the report describing Cleomenes and his followers continues by applying, as the author of the *Refutation* puts it, "the same reasoning," to conclude that the God depicted by such theology must be the subject of contrary predicates—"tangible and intangible, unbegotten and begotten, immortal and mortal"—and that it is therefore clear that the proponents of such a position must be disciples of Heraclitus (*Ref.* 9.10.10). This combination of opposites is also evident, it is claimed, in Noetus's identification of Father and Son, the Father undergoing birth to become his own Son. From all of this, the author of the *Refutation* concludes that "in this way he thinks he can construct the monarchy," by maintaining that the Father and Son are "one and the same" (ἓν καὶ τὸ αὐτὸ) differing only in the names being used for the same God at different times, "confessing to those who saw him that he was Son because of the birth, yet not concealing that he is Father for those who can comprehend this" (τοῖς χωροῦσιν).[21] That this is all presented as the author of the *Refutation* himself applying "the same reasoning," suggests a polemical distortion, twisting an affirmation that Christ is truly God into the assertion that Christ is God himself, to whom the names of

19 Irenaeus, *AH*, 4.6.6. Tertullian, who would have the Logos-Son alone to be visible (before the Incarnation as after it, the flesh simply making the Son more visible, *Against Praxeas*, 15), in distinction to the invisible Father, also criticizes the "monarchians" for wanting "the visible one and the invisible one to be taken as identical, in the same way as [they do] Father and Son" (*Against Praxeas*, 14).

20 *AH* 4.4.2: "The Son is the measure of the Father, since he also comprehends him (*capit* [Rousseau suggests: χωρεῖ] *eum*)."

21 *Ref.* 9.10.11. That the "one" is given in neuter is significant, and probably derives from Jn 10:30, "I and the Father are one (ἕν)."

Father and Son are applied at different times. However, the report also seems to acknowledge their attempt to differentiate between, on the one hand, what is merely seen, the Son born from a woman, and, on the other hand, the understanding of the divinity of this Son, presented polemically as an identification with the Father. On the basis of this position, now associated with the concern for the "monarchy" of God, the author of the *Refutation* continues by describing a patripassianist position, which, as Heine notes, "is shot through with sarcasm" such that "it seems unlikely … that anyone presented the doctrine in the way it is related here."[22] Heine further points out that rather than applying the contrary adjectives "mortal-immortal" (θνητὸν ἀθάνατον) to the same subject as Heraclitus had done (cf. *Ref.* 9.9.1), the account describes God as "dying and not dying" (ἀποθανόντα καὶ μὴ ἀποθανόντα, *Ref.* 9.10.12), which, as referring to actions, again seems to be an attempt to differentiate between one who underwent death and another who did not.[23]

The likelihood of this is strengthened by the fact that it was this very point that was unambiguously made by Zephyrinus soon after. According to the *Refutation*, Zephyrinus was a "foolish and illiterate man" who was led into the doctrine of Cleomenes by Callistus, while the latter was "fishing for the episcopal throne" (*Ref.* 9.11.1). Only two statements of Zephyrinus are recorded in the *Refutation*, and they are presented as being public statements made, on different occasions, at the prompting of Callistus (*Ref.* 9.11.3). The first reiterates the christocentric focus of this tradition of theology, "I know one God, Jesus Christ, and apart from him no other that is subject to birth and suffering." The second, however, specifically denies the patripassianist charge laid against them, "It was not the Father who died but the Son." The patripassianist position is thus explicitly denied, while a christocentric monotheism is maintained. How Zephyrinus reconciled monotheism with this distinction between Father and Son is, however, not made clear in his opponent's report.

Zephyrinus was succeeded by Callistus, and it is the controversy with Callistus that is regarded by the author of the *Refutation* as his

22 Heine, "Callistus," 89.
23 Ibid.

"greatest struggle."[24] It is also here that Sabellius first makes his appearance. Originally Sabellius appears to have been associated with the author of the *Refutation*, for while Sabellius was being advised by him, he "had not hardened his heart," but when Sabellius began to spend time alone with Callistus, he began to incline towards the doctrine of Cleomenes (*Ref.* 9.11.1-2). However, when Callistus succeeded Zephyrinus, Callistus expelled Sabellius "as one who did not think correctly" (*Ref.* 9.12.15). The author of the *Refutation* claims that Callistus did this "fearing me and thinking that in this way he would be able to rub off the accusation [made] to the churches (τὴν πρὸς τὰς ἐκκλησίας κατηγορίαν) that he thought no differently from Sabellius" (*Ref.* 9.12.15). The accusation that Callistus held to the same position as Sabellius clearly belies the previous accusation that Callistus was responsible for perverting him; Sabellius now appears as the leader of a recognizable heresy, with whom the author of the *Refutation* wants to associate Callistus. Yet Sabellius' teaching is not even mentioned in the *Refutation*; he is only brought in by the *Refutation* to blacken the reputation of Callistus by tarring him with a brush presumably already known to be black. It is probably in response to this charge that Callistus distanced himself from Sabellius, who, in turn, accused Callistus of "transgressing his first faith" (τὴν πρώτην πίστιν, *Ref.* 9.12.16). By the fourth century, Sabellius is ubiquitously known as the one who taught the complete identification of Father and Son as "one person."[25] The validity of this description is now impossible to determine; all that can be said is that the figure of Sabellius described in this way cast a long shadow on future theological reflection.

After describing these intrigues, the *Refutation* provides a short account of Callistus' teaching, from which it concludes that at times Callistus fell into the doctrine of Sabellius and at other times into that of Theodotus, evidently unable to understand the coherence of Callistus' position (*Ref.* 9.12.19). The account begins by describing

24 Marcovich describes *Ref.* 9.11-12 as "a regrettable vitriolic 'character assassination,' written with a pen dipped in gall, not in ink... Hippolytus' [he accepts his authorship] μέγιστος ἀγών is actually his only real ἀγών—to refute the *contemporary* Trinitarian modalists, Cleomenes, Sabellius and, above all, Callistus." (*Hippolytus: Refutatio Omnium Haeresium*, ed. M. Marcovich, PTS 25 [Berlin: De Gruyter, 1986], 40).
25 Cf. Epiphanius, *Panarion*, 62.

how Callistus "said the Logos himself is Son, and is himself called by
the name Father, but is one indivisible spirit" (*Ref.* 9.12.16). This is the
first, and only, time that the term "Logos" has appeared in the accounts
of this tradition of theology, and seems to indicate the inability of
Callistus' adversary to understand Callistus' account of the Son in any
other manner than that of his own.[26] Yet from what follows it is clear
that Callistus does not begin his account of the Son with an already
conceived notion of a "Logos," but rather starts from the incarnate, visible, Jesus Christ. After citing Christ's words to Philip, that he is in the
Father and the Father in him (Jn 14:10), which explain how it is that
in seeing Christ one can see the Father, Callistus comments, "For that
which is seen, which is man, that is the Son, but the spirit contained
within the Son is the Father" (*Ref.* 9.12.18): the locus of revelation is
the man, Jesus Christ; he is the Son, and in him we see the Father. The
presence of the Father in the Son as "spirit" perhaps echoes John 4:24,
so that the divinity of the Son, which is not other than the divinity of
the Father, is described simply as "spirit," and perhaps also picks up the
need to reflect on Christ "according to the Spirit" as well as "according
to the flesh," to see Christ as God.[27] On this basis Callistus continues
by asserting "I will not speak of two Gods, Father and Son, but of one"
(*Ref.* 9.12.18), not because the Son is merely a man, the visible Jesus
Christ, which would be the position of Theodotus that the *Refutation*
also attributes to Callistus, but because it is the Father who is revealed
in him, when viewed "according to the spirit," not an other or a second
God. The account of Callistus' teaching continues by accusing him of
saying that the Father was born in the flesh, so that the one God should
be called Father and Son, because they are "one person," though again
the author of the *Refutation* seems to be using his own more philosophical framework to present Callistus's thought, or is perhaps trying to

---

26 A point made by Heine ("Callistus," 63-8). Heine's own attempt to read Callistus' Christology in terms of the Stoic distinction between λόγος προφόρικος and λόγος
ἐνδιάθετος, however, also seems to be based upon the interpretations offered by
Tertullian and Origen, given in the categories with which they were familiar, rather than
derived from the reports presented in the *Refutation*, and thus is equally open to misinter-
pretation. If Callistus is indeed following in a more Irenaean position, it is very unlikely
that he would have employed this distinction (cf. *AH* 2.28.5-6).

27 Cf. Heine, "Callistus," 69; Heine also suggests the plausible emendation to the text of *Ref.*
10.27.3, to bring out a possible reference by Callistus to Jn 4:24 (ibid. 70).

associate him once more with Sabellius.[28] Finally, the account concludes by acknowledging that Callistus "does not want to say that the
Father suffered," yet nevertheless teaches that "the Father co-suffered
with the Son."[29] As with Zephyrinus, Callistus seems to be trying to
find a way to affirm that God really is involved in the death of Christ,
that the Passion does express the wisdom and the power of God, yet at
the same time maintain the distinction between the Son, who died,
and the Father revealed by the Son.[30]

The "True Discourse" of the Refutation

The theological outlook of the author of the *Refutation*, as presented
in his own "True Discourse on the Divine," which concludes his
lengthy discussion of all the heresies (*Ref.* 10.32-4; at 34.1), is very
different from that of his opponents. Although we do not know how
they would have presented their theology given the opportunity to do
so, it is clear, despite the polemical depiction of them, that their central concern, and probable starting point, was Jesus Christ, who
through his Passion reveals God the Father. The starting point of the
"True Discourse," on the other hand, is not the scriptural interpretation of Jesus, whose name is not even mentioned, but is much more
abstract, beginning, in a philosophical manner, by setting a framework relating God, the Logos and creation. It begins by describing
"the first and only, one God," the creator and Lord of all, who "was
one, alone by himself" (*Ref.* 10.32.1). There was nothing eternal
alongside this God, but he brought all things into being by his will,
beings which, composed of diverse elements, are liable to disintegra-
tion and death (*Ref.* 10.32.1-4). Having described God and creation,
Platonic and Stoic elements are then brought together to explain
how, in fact, this God was not alone, but had with him the Logos
who effected the creation of the world:

---

28 *Ref.* 9.12.18-19. Cf. Heine, "Callistus," 72-4
29 *Ref.* 9.12.18-19: τὸν πατέρα συμπεπονθέναι τῷ υἱῷ.
30 Heine points to the Stoic background of the term συμπάσχειν, where it can be used to
    describe the relation between the soul and the body (cf. Cleanthes, *SVF* I, 518), to con-
    clude: "Just as the soul, though it interacts (συμπάσχει) with the body when the latter is
    cut, does not bleed, so the Roman modalists could have thought of the Father's interaction
    with the Son in the Son's suffering." ("Callistus," 78).

The sole and supreme God, taking thought, begot the Logos first (λόγον πρῶτον ἐννοηθεὶς ἀπογεννᾷ), not a Logos as voice (οὐ δὲ λόγον ὡς φωνήν), but the immanent reason of the whole (ἐνδιάθετον τοῦ παντὸς λογισμόν). This one alone he begot from what was in existence, for it was the Father himself who was existence, from whom he was begotten. And the Logos was the cause of all created things, bearing in himself the will of the one who begot him, not being unacquainted with the thought of the Father. And proceeding from the begetter, he was the first-begotten of this one, as a voice containing in himself the ideas conceived in the paternal mind. And thus, when the Father ordered the world to be made, the Logos completed each thing pleasing to God. (*Ref.* 10.33.1-2)

Without doubt, the Logos of God is understood here not simply as the expression of God, his voice, but as an independent agent capable of knowing the Father and fulfilling his will; if he can be compared to a voice, it is as one who can hold the ideas contained in another's mind. It is this Logos who brought all of creation into being, the earth and heavens, the animals and their ruler, man (*Ref.* 10.33.3-10). The "True Discourse" asserts that God could also have created man "a god," as he did the Logos, but chose to make human beings who, if they desire to "become god," can do so through obedience.[31] While all other things were created out of nothing (ἐξ οὐδενός), the Logos alone is from God, "and therefore God, being a thing of God,"[32] and "the first-begotten child of the Father" (ὁ πρωτόγονος πατρός παῖς) who controls all things within creation (*Ref.* 10.33.11).

Having established the basic structure within which to theologize, the "True Discourse" continues by describing briefly how man was guided by the Law and the Prophets until the last days, when the Father "sent forth this Logos to speak no longer by a prophet, not wishing [the Logos] to be conjectured because obscurely proclaimed, but to be visibly manifest," so that, by seeing "the speaker himself present," rather than giving commands through a prophet or causing fear by an

31 *Ref.* 10.33.7. This is similar to a point made by Irenaeus, but for Irenaeus while God could have created man perfect from the beginning, man, as newly created, would not have been able to receive or retain this gift (*AH* 4.38.1-2).
32 *Ref.* 10.33.8: διὸ καὶ θεός, οὐσία ὑπάρχων θεοῦ. Here οὐσία does not have the later sense of the common nature or essence of Father and Son, but is used in a looser sense, to indicate that the Logos is "something" which is "of God" and "God" himself. Cf. P. Nautin, *Hippolyte et Josipe* (Paris: Cerf, 1947), 116, n. 2.

angel, the world might finally be persuaded of him (*Ref.* 10.33.14). In the ensuing analysis of how the Logos is present and what this effects, the emphasis is almost exclusively on the model established by the Logos for imitation. Having received a body from the Virgin, the Logos passed through every stage of life, exhibiting a model for all, an idea found earlier in Irenaeus, who, however, sees the action of Christ in broader terms, as sanctifying and saving each age.[33] "This man" was of the same nature as we are, so that it is not in vain that man is instructed "to imitate the teacher" (*Ref.* 10.33.16). Moreover, "lest he be supposed to be different to us, he underwent toil, and willed to be hungry, and did not refuse to be thirsty, and sunk into sleep, and did not protest his Passion, was obedient unto death and manifested the Resurrection, offering as first fruits in all these things his own man" (τὸν ἴδιον ἄνθρωπον), and all this was undertaken so that we might not be disheartened in our own suffering, but "confessing yourself to be a man, you also might expect what God has bestowed upon him" (*Ref.* 10.33.17). Those who are instructed in this knowledge of the true God are able, according to the "True Discourse," to avoid the torments of Tartarus; those who have known the heavenly kingdom while living on this earth will become a "co-heir with Christ," with an immortal and incorruptible body, subject neither to suffering, passion or disease, for they will have "been deified" and "rendered immortal," having "become a god" (*Ref.* 10.34.2-4).

Becoming a god is evidently a key theme in the "True Discourse," from its initial discussion of the creation of man (*Ref.* 10.33.7) to its closing words: "For God is not poor, and will make you a god to his glory" (*Ref.* 10.34.5). This provides the context for the bold reinterpretation it offers of the injunction of the Delphic oracle: "this is to 'know yourself,' to know the creator God; for the one called by him, to know himself [34] is to be known [by him]" (*Ref.* 10.34.4). God is now the object of knowledge, but he is known, to those called, by their knowledge of themselves and the work of God in creating them, making them gods. The model for all this is certainly provided by the Incarnate

---

33 *Ref.* 10.33.15; cf. Irenaeus, *AH* 2.22.4.
34 Marcovich, following Nautin (*Hippolyte et Josipe*, 125 and 126, ftn. 2), prefers αὐτὸν, rather than the ms ἑαυτὸν.

Logos, making clear what the prophets had spoken obscurely, but the attempt to understand Jesus Christ and his revelation of the Father through an interpretative engagement with the Scriptures, beyond the briefest of allusions, is almost completely absent. The presentation in fact has more in common with a gnostic myth describing the sojourn of a divine aeon sent to instruct the elect with a knowledge that can effect salvation and deification. In comparison with the glimpses we are given of the concerns of his opponents, Zephyrinus and Callistus, the contrast could not be more stark.

Hippolytus

An attempt at mediating between these two positions seems to be elaborated in the work *Contra Noetum*, which is generally accepted to be by Hippolytus and probably written within the same "school" as the *Refutation*. The first part of this work deals with the error of the Noetians, but already in his refutation of them, Hippolytus demonstrates the crux of what will be his own position: he accuses them of having used the Scriptures arbitrarily, not understanding the harmony that exists between the prophets and the apostles, both speaking of the same Christ Jesus, the Father's Word (*CN* 4.5). After dealing with Noetus, as discussed above, Hippolytus opens his own "Demonstration of the Truth" with an emphatic statement that sets his whole theological project on a trajectory quite different to that followed in the *Refutation*: "There is one God, and we acquire knowledge of him from no other source, brethren, than the Holy Scriptures" (*CN* 9.1). It is, therefore, these Scriptures that have to be investigated, to see how they speak of the Father, Son and Holy Spirit, so that we might believe in the Father, glorify the Son and receive the Spirit in the manner that the Father willed that the Son be glorified and the Spirit be imparted—"the way God himself resolved to reveal them [i.e. the Son and the Spirit] through the Holy Scriptures" (*CN* 9.2-3). The God proclaimed by the Scriptures "exists alone, with nothing contemporaneous with himself," for all things were created by him as he willed (*CN* 10.1). Yet he was not fully alone, "for he was manifold" (πολὺς ἦν) not being word-less or wisdom-less, power-less or mind-less, but everything was in him and he was everything (*CN* 10.2). More concretely, "when he willed, as he willed, at the times determined by himself, he showed his Word (ἔδειξεν τὸν λόγον αὐτοῦ), through whom he made all thing" (*CN* 10.3). The primary reference point for Hippolytus is the Word who is thus "demonstrated"—it is Christ Jesus who is the Father's Word (*CN* 4.5)—and it is this one through whom God originally created the world. "He begot the Word," Hippolytus continues, as the "Leader" (cf. Acts 3:15), the "Counselor" (cf. Is 40:13) and "Craftsman" (cf. Prov 8:22) for the world; "uttering what was previously a sound" (προτέραν φωνὴν φθεγγόμενος), God sent into creation the Lord, "his own Mind," making visible what had previously only been seen by himself, "so that through his appearance the world might be able to see and be saved" (*CN* 10.4). The departure point for theological reflection is emphatically the salvific manifestation of the Lord, the Mind of the Father and his Word, who prior to this revelation was known only to the Father, being but a "sound" to the world. In this way, Hippolytus continues, "another took his stand besides him" (οὕτως αὐτῷ παρίστατο ἕτερος), and he specifies that by saying "other" he is not speaking of "two gods" (*CN* 11.1). Rather, as light from light, water from a spring and the sunbeam from the sun, there is only one Father and one Power or Word from him (*CN* 11.1), so that the light seen in the Word is not other than the light of the Father himself. Along with this denial of being a "ditheist," Hippolytus is also keen to dissociate himself from Valentinus and others, who "propose a whole crowd of gods, being emitted at different times."[35]

Having specified that theological reflection should begin from the visible manifestation of the Word in Scripture and what this reveals of God, Hippolytus continues by describing how the Law and the Prophets do in fact testify of him. The Prophets, in particular, inspired by the Spirit "caught a breath of the Power of the Father" so that they

---

35 *CN* 11.3. Brent argues that the recollection of the bishops gathered at Philippopolis in 347, that Callistus had expelled Hippolytus from the Church on the grounds of being a Valentinian (*apud* Hilary, *ex oper. hist. frag.* III.ii.662, ed. Veron), should be taken as referring to the author of the *CN* (*Hippolytus*, 357-9); it would seem, however, that Hippolytus is here (at *CN* 11.3) responding to an earlier accusation, and given what we have seen of the "True Discourse" in the *Refutation*, it would seem more plausible to refer the charge to its author. Cf. J. J. I. von Döllinger, *Hippolytus and Callistus*, trans. A. Plummer (Edinburgh: T. and T. Clark, 1876), 202-4.

could announce his Counsel and Will (*CN* 11.4); in turn, the Word "dwelt (πολιτευόμενος) in them, speaking (ἐφθέγγετο) about himself, already being his own herald in demonstrating how the Word would appear among men" (*CN* 12.1). The Word is made manifest through this scriptural texture, and this is indicated, for Hippolytus, by the words of Isaiah, "I was being made manifest to those who did not seek me" (Is 65:11; *CN* 12.1-2). John also "recapitulates" what was said by the Prophets in the beginning of his prologue (*CN* 12.3). It is therefore only the "enfleshed Word that we contemplate" (*CN* 12.5), but it is not strictly speaking or merely the "flesh" that is contemplated: the Word of God was already being revealed prior to his enfleshment. Jeremiah, for instance, spoke of standing in the presence of God and "seeing his Word" (Jer 23:18), announcing "the Word who would be made manifest" (*CN* 13.1). Unlike human speech that is audible, the Word of God, Hippolytus argues, is itself visible (*CN* 13.2). Most important, however, is the fact that the "visible Word" that has been sent out by the Father, was sent out specifically through "the preaching of Jesus Christ" (Acts 10:36, cited in *CN* 13.3). In other words, the Word of God made "manifest" (ἐμφανής, *CN* 13.1) is the preaching of Jesus Christ, in which we can behold "the enfleshed Word," and it is this "visible Word" that is the subject of the audible words of the prophets from the beginning. Hippolytus puts this in striking terms a few chapters later, when he asserts that "in the very same way in which he was proclaimed, he became present as well" (*CN* 17.4). The "enfleshed Word," who is both earthly and heavenly (*CN* 17.4), is made manifest in the preaching of the apostles, which is itself composed of the fabric of Scripture. In his treatise *On Christ and the Antichrist*, Hippolytus develops this insight through an extended metaphor:

> For the Word of God, being fleshless, put on the holy flesh from the holy virgin, as a bridegroom a garment, having woven it for himself in the sufferings of the Cross, so that having mixed our mortal body with his own power, and having mingled the corruptible into the incorruptible, and the weak with the strong, he might save perishing man.
> The web-beam, therefore, is the Passion of the Lord upon the Cross,
> and the warp on it is the power of the Holy Spirit,
> and the woof is the holy flesh woven by the Spirit,

and the thread is the grace which by the love of Christ binds and unites the
two in one,
and the rods are the Word;
and the workers are the patriarchs and prophets who weave the fair, long,
perfect tunic for Christ;
and the Word passing through these, like the combs (or rods), completes
through them that which his Father wills.[36]

The flesh of the Word, received from the Virgin and "woven in the sufferings of the Cross," is woven by the patriarchs and prophets, whose actions and words proclaim the manner in which the Word became present and manifest. It is in the preaching of Jesus Christ, the proclamation of the one who died on the Cross, interpreted and understood in the matrix, the womb, of Scripture, that the Word receives flesh from the virgin. The virgin in this case, Hippolytus later affirms following Revelation 12, is the Church, who will never cease "bearing from her heart the Word that is persecuted by the unbelieving in the world," while the male child she bears is Christ, God and man, announced by the prophets, "whom the Church continually bears as she teaches all nations."[37]

To explain how the Son, proclaimed in this manner, relates to the one God and Father, Hippolytus employs the idea of "economy."[38] The confession that there is one God does not entail that one should abandon the economy (*CN* 3.4), in which there are clearly three "persons" (πρόσωπα), Father, Son and Spirit (*CN* 14.1-3), not simply different modes of appearance but "really three" (ὄντως τρία, *CN* 8.1). God is unquestionably one, and this is shown in the fact that the activity of God is single; yet the demonstration of this activity in the economy is "triple" (τριχής, *CN* 8.2), for the Father orders, the Son executes these orders and this is revealed in the Spirit (*CN* 14.4-5). It is Jesus Christ himself, the Father's own Word, who is the heart of this demonstration, for he is "the mystery of the economy" (*CN* 4.5). The words of Isaiah misunderstood by the Noetians, that "In you is God" (Is 45:14),

---

36 *On Christ and the Antichrist*, 4; see also the extended metaphor in *Antichrist*, 59.
37 *Antichrist*, 61: . . . ὃν ἀεὶ τίκουσα ἡ ἐκκλησία διδάσκει πάντα τὰ ἔθνη.
38 In the *Refutation*, the term "economy" only appears in connection with the Marcosans, (*Ref.* 6.47.1, 3; 51.1, 4-5; 52.9); it was also used, in a similar manner to the *CN*, by Irenaeus, e.g., *Dem.* 47.

demonstrates "the mystery of the economy," for it speaks of the Father being in the Son and the Son in the Father, when the Word was enfleshed and dwelt among men (*CN* 4.7, cf. Jn 14:10). Reflecting on the gradual revelation of Father, Son and Spirit, Hippolytus concludes that the Jews did not know the Son and so were not able to give thanks to the Father, while the disciples knew the Son, but not in the Spirit, and so even they denied him. The confession of the one God in the proper manner requires the ability to see the Father in the Son by means of the Spirit: "by means of this triad (τριάδος), the Father is glorified; for the Father willed, the Son enacted [it], and the Spirit made [it] manifest. Now the whole of the Scriptures proclaim this" (*CN* 14.8). It is only by the Spirit that the proclamation of Christ in Scripture is manifest so that the Father can be glorified through the Son who has fulfilled his will; it is, as Paul put it, only by the Spirit that one can speak of Jesus Christ as Lord (cf. 1 Cor 12:3), so acknowledging how the Scriptures speak of Christ and how, as Son, he reveals the Father.

Before concluding with a long, eloquent peroration, Hippolytus deals with a possible objection: "'But,' someone will say to me, 'it sounds strange to me when you call the Son "Word."' John indeed says "Word," but he is speaking, rather, allegorically" (ἀλλ᾽ ἄλλως ἀλληγορεῖ, *CN* 15.1). Hippolytus emphatically denies that the term "Word" is to be taken figuratively. His presentation, as we have seen, begins with the preaching of Jesus Christ, and it is this one that Hippolytus describes as the Word of God. He points out that this is the way that "John" himself speaks when, in Revelation, it is the rider on the white horse, clad in a robe dipped in blood, who is called the Word of God (*CN* 15.2; Rev 19:11-13). Similarly, the prophets also spoke of his suffering in the flesh (*CN* 15.4, Mic 2:7-8), as did the Apostle (*CN* 15.5, Rom 8:3-4). This is the message spoken by the Word through the prophets from the beginning, which becomes enfleshed in the apostolic preaching of Jesus Christ; to take the term "Word" in any other sense would be an allegory, according to Hippolytus. Prior to its actualization, however, it is only spoken about as something yet to happen, and as such, the Word was addressed by the Father as "Son, in view of what he was to be in the future,"[39] for it is Jesus Christ who is the eternal Son of God. Reflecting on this, Hippolytus then comments:

39 *CN* 15.6: … ὃν υἱὸν προσηγόρευε διὰ τὸ μέλλειν αὐτὸν γενέσθαι.

Neither was the Word, without flesh and by himself, perfect Son, although being Word he was perfect *Monogenes* [unique]; nor was it possible for the flesh, by itself, to exist without the Word, for it has its subsistence in the Word. So in this way a single perfect Son of God was made manifest.[40]

The point Hippolytus is making here, which epitomizes his whole approach to theological reflection, is simply that one can only understand the Word of God as it is revealed in the preaching of Jesus Christ, the enfleshed Word, yet, at the same time, one must not remain at the flesh itself, for the flesh only exists as the flesh of the Word. As we have seen, the Son of God, the enfleshed Word, is only made manifest in the preaching of the apostles. The flesh did not exist prior to this, "in heaven" where dwelt "the fleshless Word" (*CN* 4.11), yet what was to come was already the subject of the Prophets' words throughout Scripture as they proclaimed the visible Word of God. The point of the distinction between the "fleshlessness" of the Word prior to the apostolic preaching and the enfleshed state thereafter, is not to sketch events in a mythical biography of the Word of God, nor to suggest that the eternal Word of God has undergone a change. Rather, the point of the contrast is ultimately antidocetic, to emphasize that despite the fact that the Word of God was always seen and spoken of in human form, foreshadowing what was to come, Jesus Christ, the Son and Word of God, was really flesh as we are, though this can only be contemplated in the apostolic preaching, as the Word of God.[41]

These debates in Rome brought several important issues to the fore, in particular the need to distinguish Father and Son, and yet in some

---

40 *CN* 15.7: οὔτε γὰρ ἄσαρκος καὶ καθ᾽ ἑαυτὸν ὁ λόγος τέλειος ἦν υἱός, καίτοι τέλειος, λόγος ὤν, μονογενής· οὔθ᾽ ἡ σάρξ καθ᾽ ἑαυτὴν δίχα τοῦ λόγου ὑποστῆναι ἠδύνατο διὰ τὸ ἐν λόγῳ τὴν σύστασιν ἔχειν. οὕτως οὖν εἷς υἱὸς τέλειος θεοῦ ἐφανερώθη.

41 A similar point is made by Brent, "His theology enabled him to articulate sharply the distinction between the vision of the λόγος in human form as it appeared before the incarnation and after the incarnation, as is made clear by the distinction between ἄσαρκος... and ἔνσαρκος ...But the theology that furnished such an instrument with which to refute Docetism was itself found faulty in terms of later Nicene orthodoxy which could never admit that the πρόσωπα of the Father and Son were only real after the incarnation and not eternally in existence." (*Hippolytus*, 227). The latter qualification, however, may be misplaced: to say that it is Jesus Christ who is the Son of God, does not deny the eternality of the Son, unless this is taken in a naively temporal sense; he is already being spoken of by the Prophets, and indeed the focus is upon him from the very beginning with the creation of Adam (cf. Rom 5:14).

manner maintain that what is seen in the Son, especially in his Passion, really does reveal God himself. If there was a truth that those charged with "patripassianism," crucifying the Father, wanted to preserve, this was it. How they combined their characteristic emphasis on the singularity of the revelation of God in Christ, a direct application of the christocentric reading of Scripture intrinsic to the preaching of the Gospel, with the necessary distinction between Father and Son is not indicated by the author of the *Refutation*, though his account of the Word, abstracted from any interpretative engagement with Scripture and elaborated in philosophical or even mythological terms, is hardly a successful alternative. A further important point, directly connected with the first, is that the native context for theological statements is Scripture, so that the identity of the Son of God is established from the apostolic preaching, in terms of which he is recognized as the eternal Word of God spoken of by the Law and the Prophets. Hippolytus' reflections on the relationship between the flesh of Christ and the Word are developed precisely within this framework: the flesh of the enfleshed Word, the Son, subsists only in the Word which is made manifest by the apostolic preaching, itself an interpretative engagement with Scripture, of Christ the eternal Son of God.

7

Origen and Alexandria

Origen (c. 185-c. 254) visited Rome during the time of Zephyrinus (*EH* 6.14.10), in the midst of the controversies taking place there. He was already established as a teacher of some importance in Alexandria. Despite Eusebius' attempts to suggest a continuity of teachers heading a "Catechetical School" in Alexandria, alongside and under the jurisdiction of a succession of bishops, the structure of early Alexandrian Christianity was probably much more akin to the situation in Rome, with various groups gathering around fairly independent teachers.[1] Early second-century Alexandrian Christianity was dominated by teachers such as Basilides and Valentinus, who are, in fact, the only figures from this period of whom we know anything.[2] Eusebius, wanting to emphasize Origen's ecclesial respectability, at least within his own fourth-century perspective, described Origen as having been appointed to lead the "school of catechesis" (*EH* 6.3.8), succeeding his teacher Clement (c. 150-c.215), who had succeeded his own teacher, Pantaenus (*EH* 6.6.1). However, elsewhere Eusebius describes Pantaenus as leading "the school of the faithful" (*EH* 5.10.1), and although Clement almost certainly studied under Pantaenus, along with many other teachers,[3] Eusebius seems to imply that Pantaenus and Clement were involved together in training in the "divine Scriptures" (*EH* 5.11.1). Moreover, while some of Clement's work is aimed at those preparing for baptism, the teaching he offers does not stop there, but develops, through a continuous pedagogy, to the highest realms of

---

1 Cf. G. Bardy, "Aux origines de l'école d'Alexandrie," *RSR* 27 (1937), 65-90, and, most recently, A. van den Hoek, "The 'Catechetical School' of Early Christian Alexandria and Its Philonic Heritage," *HTR* 90.1 (1997), 59-87.

2 For a blunt statement of the Gnostic tendency of early Egyptian Christianity, see W. Bauer, *Orthodoxy and Heresy*, 44-60; for a more balanced assessment see C. H. Roberts, *Manuscript, Society and Belief in Early Christian Egypt* (London: Oxford University Press, 1979).

3 Cf. Clement, *Strom.* 1.1.11.1-2.

esoteric exegesis and theological speculation: Clement, just like Pantaenus, taught the faithful, in particular those interested in a deeper understanding of Christianity. In addition, both Pantaenus and Clement are described as "presbyters," which seems to imply a full priestly function.[4] Clement himself can use the term "presbyter" interchangeably with "bishop," and when he writes of those who have preserved "the true tradition of the blessed doctrines derived directly from the holy apostles" he is referring specifically to the "teachers."[5] Despite this earlier fluidity of terminology, Jerome suggests that it was the custom, until the mid-third century, for the presbyters of the various communities in Alexandria to elect one from their own ranks to receive a "higher position as bishop."[6] The first "bishop" of Alexandria about whom Eusebius records any information beyond a mere name and conjectured dates is Demetrius, who "received the episcopate of the communities there" probably in 189.[7] It is, however, only much later that Demetrius plays any role in Eusebius' narrative.[8] After Origen's father was martyred during the persecutions under the prefect Laetus (201-3) and his family was left destitute, a wealthy lady took Origen into her house and made it possible for him to continue in his studies until he was able to support himself by teaching (*EH* 6.2.2-13). She also treated as her "adopted son" a certain heretic from Antioch called Paul, whose teaching had attracted "a multitude not only of heretics but also of our people," though Eusebius is emphatic that Origen never joined Paul in prayer (*EH* 6.2.13-14). Eusebius' account does not suggest that this

4   For references and discussion, see van den Hoek, "The 'Catechetical School,'" 77.
5   Clement, *Strom.* 1.1.11.3. In *Who is the Rich Man that shall be Saved?* 42.3-4, Clement describes the same person as "bishop" and then "presbyter," and he occasionally pairs "presbyter" with "deacon" rather than "bishop" (*Strom.* 3.12.90.1; 7.1.3.3). It is also interesting to note that it was the "presbyters and teachers" of the region of Arsinoë that Dionysius of Alexandria gathered together, in the middle of the third century, to convince them of the errors of Nepos (*EH* 7.24.6).
6   Jerome, *Epistle* 146.1.
7   *EH* 6.2.2; here Eusebius places this event around the year 203, though the date of 189, suggested by *EH* 6.26, seems preferable. R. M. Grant suggests that this confusion results from Eusebius "finding it difficult to correlate his legends about Origen with his legendary bishop list" ("Early Alexandrian Christianity," *CH* 40 [1971], 142).
8   Neither is Demetrius mentioned by Clement, whose pedagogic activity would have coincided with the first decade of Demetrius' episcopacy. It is possible that Clement too had left Alexandria because of difficulties with Demetrius. Cf. P. Nautin, *Lettres et écrivains chrétiens*, 118.

rather eclectic group met in the house of their benefactress in addition to, or instead of, gathering elsewhere in an otherwise constituted church. He gives the impression, rather, that even at this period there were a number of such communities coexisting in Alexandria, and that the relationships, and boundaries, between these house churches were somewhat hazy, a situation that seems to have prevailed until the middle of the third century.[9] When the persecutions were renewed under the prefect Aquila (206-11), all the teachers of Christianity fled Alexandria, and so Origen took it upon himself to instruct those who turned to him "to hear the Word of God."[10] He soon had a number of disciples, many of whom were martyred. Origen fearlessly accompanied them to their trials and was continually harassed, but was never himself arrested (*EH* 6.3-5). When Demetrius returned, after the persecutions had ceased (c. 211), he was clearly obliged to praise Origen's efforts, but he also seems to have tried to appropriate Origen's activity under his own auspices by "entrusting him alone with the school of catechesis."[11] It is really only from this period, when the pedagogic activity of previously independent teachers was placed at the service of a newly emerging monarchical style of episcopacy, that one can begin to speak of a "Catechetical School" in Alexandria.[12]

9   Cf. *EH* 7.9, and the comments of R. D. Williams, "Origen: Between Orthodoxy and Heresy," in W. A. Bienert and U. Kühneweg (eds.), *Origeniana Septima* (Leuven: Peeters, 1999), 6.

10 *EH* 6.3.1. On Eusebius' conflation of the two phases of the persecutions, see Nautin, *Origène: Sa vie et son œuvre* (Paris: Beauchesne, 1977), 363-5. Eusebius states that it was "some of the heathen" who came to Origen, though he assumes that Pantaenus, Clement and Origen were only ever involved in catechesis. In *HomJer.* 4.3 (2) Origen describes how during the times of martyrdom "we came to the gathering, and the entire Church was present" (ἐπὶ τὰς συναγωγάς, καὶ ὅλη ἡ ἐκκλησία. . . παρεγίνετο). Nautin refers this to the persecution under Aquila; his conclusion, however, that some priests must have remained in the city, seems unnecessary (*Origène*, 416, ftn. 11).

11 *EH* 6.3.8. It is while describing Origen's work of instruction in this period that Eusebius relates the story of Origen's act of self-castration (*EH* 6.8), suggesting that it was done so as to avoid charges of misconduct from pagans regarding his dealings with women (though Eusebius also claims that he kept it secret!), and that it resulted from an over-literal interpretation (!) of Matt 19. Epiphanius, on the other hand, records a tradition that attributed Origen's amazing chastity to drugs (*Panarion*, 64.3.12). H. Chadwick suggests that both stories are "malicious gossip" (*Early Christian Thought and the Classical Tradition* [Oxford: Clarendon Press, 1987 (1966)], 68).

12 For Demetrius' place within the emerging monarchical episcopacy, and the reaction it provoked from Origen, see J. W. Trigg, "The Charismatic Intellectual: Origen's Understanding of Religious Leadership," *CH* 50 (1981), 5-19.

However, if there was a new collaboration, it also produced an uneasy tension. In a letter he wrote after his final departure from Alexandria, a passage of which is preserved in Eusebius (*EH* 6.19.12-14), Origen felt obliged to defend the propriety of studying philosophy and investigating heretical doctrines. But according to Eusebius, Origen, in his new relationship with Demetrius, abandoned his former teaching of grammar and literature, partly because of the number of disciples, but mainly because it was not considered "consonant with divine training," and he even parted with his cherished volumes of ancient literature in exchange for a meager fixed income to support himself in his new occupation (*EH* 6.3.8-9). The relations between the Christian teacher and the Christian bishop were already "smouldering."[13] It was in this period that Origen visited Rome, perhaps looking for a more congenial milieu in which to pursue his studies and teaching.[14] When he returned from Rome, his teaching activity was reorganized. According to Eusebius, Origen entrusted "his pupil" Heraclas with "the preliminary studies of those just learning the elements," while he taught only the more advanced (*EH* 6.15). It is more likely, however, that Demetrius was more directly involved and that Origen was ousted from his previous role.[15] The issue was probably primarily personal, rather than concerning the propriety of study and philosophy, for Heraclas himself was in fact already a philosopher of great repute, perhaps more so than Origen.[16] In the letter he composed after his final departure from Alexandria (c. 232), Origen points out that Heraclas had attended the lectures of the famous philosopher Ammonius Saccas for five years longer than himself, and he notes somewhat wryly that even though he now "sits in the presbyterate of Alexandria," Heraclas

13 The description is that of R. Heine, *Origen: Homilies on Genesis and Exodus*, FC 71 (Washington: Catholic University of America, 1982), 12-13.

14 Nautin suggests this motive and places the visit around 215 (*Origène*, 365, 418).

15 R. L. Wilken speaks of Origen being "relieved of his duties by the bishop" ("Alexandria: A School for Training in Virtue," in P. Henry [ed.], *Schools of Thought in the Christian Tradition* [Philadelphia: Fortress, 1984], 17).

16 Knowing of the great learning of Heraclas, Julius Africanus visited Alexandria sometime prior to 221 (*EH* 6.31.2). Eusebius obscures the implication, that at this time Heraclas was more famous than Origen, by recounting this visit at a later point in his narrative, so that it is as "bishop" of Alexandria that Heraclas is known. Cf. Grant, "Early Alexandrian Christianity," 135.

still wears the philosopher's mantle and studies the books of the Greeks (*EH* 6.19.13-14). In Eusebius' reckoning Heraclas succeeded Demetrius as "bishop" of Alexandria (*EH* 6.26), and the following head of the Catechetical School, Dionysius, another "pupil" of Origen, also succeeded to the episcopacy after Heraclas (*EH* 6.29.4; 6.35). This integration of "School" and "Church" seems to have continued until the death of Theonas (300 A.D.), when Pierius, the head of the School, was passed over in preference for Theonas' protégé, Peter.

Back in Alexandria after his visit to Rome, Origen, supported by his wealthy patron Ambrose, whom he had converted from Valentinianism (*EH* 6.18.1), began writing his *Commentary on the Psalms* and other works concerned with more speculative and philosophical issues. The tension between Origen and Demetrius increased when Origen presented an allegorical interpretation of the creation story in his *Commentary on Genesis*. His attempts to defend the integrity of his faith and to justify his method of scriptural interpretation in *On First Principles* only exacerbated the situation further, to the point that "no small warfare broke out in the city."[17] Origen left the city for Palestine (c.230), where he took refuge with Alexander of Jerusalem. While he was there, the bishops of that region invited Origen to preach and expound the Scriptures in public. What seemed normal in Palestine, however, ran counter to Demetrius' developing sense of the episcopal role, and he protested that it was unheard of for a layman to preach in the presence of bishops. To this claim, Alexander simply replied, "I know not how he [Demetrius] comes to say what is plainly untrue," and gave precedents for this practice (*EH* 6.19.17). Persuaded by deacons sent by Demetrius, Origen eventually returned to Alexandria (*EH* 6.19.19). Their respective visions of the Church, however, were markedly different. When Origen, back in Alexandria, began his magisterial *Commentary on John*, he opened the first book with the assertion that true Levites, the priests and high priests, are "those who devote themselves to the divine Word and truly exist by the service of God alone,"[18] words which Origen later used to

17 *EH* 6.19.16. Cf. Nautin, *Origène*, 366.
18 *ComJn.* 1.10-11. Cf. J. A. McGuckin, "Structural Design and Apologetic Intent in Origen's *Commentary on John*," in G. Dorival and A. Le Boulluec (eds.), *Origeniana Sexta* (Leuven: Peeters, 1995), 441-57.

describe himself (*EH* 6.19.12) and a piety which infuses the whole of Eusebius' characterization of him. Whatever truce there had been between Demetrius and Origen did not last, and, probably in 232, Origen left Alexandria for good.

After a brief sojourn in Athens, Origen settled in Caesarea in Palestine.[19] Here he continued teaching, preaching and writing, completing his *Commentary on John*, composing numerous other commentaries and homilies on books of Scripture, and undertaking works such as the *Contra Celsum*, as well as being called upon to settle theological disputes at various ecclesiastical gatherings, the nature of which will be considered in the following chapter, until his death, either as a martyr under Decius (c. 250-1) or a few years later. Origen's literary output was prodigious; he was reported to have written between two and six thousand works. Partly because of its sheer volume, there simply being too much to copy, but mainly as a result of the controversy which the man and his works provoked during his own lifetime, and increasingly thereafter, until he was finally condemned as a heretic at the Second Council of Constantinople (in 553), the corpus has not survived intact.[20] A small number of works survive, in varying degrees of completeness, in Greek,[21] a larger number are extant in the Latin translations of Jerome and Rufinus, while the majority of the works are simply lost.[22] Due caution has to be taken when using those works that only exist in Latin, especially the work *On First Principles*, though with this work even more care is needed for the passages in Greek produced by Justinian and other later critics of Origen. Given the diversity of texts that have been preserved, it is not surprising that modern

19 For details of Origen's life outside of Alexandria, his ordination and his death see H. Crouzel, *Origen*, trans. A. S. Worrall (Edinburgh: T. and T. Clark, 1989), 17-36.

20 On the many dimensions of the controversy regarding Origen during the fourth century, see E. A. Clark, *The Origenist Controversy: The Cultural Construction of an Early Christian Debate* (Princeton: Princeton University Press, 1992).

21 These include eight books of the *Commentary on John*, eight books of the *Commentary on Matthew*, twenty *Homilies on Jeremiah*, *Contra Celsum*, extracts from various works, including *On First Principles*, preserved in the *Philokalia* compiled by Basil of Caesarea and Gregory of Nazianzus, *On Prayer*, the *Exhortation to Martyrdom*, the *Dialogue with Heraclides*, and fragments from the *Commentary on Romans* and *On Pascha*.

22 For further details, and an assessment of the value of the Latin translations, see Heine, *Origen: Homilies on Genesis and Exodus*, 25-39; Crouzel, *Origen*, 37-49.

assessments of Origen have differed widely.[23] An earlier tendency to present Origen as a systematic and speculative theologian, based upon *On First Principles* and the version of "origenism" condemned in the sixth century, has generally given way to a more sympathetic picture of Origen as an exegete. But such a contrast would not have been intelligible for Origen, for whom all theological reflection is ultimately exegetical in character. The *Commentary on John*, begun already in Alexandria and preserved in Greek, makes this point abundantly clear, and is thus the point of departure for this chapter.

Jesus Christ, the Gospel and Scripture

In the opening books of his *Commentary on John*, Origen directly addresses issues that had been discussed in Rome at the time of his visit there, and which had already informed his *On First Principles* and would continue to engage him to his final years, when writing the *Contra Celsum*. Origen's primary concern is that theological reflection should not remain at the level of the flesh, neither that of Jesus himself nor that of Scripture, its letters and their literal sense, but should penetrate these veils to discern the very Word of God. Equally important for Origen is that, understood in this manner, the Son of God should be affirmed to have his own distinct subsistence, alongside the Father, from all eternity. This second affirmation is bound up with the first for, according to Origen, those who hesitate to ascribe subsistence (ὑπόστασις) to the Son, or to clarify his being (οὐσία), take refuge in his designation "Word," and of all the various titles applied by Scripture to the Son of God, only in the case of this one do they refuse to analyze the manner in which it is applied (*ComJn.* 1.151-3). For Origen, theological reflection and affirmation require an awareness of the exegetical dimension in which such activity is carried out.

In the *Commentary on John*, Origen sets out the exegetical framework for his theological reflection by beginning the work with an extended analysis of the relation between Scripture, the Law and the Prophets, and the Gospel.[24] By "Gospel" Origen does not primarily

---

23 Cf. E. Osborn, "Origen: The Twentieth Century Quarrel and Its Recovery," in R. Daly (ed.), *Origeniana Quinta* (Leuven: Peeters, 1992), 26-39.

24 For the exegetical setting of the more systematic account of theology given in *On First*

mean "the narrative of the deeds, suffering and words of Jesus" (*ComJn.* 1.20), but all the writings which "present the sojourn (ἐπιδημία) of Christ and prepare for his coming (παρουσία) and produce it in the souls of those who are willing to receive the Word of God who stands at the door and knocks and wishes to enter their souls" (*ComJn.* 1.26). The Gospel thus is an "exhortatory address" (*ComJn.* 1.18), presenting the Word of God to the hearers in such a way that they receive the Word, who then dwells in them. If this definition can also be applied to the writings of the Law and the Prophets, Origen insists that this is possible only retrospectively:

> Before the sojourn of Christ, the Law and the Prophets did not contain the proclamation which belongs to the definition of the Gospel, since he who explained the mysteries in them had not yet come. But since the Savior has come and has caused the Gospel to be embodied, he has by the Gospel made all things as Gospel.[25]

So strong is Origen's emphasis upon the distinctiveness of the revelation brought by Christ that it leads him to suggest that heretics such as Marcion may have had a point: "It is indeed possible to agree with the heterodox view, that Moses and the prophets did not know the Father" (*ComJn.* 19.27). As Origen points out, though there are countless prayers in the Psalms and the Prophets, none of them address God as Father, but only as Lord and God.[26]

He is not, however, prepared to concede the ontological disjunction introduced by the heterodox between the God of the Old Testament and the God of the New Testament. Rather, having apparently conceded ground to Marcion, Origen makes a qualification which invests the designation of God as "Father" with new significance. When Christ explained the mysteries hidden in the writings of the Law and the Prophets, he revealed the spiritual sense of Scripture, and as the true meaning of their words this is, according to Origen, the meaning truly

---

Principles see K. J. Torjesen, "Hermeneutics and Soteriology in Origen's *Peri Archon*," *St. Patr.* 21 (Leuven: Peeters, 1989), 333-48.

25 *ComJn.* 1.33. The point is repeated a few lines later: "Nothing of the ancients was Gospel, then, before that Gospel which came into existence because of the sojourn of Christ" (*ComJn.* 1.36). Cf. *FP* 4.1.6: "We must add that it was after the advent of Jesus that the inspiration of the prophetic words and the spiritual nature of Moses' law came to light."

26 *ComJn.* 19.28. Cf. *On Prayer*, 22.

intended by those who wrote the Scriptures. So, Origen claims, they already

> spoke or wrote about God as Father in secret and not in a manner intelligible to all, so that they might not anticipate the grace that is poured out to all the world through Jesus, who calls all people to adoption so that he may declare the name of God to his brothers and praise the Father in the midst of the assembly in accordance with what has been written.[27]

That is, if Moses and the Prophets already knew God as Father, this knowledge is nevertheless dependent upon the grace granted only through Jesus. In this way, Origen ensures the constancy of the revelation of God, and does so by viewing it exclusively through Jesus Christ. Moreover, although Origen occasionally classifies the designation "Father" along with titles such as "Lord," "Creator," and "Judge" as "aspects" (ἐπίνοιαι) of God, here he suggests that the term "Father" should actually be considered as the very *name* of God, revealed for the first time by the Son.[28] Thus, for Origen, not only is it the relationship to the only-begotten Son, Jesus Christ, that defines God as Father, rather than the more general relationship of God to creation described by the Platonic designation "Father of all,"[29] but as the very name "Father" depends upon this relationship to the Son, the existence of the Son is now, as it were, constitutive of what it is to be God.[30] The Gospel which proclaims this fatherhood of God and opens up for all the possibility of adoption to sonship is the universal content of Scripture. This is the deeper, spiritual sense of Scripture, revealed in the exegesis taught by the Savior in the Gospel he caused to be embodied. The theological affirmation, that there is only one God, the Father of his Son Jesus Christ and those adopted as sons in him, is inextricably related for Origen to the exegetical setting in which the scope of the Gospel extends throughout Scripture.

In his *Commentary on Matthew,* Origen illustrates this ascendancy of the Gospel in terms of the transfiguration on Mount Tabor. According to Origen, when the disciples, seeing the Son of God on the

---

27 *ComJn.* 19.28, which concludes by citing Ps 21:23 (LXX), already applied to Christ in Heb 2:12.
28 Cf. P. Widdicombe, *The Fatherhood of God from Origen to Athanasius* (Oxford: Clarendon Press, 1994), 84.
29 Plato, *Timaeus,* 28c; Justin Martyr, *App.* 10.6.
30 Cf. Widdicombe, *Fatherhood,* 78-9.

mountain speaking with Moses, understood that it was he who said "A man shall not see my face and live" (Ex 33:20), they were unable to endure the radiance of the Word, and so fell on their faces, humbling themselves under the hand of God. However, he continues,

> after the touch of the Word, lifting up their eyes they saw Jesus only and no other. Moses, the Law, and Elijah, the prophetic element (ἡ προφητεία), became one only with the Gospel of Jesus; and they did not remain three as they formerly were, but the three became one. (*ComMatt.*12.43)

In this elevated state, to which we must return later, not only are the Law and the Prophets seen by the disciples as nothing other than the Gospel of Jesus, but this very vision is what it is to behold the transfigured Jesus himself. Scripture, the Law and the Prophets, are not made redundant by the proclamation of the Gospel, nor is the Gospel arbitrarily imposed as the true meaning of Scripture. The Law and the Prophets are the "basic discipline" (στοιχείωσις), without the knowledge of which it is impossible to understand the Gospel. Yet, when exegeted properly and understood fully, they lead "to the perfect comprehension of the Gospel and all the meaning (νοῦν) of the words and acts of Jesus Christ."[31] Origen continues his analysis of the transfiguration account by drawing attention to Jesus' injunction that the disciples should not speak of this vision until the Son of Man is raised from the dead (Matt 17:9). According to Origen, this indicates that Christ's glorified state in the Resurrection is akin (συγγενές) to that of the transfiguration (*ComMatt.*12.43), in which Jesus became one with his Gospel. Though anticipated in the transfiguration, the full revelation of the Gospel is nevertheless only actualized in the Resurrection, and only at this point do the patriarchs finally come to know God as Father (*ComMatt.* 17.36).

By pivoting theological reflection around this turning point, Origen secures two fundamental positions. First, that it is the humanity of the Savior which creates the very possibility for the Word of God to be made known.[32] Second, that it is this crux which ensures

---

31 *ComMatt.* 10.10. Nautin points out how the three-year catechumenate, reading through the Old Testament in preparation for the Gospel heard at baptism and Eucharist, developed in this time and is reflected in the structure of Origen's commentaries and homilies (*Origène*, 389-409).

32 K. J. Torjesen comments that "the incarnation is not only universal in its comprehensive disclosure of the divine Logos, but it is also universal in that in the taking on of flesh the

the eternal, unchanging, identity of the Word of God: "Jesus is proved to be the Son of God both before and after his Incarnation."[33] It is furthermore important to note that the revelation of the Word of God is focused specifically on his saving death on the Cross.[34] According to Origen, while the various miracles performed by Christ can be passed by in silence, "it is necessary to the proclamation of Jesus as Christ that he should be proclaimed as crucified" (*ComMatt.* 12.19). In another place Origen employs the imagery of Philippians 2 in a surprising manner to claim that by dying on the Cross "the goodness of Christ appeared greater and more divine and truly in accordance with the image of the Father," than if he had remained "equal to God" and had not become a servant for the salvation of the world.[35] It is therefore by the "economy" of the Passion that Christ reveals the Father (*ComJn.* 32.359). In fact, for Origen, "the high exaltation of the Son of Man which occurred when he glorified God in his own death consisted in the fact that he was no longer any different from the Word, but was the same with it" (*ComJn.* 32.325). In a similar manner to the vision of the transfigured Jesus as the Gospel which embraces the Law and the Prophets, anticipating his resurrectional existence, here the identity between Jesus and the Word of God turns upon the Passion, for it is as the crucified and risen one that he opens up the hidden sense of Scripture, the Word of God embodied in the Gospel. That this identity hangs upon the Cross means, in reverse, that the full revelation of the Word of God occurs through the saving death of Christ.

If the Law and the Prophets, when exegeted properly, refer to this Christ and his Gospel then, Origen concludes, he was already present

Logos makes himself comprehensible to all those who wear flesh... in the incarnation he has created the human conditions of his own perfect intelligibility for all time." (*Hermeneutical Procedure and Theological Method in Origen's Exegesis*, PTS 28 [Berlin: De Gruyter, 1986], 115).

33 *CC* 3.14. In *ComJn.* 1.236, Origen similarly suggests that in some way the Word of God must always be recognized as human, that "the human nature of the Son of God which was united with his divinity antedates his birth from Mary."

34 Cf. H. de Lubac, *Histoire et Esprit: L'intelligence de l'Écriture d'après Origène* (Paris: Aubier, 1950), 77-91.

35 *ComJn.* 1.231. Cf. *ComJn.* 10.25. In *FP* 1.2.8 the revelation of the Father by the Son's abasement is used to explain how Christ is the "express image" of God's being (cf. Heb 1:3).

to the righteous of old. Thus, in the passage considered earlier, before claiming that the writers of Scripture knew God as Father and wrote about this secretly, Origen suggests that "Christ sojourned spiritually in them and they had the Spirit of adoption," for only in this way could they speak, even if enigmatically, of God as Father.[36] The presence of Christ to Moses and the Prophets, sojourning in them and teaching them about God, is implied by the universal testimony of Scripture to Christ, as is the claim that when writing the books of Scripture they already saw the spiritual meaning that Christ would draw out from them.[37] Yet, just as it is only possible to see the Law and the Prophets as referring to Christ once they have been expounded by Christ himself in his bodily sojourn, so also the spiritual sojourn of Christ amongst the righteous of old is a consequence of the universal import of his bodily Incarnation. Origen maintains this order, and so preserves both the distinctiveness of Christ's Incarnation and its paradigmatic function. It is thus by analogy with the Incarnation of the Word from Mary that Origen, in his *Homilies on Leviticus*, describes the sojourn of the Word of God through Moses and the Prophets:

> As in "the last days," the Word of God, which was clothed with the flesh from Mary, proceeded into this world, and what was seen in him was one thing, and what was understood was another—for the sight of his flesh was open for all to see, but the knowledge of his divinity was given to the few, to the elect—so also, when the Word of God was brought to humans through the Prophets and the Lawgiver, it was not brought without proper clothing. For just as there it was covered with the veil of the flesh, so here with the veil of the letter, so that indeed the letter is seen as flesh but the spiritual sense hiding within is perceived as divinity. (*Homilies on Leviticus*, 1.1)

The Word of God is "incarnate" in the writings of the Law and the Prophets. Though the words of Scripture veil the Word of God, yet at

---

36 *ComJn.* 19.28. The same point is made in *ComJn.* 1.36-40.

37 Cf. *ComJn.* 6.19: "They lived because they shared in him who said, 'I am the life' [Jn 11:25]. And as heirs of such great promises, they received a manifestation, not only of angels but also of God in Christ. And perhaps because they saw the image of the invisible God [Col 1:15], since he who has seen the Son has seen the Father [Jn 14:9], they have been recorded to have seen God and to have heard him, having known God and heard his words in a divine manner." Origen continues in *ComJn.* 6.22: "It is clear that Moses saw in his mind the truth of the Law and the allegorical meanings, according to the anagogical sense, of the stories recorded by him."

the same time they alone provide the means by which the Word is known. It is not possible to arrive at the spiritual sense of Scripture in any other way than through the words of Scripture themselves. Thus, in his scriptural exegesis, Origen always begins with the literal or lexical sense (τὸ ῥητόν), before exploring its spiritual sense.[38] And, as we have seen, the veiled content of Scripture is identical to the truth taught by Christ, which is Christ himself. The importance of this for Origen, as the basis of all theological reflection, is amply shown by the emphatic manner in which he states this principle as the opening words of his *On First Principles*:

> All who believe and are certain that grace and truth came by Jesus Christ and that Christ is the truth according to his own saying, "I am the truth" [Jn 14:6], receive the knowledge which invites men to a good and blessed life, from nowhere else than the very words and teachings of Christ. By the words of Christ we do not mean only those which he taught when he was made man and dwelt in the flesh, since even before that Christ, the Word of God, was in Moses and in the prophets. (*FP* 1.Pref.1)

The Incarnation of Christ clearly has tremendous retrospective power for Origen. Using the sojourn of Christ in the flesh, and the exegesis taught by the risen Christ, as his paradigm, Origen finds Christ throughout the Scriptures, sojourning in the righteous figures of old and present as the spiritual sense of their writings.

Though present throughout Scripture, prior to his bodily sojourn Christ speaks indirectly, through the various figures of old.[39] In the writings of the apostles and evangelists, on the other hand, the Incarnate Word speaks directly, and, after his ascension, he bestows the Spirit, whose power is demonstrated in the discernment of all those now able to read the Scriptures and understand the spiritual sense intended by Moses and the Prophets who wrote under the inspiration of the same Spirit.[40] Nevertheless even in the case of the writings of the apostles and evangelists, it is important, for Origen, that theological reflection should not remain at the level of the letter or the flesh. As he

38 Regarding Origen's understanding of the "literal sense," Crouzel comments, "Origen means by it the raw matter of what is said, before, if that were possible, any attempt at interpretation is made." (*Origen*, 62).
39 Cf. Torjesen, *Hermeneutical Procedure*, 111-13.
40 *FP* 2.7.2.

points out, in the passage from the *Homilies on Leviticus* cited above, it is not enough to see the flesh of Christ to see his divinity.[41] Origen is concerned that the Word of God should not be reduced to the flesh which he assumed to make himself known, through his salvific death, nor that his presence should be restricted in this way to the past. Origen extends the paradigm of the Incarnation not only backwards but forwards, so that there is a third aspect to the sojourn of the Word. These three dimensions are brought together in a striking passage from his *Homilies on Jeremiah*:

> According to the coming of our Lord Jesus Christ as narratively told (κατὰ μὲν τὴν ἰστορουμένην παρουσίαν), his sojourn (ἐπιδημία) was bodily and something universal, illumining the whole world, for "the Word became flesh and dwelt among us" [Jn 1:14]. "He was the true light that enlightens every man who comes into the world. He was in the world and the world was made through him, yet the world knew him not. He came to his own, and his own received him not" [Jn 1:9-11]. However, it is also necessary to know that he was also sojourning prior to this, though not bodily, in each of the holy ones, and that after this visible sojourn of his, he again sojourns in us… It is necessary for us to know these things, because there is a sojourn of the Word with each, especially for those who would benefit from it. For what benefit is it to me, if the Word has sojourned in the world and I do not have him?[42]

What is brought about in the coming of Jesus Christ is thus extended to the sojourn of the Word in the righteous of old and is continued in those who now turn to the Word. The significance of the Incarnation is thus not limited to the coming of Jesus Christ, but is extended to all those in whom the Word sojourns. To see the sojourning of the Word in such universal terms clearly takes us beyond the flesh of Christ himself, the Incarnate Word, just as it takes us beyond

---

41 Cf. *Homilies on Luke*, 1.4: "The apostles themselves saw the Word, not because they had beheld the body of our Lord and Savior, but because they had seen the Word. If seeing Jesus' body meant seeing God's Word, then Pilate, who condemned Jesus, saw God's Word; so did Judas the traitor, and all those who cried out, 'crucify him, crucify him, remove such a one from the earth.' But far be it that any unbeliever should see God's Word. Seeing God's Word means what the Savior says, 'He who has seen me has also seen the Father who sent me.'"

42 *HomJer.* 9.1. Cf. *ComJn.* 20.91-4, where the presence of Christ, both before and after his coming, is related specifically to the crucifixion, for "there is no period when the spiritual economy concerning Jesus [i.e. the Passion] was not present to the saints" (*ComJn.* 20.94).

the literal or lexical (τὸ ῥητόν) sense of the four Gospels. But, Origen points out, there are so many discrepancies in the accounts presented by the Gospels, that one must admit that their truth does not lie in their literal sense.[43] The four evangelists, according to Origen, even allowed a certain degree of distortion in their accounts of Jesus, in order to present the spiritual truth where it was not possible to speak the truth both materially and spiritually.[44] It is thus necessary to "adapt the events of the narrative account (τὰ τῆς ἱστορίας)," if we are to preserve "the good things given once for all to the saints" (Jude 3) and so maintain "the harmony of the exposition (τὴν συμφωνίαν τῆς διηγήσεως) of the Scriptures from beginning to end" (*ComJn.* 10.290). So, just as the humanity of Christ and his human story needs to be interpreted to see in it the divinity of the Word of God, so also it is necessary to interpret the words of the Gospels. It is certainly necessary to begin with the humanity of Christ as recorded in the letters of the Gospels, for it is in and through this that his divinity is revealed.[45] But theological reflection cannot remain at the level of the flesh, otherwise it will never contemplate his divinity nor will it produce the sojourn of the Word in the believer, an effect which, as we have seen, lies at the heart of the definition of the "Gospel." Origen thus differentiates "in aspect" (τῇ ἐπινοίᾳ) the "bodily" Gospel, which is "perceptible to the senses," and the "spiritual" Gospel, arrived at by interpretation. At the literal level, the Gospels present narratives describing the human story of Jesus. Those who remain at this level "know nothing apart from Christ and him crucified," and for these it is necessary to preach the "bodily" Gospel. However, to see the divinity in this, to "restore the Word from being made flesh to what 'he was in

---

43 Cf. *ComJn.* 10.14. In *FP* 4.2.9 Origen suggests in Scripture there are certain "stumbling-blocks," placed there providentially by the Word of God, to make it clear that they possess a deeper meaning beyond the literal sense, and that the Spirit dealt in like manner with the Gospels and writings of the apostles.

44 *ComJn.* 10.18-20: "The spiritual truth is often preserved in the material falsehood, so to speak" (*ComJn.* 10.20).

45 Cf. *ComJn.* 1.107, where Origen analyzes the twofold character of Christ as "beginning": in his own nature, his divinity is his beginning; in relation to us, the beginning "is his humanity, according to which Jesus Christ, and he crucified, is proclaimed to infants," proclaimed as having become flesh "that he might dwell among us who are able to receive him only in this manner at first." See also *ComJn.* 19.38.

the beginning with God,'" it is necessary to "translate" the "perceptible gospel" into its "spiritual" form, the Gospel, in which the Word is
universally present and seeking to abide in those ready to receive
him.[46] Such exegesis does not abandon the humanity of Christ any
more than discerning the meaning of a text abandons the letters
read: "even if in some way we attain the most sublime and highest
contemplation of the Word and of the truth, we shall not forget
completely that we were introduced to him by his coming in the
body" (*ComJn.* 2.61). Exegeted in this manner, the narratives of the
Gospels, recounting the human story of Jesus, find their place
alongside the epistles as exhortatory addresses, fulfilling the proper
role of a Gospel.[47]

The interpretative movement involved in discerning the spiritual
Gospel, and the Word of God it presents, is described in the compila-
tion of extracts from the *Contra Celsum* assembled by Basil the Great
and Gregory the Theologian as the fifteenth chapter of their anthology
of Origen's writings entitled *The Philokalia.* The first eleven sections of
this chapter are devoted to replying to Celsus' disparagement of the
Christian Scriptures for their "poverty of style" compared to the writings of the Greeks who have expressed the same things more elo-
quently. Origen argues that this very poverty is its advantage, for with
its common idiom the Christian Scriptures are able to nourish those
who lack formal education, so demonstrating that its power resides not
in persuasive words but in the "demonstration of the Spirit and of
power" (1 Cor 2:4).[48] Origen further explains Scripture's poverty of
style by analogy to the coming of the Word in the flesh: the divine
nature is not concerned only for the educated, but has condescended to
the level of the multitude, "that by using a style familiar to them it

---

46 *ComJn.* 1.43-5. It is important to note how he prefaces these reflections by stating "We
    must live as a Christian in a spiritual and bodily fashion."
47 Torjesen puts it this way: "Here is the underlying unity between the Gospels and the epis-
    tles: Both have the same subject matter, the universal coming of the Logos to the soul
    through the incarnation, but in the Gospels under the allegorical aspect of the human his-
    tory of Jesus, the epistles in the direct form of teaching about the divine Logos."
    (*Hermeneutical Procedure*, 129).
48 *Phil.* 15.2 = *CC* 6.2. By "the demonstration of the Spirit" Origen understands the exposi-
    tion that shows how the prophecies refer to Christ, for this "is capable of convincing
    anyone who reads them" (*Phil.* 15.3 = *CC* 1.2). Cf. *FP* 4.1.6; 4.2.3.

might encourage the mass of common people to listen."[49] Yet at the same time, as we have already seen, this style directs the reader to the deeper meaning of Scripture, for "even an ordinary reader soon discovers that many passages have a deeper significance than appears on the surface, a significance revealed to devoted students of the Word."[50] The remaining sections continue the same dialectic, but consider it in relation to Celsus' charge that the Lord's body was unsightly. Origen notes that while there are passages in Scripture which describe the body of Jesus as having no form or beauty, such as the prophecy of Isaiah (Is 53:1-3), there are other passages that speak of his beauty and grace, such as Psalm 44 (LXX), or describe Christ appearing transfigured in glory.[51] From these various descriptions, Origen concludes that Christ's body "varied according to the capacity of the observers," a teaching that he regarded as being thoroughly traditional.[52] The variability to which he is referring is not simply that of the instability of all matter, for that would be nothing remarkable.[53] Rather "the different forms of Jesus are to be applied to the nature of the divine Word."[54] Thus Origen's use of the idea of the changing forms of Jesus is not ultimately docetic, for its point is not to question the bodily reality of Jesus, but to indicate, on the one hand, the willingness of the divine Word to make himself comprehensible to all, and, on the other hand, the varying ability of people to comprehend the divine Word. To those who are not even ready to ascend the mountain with Christ, who are attracted by the beauty of human words, such as the teachings of the philosophers, rather than the Word of God, he only shows "the foolishness of the preaching," so that because of this apparent foolishness they say "we saw him and he had not form nor beauty."[55] But to those who by following him have

49 *Phil.* 15.10 = *CC* 7.60.
50 Ibid.
51 *Phil.* 15.12 = *CC* 6.75-6.
52 *Phil.* 15.14 = *CC* 6.77. On the variability of the form of Jesus, see *ComMatt.* 12.36-8; *Homilies on Genesis*, 1.7; *CC* 2.64-6; 4.16; 6.68; 6.75-7. For the claim that this teaching is traditional, see *Comm. ser. in Matt.* 100 (GCS 11.2, 218-19). For a heterodox use of this idea, see *Acts of John* 93. Cf. J. A. McGuckin, "The Changing Forms of Jesus," L. Lies (ed.), *Origeniana Quarta* (Innsbruck-Vienna: Tyrolia, 1987) 215-22.
53 Cf. *Phil.* 15.14 = *CC* 6.77.
54 *Phil.* 15.18 = *CC* 6.77.
55 Ibid. Cf. 1 Cor 1:21; Is 53:2.

received the strength to ascend the mountain, he appears in a "more divine form," and those capable of such vision are indeed a "Peter, allowing the Church to be built in them by the Word."[56] The chapter then continues with a passage from Origen in which he makes clear the exegetical dimensions of this ascent of Tabor:

> Down below the Word has other garments; they are not white, they are not as the light. If you ascend the high mountain, you will see his light as well as his garments. The garments of the Word are the phrases of Scripture; these words are the clothing of the divine thoughts. As then down below he appears different, but having ascended he is transfigured, his face having become as the sun, so it is with his clothing, so it is with the garments, when you are below, they do not shine, they are not white, but if you ascend, you will see the beauty and the light of the garments, and will marvel at the transfigured face of Jesus.[57]

The difference between seeing Jesus as an ordinary man and contemplating him transfigured in divine glory is that of merely reading the words of Scripture, expressed in the common idiom, and understanding their divine content. The Gospels themselves indicate this difference, Origen suggests, in the contrast they make between the particulars of Jesus' human existence, "The book of the generation of Christ" (Matt 1:1), and the divine things to be said about him, which would fill so many books that the world could not contain them (Jn 21:25). To learn the more divine things, Origen continues, Paul was rapt into the heavens (2 Cor 12:2-4), while what is spoken about down here is the Word who has emptied himself of equality with God and become flesh and been seen, in a human manner, as man. But, again, it

---

56 Ibid. Cf. *ComMatt.* 12.10-14, where this role of "Peter" is discussed in relation to the episcopate.

57 *Phil.* 15.19. Section 15.19 is the only passage from *Philokalia* 15 that does not appear in any mss of the *Contra Celsum*, and so was printed in brackets by Koetschau in his edition of *Contra Celsum* (GCS 2-3, 1899); for the authenticity of this passage, and its place in *CC* 6.77 see R. P. C. Hanson, "The passage marked 'Unde?' in Robinson's *Philocalia* XV,19," in H. Crouzel and A. Quacquarelli (eds.), *Origeniana Secunda* (Rome: Ateneo, 1980), 293-303. The same point is made in *ComMatt.* 12.38: "The garments of Jesus are the expressions and letters of the Gospels with which he invested himself; and I think that even the things indicated by the apostles concerning him are garments of Jesus, which become white to those who go up into the high mountain with Jesus." Those who see Jesus with transfigured garments, Origen continues, will simultaneously see Moses, representing the Law, and Elijah, representing the Prophets.

is only through the flesh, the garments of the Word, that the divinity of the Word is made manifest, when they are understood and interpreted no longer in a merely human manner, but in a manner befitting God. Thus, Origen adds, "since he became man, we see the Word of God in human form on earth, for always in the Scriptures the Word became flesh, so that he might dwell among us," but those able to recline upon his breast, as did the beloved disciple, or follow him as he ascends the mountain, come to see the glory of the only-begotten.[58] Those able to contemplate the Word in this manner, ascending Tabor or laying on his breast, "see his transfiguration in every Scripture," both those in which Jesus appears to the multitude in the literal sense of the text, and when he is transfigured on the mountain, and this, Origen concludes, "is the work of the highest and most sublime sense, containing the oracles of the wisdom hidden in a mystery, which 'God foreordained before the worlds unto the glory of his righteous ones.'"[59] The chapter is finished by a passage in which Origen makes the qualification that when speaking of the different forms of Jesus, he is specifically referring to "anything he did before the Passion and whatever happened after his Resurrection from the dead."[60] That is, the unchanging identity of the Word of God, as we have seen, is revealed through the Cross, and everything else is understood as patterned upon this. Though the arrangement of the passages is not that of Origen himself but his Cappadocian editors, the vision it expresses certainly captures the heart of Origen's theology and also indicates what inspired the young Basil and Gregory.[61]

Closely related to his teaching about the varying form of Jesus, is Origen's analysis of the titles applied by Scripture to Jesus in terms of his various "aspects" (ἐπίνοιαι).[62] Jesus is certainly one, but he refers to himself in many ways, for instance as "the way, the truth and the life"

---

58 *Phil.* 15.19: ἀεὶ γὰρ ἐν ταῖς γραφαῖς ὁ λόγος σὰρξ ἐγένετο, ἵνα κατασκηνώσῃ ἐν ἡμῖν· Cf. Jn 1:14.
59 *Phil.* 15.19; cf. 1 Cor 2.7
60 *Phil.* 20 = *CC* 6.77.
61 Elsewhere Basil expresses caution with regard to Origen's views on the Holy Spirit (cf. *On the Holy Spirit* 29.73); for his attitude to Origen when compiling the *Philokalia*, see P. Rousseau, *Basil of Caesarea* (Berkeley: University of California Press, 1994), 11-14, 82-4.
62 Origen connects these two ideas in *CC* 2.64.

(Jn 14:6), and he is described in Scripture in many other ways (Origen claims that it would be possible to collect ten thousand such titles, *ComJn.* 1.136), so that Jesus himself is the "good things" of the apostles' proclamation.[63] These aspects are, again, revealed through the Incarnation, which acts as a prism, refracting the incomprehensible, undivided nature of God into a spectrum of comprehensible aspects. The larger part of the first two books of the *Commentary on John* is devoted to examining the meaning and content of these aspects. Most attention is devoted to the designation of Jesus as the "Word," for, as mentioned earlier, Origen is particularly concerned about those who refrain from investigating "the meaning of what is indicated by the term 'Word,'" so that they do not have to affirm the independent subsistence of the Son (*ComJn.* 1.125, 151). He also notes how others hesitate to apply the term "God" to the Son, lest they fall into ditheism (*ComJn.* 2.16). In reply, Origen points out how John was very careful in his use of articles with the noun "God," using an article when it refers to the uncreated cause of the universe, but omitting it when referring to the Word as "God."[64] There is, therefore, only "one true God" (Jn 17:3), the "God of gods" (Ps 49:1, LXX), of those, that is, who are made gods by participation in him. However, while there are many to whom the anarthrous noun "god" can be applied, the "Firstborn of every creature" (Col 1:15) is more honored than them all, for "it was by his ministry that they became gods, for he drew from God that they might be deified" (*ComJn.* 2.17). It is only through the mediation of the Word, who alone knows the Father and reveals him to men, that others participate in divinity, so that the Word is "the minister of deity to all the other gods" (*ComJn.* 2.19). Origen explains the term "Word" in a similar manner, differentiating between the absolute sense in which it is applied to the Son and the way in which human beings share in this aspect of Christ: "He is called 'Word' because he removes everything irrational from us and makes us truly rational beings who do all things for the glory of God."[65] Unless they have

---

63 *ComJn.* 1.51-65; referring to Is 52:7, as cited in Rom 10:15.
64 *ComJn.* 2.12-15. Cf. *supra* 57-8.
65 *ComJn.* 1.267. The definition of "rational" (λογικός) here is totally shaped by the Word (λόγος) of God. Cf. *ComJn.* 2.114: "we could also say that the saint alone is rational."

fallen away to so-called words, which are totally foreign to *the* Word, human beings share in this aspect of Christ in varying degrees, depending on whether they know the Word as he is with God, or as flesh, or only through others who have partaken in the Word (*ComJn.* 2.22). As we have seen, Origen is emphatic that the proper understanding of Christ as Word entails being able to see the divinity of Christ, rather than remaining at the level of the flesh or letters. Thus some aspects, such as Word, Truth and Wisdom, pertain to Jesus as he is in his divinity, with the Father. Others, however, are ones that Jesus has taken upon himself for the benefit of those yet unable to contemplate his divinity, such as Physician and Redemption (*ComJn.* 1.123-4). The path to knowing God begins with the elementary aspects, such as Door, so that one may enter on the Way, in which one is led by Jesus as Shepherd, and ruled by him as King, and benefit from him as Lamb, until we also come to know the Father (*ComJn.* 19.39). Being himself all these aspects, "our Savior is the whole of the steps" to God (*ComJn.* 19.38).

Origen's understanding of the Savior, Jesus Christ, and what is meant by the Incarnation of the Word, is clearly broader than can be encapsulated in brief dogmatic formulae. It is a theology which begins and ends with Jesus, who, as crucified and risen, is one with the Word of God, rather who *is* the Word of God, for he reveals the mysteries contained in Scripture, explaining how they refer to himself and so clothing himself with its words, an investiture which continues in the apostolic depiction of Christ. Beginning with the flesh that Christ assumes in Scripture to make himself known, Origen's theology leads to the point where the exegete can see in the flesh of the literal sense, rather than elsewhere, the eternal Word of God. Christ is thus present throughout Scripture, and continues to be present in those who devote themselves to the Word and follow him. This is the "eternal Gospel" or the "spiritual Gospel" (Rev 14:6; *ComJn.* 1.40), and it is found most clearly in the loftiest of the four Gospels, that of John:

> We might dare say, then, that the Gospels are the firstfruits of all Scriptures, but that the firstfruits of the Gospels is that according to John, whose meaning no one can understand who has not leaned on Jesus' breast nor received Mary from Jesus to be his mother also. But he who would be another

John must also become such as John, to be shown to be Jesus, so to speak. For if Mary had no son except Jesus, in accordance with those who hold a sound opinion of her, and Jesus says to his mother, "Behold your son," and not, "Behold, this man also is your son," he has said equally, "Behold, this is Jesus whom you bore." For indeed everyone who has been perfected "no longer lives, but Christ lives in him," and since "Christ lives" in him, it is said of him to Mary, "Behold your son," the Christ. (*ComJn.* 1.23)

Exegesis lies at the heart of Origen's understanding of the Incarnation of the Word, extending the presence of Jesus Christ to all those who are devoted to the Word. This is ultimately not concluded until the eschaton, when those devoted to the Word will have reached the stature of Christ (cf. Eph 4:13), and so will no longer see the Father through the mediation of the Son, but "will see the Father and the things with the Father as the Son sees them," when the Son delivers the kingdom to the Father, so that "God becomes all in all" (*ComJn.* 20.47-8; 1 Cor 15:28).

The Distinct Subsistence, Divinity and Eternity of the Son of God

Within this vision, Jesus Christ is both the beginning and the end for theological reflection as it ascends from the literal, fleshly sense of Scripture to its spiritual sense, the eternal Gospel proclaiming the Word of God. He is the beginning as the one through whom the revelation of God in Scripture is understood, and the end as the model for all those who, through their devotion to the Word, would come to know God as he knows his Father. For Origen, as Rowan Williams puts it, the Word of God is not simply a "cosmological convenience," introduced to mediate between a transcendent God and created reality, but is "the paradigm for our knowing and loving the Father."[66] As such, alongside his insistence that theological reflection should not remain at the level of the flesh, Origen is equally emphatic, as mentioned earlier, that the independent, concrete subsistence (ὑπόστασις or ὑποκείμενον) of the Son should be explicitly affirmed,[67] and these

---

66 Williams, *Arius*, 139.

67 For the possibility that Origen learnt the value of such language from the Valentinians in Rome, but turned it to other purposes and opponents, see A. Logan, "Origen and the Development of Trinitarian Theology," in L. Lies (ed.), *Origeniana Quarta* (Innsbruck-Vienna: Tyrolia, 1987), 424-9.

two points are closely related. Thus Origen singles out for particular criticism those who refuse to analyze what is meant by calling the Son "Word" but remain at a superficial understanding of this term, thinking of the Son merely as an "utterance of the Father existing in syllables," for in this way they "neither ascribe to him subsistence (ὑπόστασιν) nor explain his essence (οὐσίαν)" (*ComJn.* 1.151). He likewise criticizes those who conflate scriptural texts to argue that the Father and Son are not numerically distinct but that "both are one, not only in essence (οὐσίᾳ) but also as subject (ὑποκειμένῳ), and that they are said to be Father and Son only in relation to certain differing aspects (ἐπινοίας) and not in relation to their subsistence (ὑπόστασιν)."[68] Against such claims, Origen would refer to texts that demonstrate that "the Son is other than the Father," a distinction, he adds, implied by the names themselves and one which necessarily entails plurality and mutuality: "it is necessary that a son be the son of a father and that a father be the father of a son" (*ComJn.* 10.246). This same point is made in the *Dialogue with Heraclides* when, in response to Origen's question whether the Son should be considered as distinct from the Father, Heraclides replies, "Of course! How can he be Son if he is also Father?"[69] Like his suggestion, considered earlier, that the name of God is "Father," Origen's appeal to a common-sense logic of relations leads to the key theological insight, a fundamental principle of later Nicene trinitarian theology, that the relationship to the Son is constitutive of what it is to be God and, moreover, that the distinct subsistence of the Son derives from the existence of God as Father rather than from his activity as Creator. Given that the Spirit is also spoken of in Scripture as a distinct being, Origen similarly affirms the Spirit's distinct subsistence, and does so by using the term "hypostasis" not simply to qualify the manner in which a being exists, as in the above quotations, but to designate the being itself: "We are persuaded that there are three hypostases, the Father, the Son and the Holy Spirit."[70]

Two related qualifications need to be made regarding Origen's

---

68 *ComJn.* 10.246. The same contrast between "aspect" and "reality" is drawn in *ComMatt.* 17.14.

69 *Dialogue with Heraclides*, 2.

70 *ComJn.* 2.75; a point noted by A. Logan, "Origen and the Development of Trinitarian Theology," 427, n. 2.

affirmation of the distinct subsistence of the Son, both relating to the desire not to postulate two independent first principles. First, that the Son is never considered in isolation from the Father. The Son reveals the Father, the one true God, and is the way to him. Origen even suggests that prayer should not be made to the Son alone, nor even to the Father and the Son, but only to the Father, in and through the Son.[71] Second, that the distinct subsistence of the Father and of the Son must not be asserted in such a manner that the divinity of the Son is thought of as other than that of the Father. Both the distinct subsistence of the Son and his divinity must be affirmed together, without either capitulating to the other. According to Origen, those who hesitate to speak of the Son as "God," fearing the error of ditheism, are not able to do this:

> Either they deny that the particularity (ἰδιότητα) of the Son is other than that of the Father, while confessing as God the one they call, at least in name, "Son"; or they deny the divinity of the Son, making his particularity and essence (οὐσίαν) as an individual to be different from the Father. (*ComJn.* 2.16)

There is no point in affirming the divinity of the Son, if he is not distinct from the Father, for then he no longer exists; nor is there any purpose in affirming the particular subsistence of the Son, if, as an individual, his essence is different than the Father, for then he would no longer be divine.[72] Origen seems to suggest here, though somewhat indirectly, that the Son should be considered as having the same "essence" (οὐσία) as the Father. So also the passage cited above, where Origen criticizes those who affirm that the Father and Son are "one, not only in essence (οὐσίᾳ) but also as subject (ὑποκειμένῳ)" (*ComJn.* 10.246), might be taken as suggesting that they should be considered as one in "essence" whilst being other in their own subsistence. Yet in other contexts Origen seems to treat the term οὐσία as a synonym of words designating the actual existence of subsisting realities, as for instance when he asks Celsus to prove the "subsistence and reality" (ὑπόστασιν καὶ οὐσίαν) of the Greek gods, that they "subsist in reality" (κατ᾽ οὐσίαν ὑφεστηκέναι)

---

71 *On Prayer*, 15.
72 A similar alternative is given in *ComJn.* 1.152: either one says that the Son is not separate from the Father, and thus neither subsists nor is a son, or that he is both separate and given existence (οὐσιωμένον).

rather than being personified abstractions (*CC* 1.23). However, it is probably not simply a matter of such synonymy when Origen alludes, in his work *On Prayer*, to having shown "elsewhere" that the Father and Son must be considered as distinct "according to essence and substance."[73] As he notes in the *Commentary on John*, someone may think that as the Savior and God are both said to be light it immediately follows that "the Father is not separate in essence (τῇ οὐσίᾳ μὴ διεστηκέναι) from the Son," but a more accurate conclusion would be that they are not the same (οὐ ταὐτὸν εἶναι) since the Son is "the light that shines in darkness," whereas the Father is the light in which there is no darkness at all.[74] In fact, Origen continues, the Father "transcends being 'true light'" altogether, in the same way that, as Father of the truth, God transcends truth (*ComJn.* 2.151). Origen's main concern here is to preserve the transcendence of the Father: He is the source of all the properties that characterize the Son as divine, and so Father and Son cannot be said to possess these properties in an identical manner. If the properties of divinity were ascribed to the Father and the Son in the same manner, they would have to be considered as equal members of the same class. To avoid this conclusion Origen intimates that perhaps they should not be said to be the same in "essence," though his obliqueness on this point surely indicates a reluctance to make a categorical statement to this effect.

The dependency of the Son upon the Father is essential for Origen. Equally important is the need not to misunderstand this relationship of derivation in a materialistic fashion. Origen specifically eschews speaking of the Son as begotten "from the essence of the Father," as such language implies for him that God is a material being whose substance is depleted after begetting the Son, as happens in human parturition. Nor does the Son "come out" from the Father in such a manner that he is thereafter external to the Father, for the Father is in the Son and the Son is in the Father (cf. Jn 14:10), a relationship which cannot be understood in corporeal terms (*ComJn.* 20.153-9). He is also extremely critical of Valentinians such as Heracleon, who seem to teach that the spirits destined for salvation are portions of the divine substance,

---

73 *On Prayer*, 15.1: ἕτερος ... κατ᾿ οὐσίαν καὶ ὑποκείμενον.
74 *ComJn.* 2.149, referring to Jn 1:5 and 1 Jn 1:5.

having come forth from God, and are therefore to be considered as of the same substance, *homoousios*, with him (*ComJn.* 13.149). Origen claims that properly understood "everything that is *homoousios* is a subject of the same attributes" (τῶν αὐτῶν δεκτικόν), that is, are members of a single class who share the same properties in the same manner, and therefore, Origen suggests, Heracleon implies that God is as capable of change and corruption as created spirits (*ComJn.* 13.150). Such unacceptable consequences would not arise if the term were to be applied to the Father and the Son, and it is possible that Origen might have used the term *homoousios* elsewhere to express the relationship between the two divine hypostases.[75] Nevertheless, the term as Origen defines it here is not applicable to his understanding of the relationship between the Father and the Son, for it lacks the essential element of derivation.[76]

Origen thus emphasizes the transcendence of the Father, such that there are no others besides him as members of the same class, yet at the same time he wants to ensure that the essence (οὐσία) of the Son, even if it cannot unequivocally be stated to be the same as the Father's, at least is not considered as separate from that of the Father, so that the divinity of the Son is affirmed. In the *Commentary On John*, Origen tries to hold these two key elements together through the notion of participation. Origen points out, as we have seen, that in Scripture it is the Father alone who is "the one true God" (Jn 17:3) and "the God of gods" (Ps 49:1, LXX), and so is referred to as "*the* God" (ὁ θεός). All the other beings called "god" in Scripture, designated by the noun without an article, are "made god by participation in his divinity."[77] This is especially the case for "the Firstborn of all creation" (Col 1:15),

75 For a positive appraisal of the occurrence of the term *homoousios* in the passage from the *Commentary on Hebrews* preserved in Rufinus' Latin translation of Pamphilus' *Apology for Origen*, see most recently M. J. Edwards, "Did Origen Apply the Word *Homoousios* to the Son?" *JTS* ns 49.2 (1998), 658-70.

76 A point made by Williams (*Arius*, 134-5), who also suggests that the definition given by Origen might be "a familiar and quasi-technical definition of the term *homoousios*" (*Arius*, 296, n.164), which would help explain why Origen did not retain the term as used by Heracleon, for whom it did imply a sense of derivation, and strip it of its materialistic overtones.

77 *ComJn.* 2.17: πᾶν δὲ τὸ παρὰ τὸ αὐτόθεος μετοχῇ τῆς ἐκείνου θεότητος θεοποιούμενον οὐχ "ὁ θεός" ἀλλὰ "θεός" κυριώτερον ἂν λέγοιτο.

who, as "the first to be with God, drawing divinity into himself," is more honored than any other god.[78] Again, this must not be understood in crude materialistic terms, as if "participating in God" meant receiving a share of some*thing*, some divine "stuff." The Son's participation in God, and so his unity with him, is conceived by Origen in active, rather than substantial terms,[79] though it is the activity of the Son, revealing the Father, that is, as Williams notes, his "essence," in the sense of the form or definition of the Son's existence.[80] It is by knowing the Father, or as Origen puts it, by his "unceasing contemplation of the depths of the Father" that the Son partakes of his divinity and so is "God" (*ComJn.* 2.18). And it is "by this ministry that the others became gods," for Son has "drawn from God to deify others," sharing ungrudgingly with them in his goodness (*ComJn.* 2.17). Although now only the Son knows the Father, it is possible for all those who have "the contemplation of God as their only activity" to be "formed in the knowledge of God" and so "become sons" (*ComJn.* 1.92). Such reflection on the Son's participation in God and his ministry towards others is perhaps a more abstract way of stating what we have seen worked out in Origen's reflections on Scripture and the Gospel, that it is in the abasement of the Cross that the Son appears as "more divine and truly in the image of the Father" (*ComJn.* 1.231) and that through Passion he is one with the Word (*ComJn.* 32.325), revealing the Father and explaining the deeper meaning of Scripture, so that those who devote themselves to the contemplation of its spiritual sense can also come to know God as Father. For Origen there is no part or aspect of the Son, clothed in flesh in the letters of Scripture, which does not, when contemplated in its spiritual sense as the eternal Word of God, reveal the Father. So, for all that he underscores the distinct subsistence of the Son, Origen never considers the Son in isolation from the Father, for the very "essence" of the Son is to reveal the Father. By speaking of the Son as divine "by participation," Origen

78 *ComJn.* 2.17. In *ComJn.* 13.219, commenting on Jn 4:32, "I have meat to eat of which you do not know," Origen describes Christ as "being eternally nourished by the Father who alone is without need and sufficient in himself."

79 Cf. *CC* 8.12: "They are two things in subsistence (δύο τῇ ὑποστάσει πράγματα), but one in mental unity, in agreement and in identity of will."

80 Williams, *Arius*, 142-3.

avoids any suggestion that the Father and Son should be thought of as two independent first principles, the error of ditheism, and also avoids making the essence of the Son, as an individual, to be other than the Father (cf. *ComJn.* 2.16). He is able to affirm both the transcendence of the Father as "the one true God" and also the divinity of the Son who reveals the Father.

However, whether Origen manages in this way to affirm satisfactorily that the divinity of the Son is not only not different than that of the Father, but the very same, so that it is indeed the Father who is revealed, is debatable. As the one who reveals the Father, the Son seems to end up in a mediating position between a transcendent God and creation. Being the first to "draw divinity into himself," the Word is "more honorable" than all the other gods besides him (*ComJn.* 2.17), and for them he is a "minister of divinity" (*ComJn.* 2.19). When explaining Christ's statement that "the Father is greater than I" (Jn 14:28) and his refusal to be called "good" (Mk 10:18), Origen suggests that "the Father exceeds the Savior as much as, or even more than, the Savior himself and the Holy Spirit exceed the rest" (*ComJn.* 13.151). Yet it is not as having some lower form of divinity, in a materialistic sense, that the Son is a mediator, but rather because he *is* the one who reveals God. Thus, prior to emphasizing the transcendence of the Father indicated by Mark 10:18, Origen explicitly affirmed that it would be "perfectly legitimate and true" to apply the title "good" to Christ, but that he "graciously offered it up to the Father and rebuked the one who wished to praise the Son excessively," for the Son always points to the Father (*ComJn.* 13.151). Nevertheless, Origen was later accused of having taught that the Son is not "good" in an absolute manner.[81] He was also accused of having taught that the Son "does not know the Father as himself," though it is clearly essential for Origen that the Son does know the Father, so that he can reveal him and be the medium and model for our relationship with the Father.[82] Again Origen's point is to emphasize the Father's transcendence by asserting that the Father knows himself in a manner which is beyond the way in which the Son

---

81 Cf. Photius, *Bibl.* 117.
82 Ibid. Nautin refers this charge to *FP* 4.4.8, which would again connect it to comments made by Origen on Jn 14:28 (*Origène*, 120-2).

knows the Father, even though the Son's knowledge of the Father is complete or perfect (cf. *ComJn.* 32.345, 350). Origen's tendency to obliqueness when speaking of the "essence" of the Father and the Son, suggests that he was aware of the difficulties of using participatory language to explain this relationship. Some of his later writings seem to indicate a tendency to lessen the gap between the Father and the Son, and in a few fragments he affirms the divinity of the Son in his essence, though the overall vision remained the same.[83]

Christ as God and Man in On First Principles

Although preserved in its entirety only in the Latin translation of Rufinus, Origen's work *On First Principles* provides a valuable sustained analysis of both the divinity and humanity of Jesus Christ. It is necessary, Origen notes, "to know that the divine nature in Christ, as he is the only-begotten Son of the Father, is one [thing], and the human nature, which he assumed in the last times for the economy, is another" (*FP* 1.2.1). These two tasks are carried out in different parts of the work (*FP* 1.2 and 2.6 respectively), though it is clear that Origen regarded them as being continuous.[84] Origen's analysis of the divinity of the Son is basically exegetical, examining the various aspects by which the Son is described in Scripture: "our first task is to see what the only-begotten Son of God is, who is called by many different names" (*FP* 1.2.1). The aspect of the Son most important for Origen here is Wisdom, for as Solomon said, in the person of Wisdom, "The Lord created me at the beginning of his ways... before all the hills he begets me" (Prov 8:22-5). Though Origen touches upon other aspects, such as Word, Truth, Life and Resurrection, which are explained as analogous to Wisdom (*FP* 1.2.3-4), most attention is given to the terms

83 Cf. *ComMatt.*15.10. Williams (*Arius*, 142-3) points to two passages, which are probably later than the *Commentary on John*, in which Origen asserts that the Savior is God "not by participation but in essence" (the *selecta in Psalmos* on Psalm 134; in the edition of Lommatsch, 13, 134.19-20), and that the Son is "He Who Is in his very essence" (a fragment on the Apocalypse, TU 38, 29).

84 Thus *FP* 2.6.1 begins: "Now that these points have been discussed, it is time to resume our inquiry into the Incarnation of our Lord and Savior." The division of *On First Principles* into four books does not reflect the actual content of the work, which is more naturally divided into two main sections, *FP* 1.1 to 2.3, and *FP* 2.4 to 4.3.

used to designate the Wisdom of God—the power of God, the glory of the Almighty, a reflection of eternal light, a spotless mirror of the workings of God, and an image of his goodness (all from Wis 7:25-6)—each of which is picked up in the apostolic depiction of Christ (*FP* 1.2.5-13). Origen insists that by speaking of the Son as the Wisdom of God he does not mean anything that does not actually exist, for the Son of God is "God's Wisdom existing hypostatically," and cautions that by this he does not mean to suggest that the Son should be thought of in materialistic terms (*FP* 1.2.2). All of the divine titles of Christ, Origen points out, derive from his activity rather than corporeal properties (*FP* 1.2.4), and as the works done by the Son are those of the Father (cf. Jn 5:19), so that "there is one and the same movement, so to speak, in all they do," the Son is called a "spotless mirror" to make it clear that "there is absolutely no dissimilarity between the Father and the Son" (*FP* 1.2.12).

As we have seen, Origen is very clear on the distinct subsistence of the Son, Jesus Christ, and on his eternity; he is present throughout all of Scripture and in those who devote themselves to the Word. Yet he avoids asserting two first principles, which for him would have been unthinkable, by pointing to the derivation of the Son from the Father. Picking up on Proverbs 8:25, "Before the hills he begets me," Origen explains this derivation in terms of an eternal, timeless, begetting. It is impossible, Origen claims, to conceive of God as ever having existed without his Wisdom, for this would imply either that God could not have begotten Wisdom before he did beget her, or that he could have begotten her, but was previously unwilling to do so. Thus by a *reductio ad absurdam*, Origen concludes:

> We recognize that God was always the Father of his only-begotten Son, who was indeed born of him and draws his being from him, but is yet without any beginning, not only of that kind which can be distinguished by periods of time, but even of that other kind which the mind alone is able to contemplate in itself and to perceive, if I may so say, with the bare intellect and reason. Wisdom, therefore, must be believed to have been begotten beyond the limits of any beginning that we can speak of or understand. (*FP* 1.2.2)

The only "beginning" that the Wisdom of God has, Origen notes later on, playing on the various meanings of "beginning" (ἀρχή), is God himself, "from whom he takes his existence and birth."[85] It is therefore impossible for someone to say that "there was [a time] when the Son was not" (ἦν ποτε ὅτε οὐκ ἦν ὁ υἱός), a conclusion of "the labor-loving Origen" cited approvingly by Athanasius a century later.[86] Origen again insists that this begetting is not to be understood in material terms, as a division of the divine nature into parts, which he thinks is suggested by those who spin "absurd fables" in which the Son is an "emanation" (προβολή) of the Father (*FP* 1.2.6). Origen suggests that "the birth from the Father" might rather be thought of as "an act of his will proceeding from the mind," for the Son does all things just as the Father does (*FP* 1.2.6). Though Origen can speak of the Father willing the existence of the Son, his point is not to assert the contingency of the existence of the Son, as if God could have been otherwise, but to emphasize that God is unconstrained by anything prior to himself, that he is the absolute first principle and, in some way at least, is an active subject whose will is sufficient to ensure the existence of his deliberations (*FP* 1.2.6). Origen also uses the imagery of Wisdom 7:26 and Hebrews 1:3, to describe this begetting in terms of light: "This is an eternal and everlasting begetting, as brightness is begotten from light; for he does not become Son in an external manner, through the adoption of the Spirit, but is Son by nature."[87] The begetting of Wisdom by the Father is not a one-time act, somehow "before" the beginning of time, but a continuous begetting, as it is also by the continuous contemplation of the Father that the Son participates in divinity (cf. *ComJn.* 2.18). It is also a relationship that extends beyond the Only-Begotten, who alone is Son by nature, to all those who receive the Spirit of adoption. Both of these points are developed most clearly in the *Homilies on Jeremiah*, 9.4. Origen begins by suggesting that in contrast to the one who commits sin and is thus "born (γεγέννηται) of

85 *FP* 1.2.9, Cf. *ComJn.* 1.204.

86 Athanasius, *On the Decrees of Nicaea*, 27, citing *FP* 4.4.1. The same formula can be found at *FP* 1.2.9 and in Origen's *Commentary on Romans* 1.5. Origen uses a similar formula to express the eternal significance of Christ's saving death, *ComJn.* 20.94: "there is no [time] when the spiritual economy of the Jesus was not present to the saints" (ἡ κατὰ τὸν Ἰησοῦν πνευματικὴ οἰκονομία οὐκ ἔστιν ὅτε τοῖς ἁγίοις οὐκ ἦν).

87 *FP* 1.2.4. That the Only-Begotten is "by nature Son from the beginning" is also stated in *ComJn.* 2.76.

the devil" (1 Jn 3:8, in Origen's version), the righteous one is begotten by God, not once, but "begotten continuously in each good act," just as in the case of the Savior, for "the Father did not beget the Son and then separate him from his generation, but always begets him." The generation of the Savior is explained by reference to the same scriptural texts utilized in *On First Principles*, describing the Savior in terms of light (Wis 7:26, Heb 1:3), and by drawing attention to the present, rather than past tense of the verse, "Before the hills he begets (γεννᾷ) me" (Prov 8:25). Origen then concludes his homily thus:

> The Savior is eternally begotten by the Father, so also, if you possess the "Spirit of adoption" [Rom 8:15] God eternally begets you in him according to each of your works, each of your thoughts. And being begotten you thereby become an eternally begotten son of God in Christ Jesus.[88]

The Son's status as the only-begotten Son by nature is not undermined by the extension of this relationship to those begotten by the Father in him, for it is precisely *in him* that those who receive the Spirit of adoption come to share in this eternal relationship of Father and Son. It is by Christ that we receive the "Spirit of adoption," so that our sonship is always based on that of Christ, who alone is Son by nature.

It is as "the beginning of his ways" that God "created" Wisdom (Prov 8:22). Origen's teaching on creation is notoriously complex and has been the subject of controversy almost from the beginning. Origen explains this verse in terms which recall both the Platonic "ideas" and the Stoic "reasons," suggesting that it refers to the way in which the Wisdom of God "contains within herself the beginnings and the reasons and the forms of the whole creation" (*FP* 1.2.2). In this prefigurative sense, creation can be said to be eternal: "In this Wisdom, who ever existed with the Father, the creation was always present in form and outline, and there never was a time when the prefiguration of those things which hereafter were to be did not exist in Wisdom" (*FP* 1.4.4). However, when examining how Wisdom is said to be "a pure effluence of the glory of the Almighty" (Wis 7:25), Origen seems

---

88 *HomJer.* 9.4: καὶ ἀεὶ γεννᾶται ὁ σωτὴρ ὑπὸ τοῦ πατρός, οὕτως καὶ σὺ ἐὰν ἔχῃς "τὸ τῆς υἱοθεσίας πνεῦμα," ἀεὶ γεννᾷ σε ἐν αὐτῷ ὁ θεὸς καθ' ἕκαστον ἔργον, καθ' ἕκαστον διανόημα, καὶ γεννώμενος οὕτως γίνῃ ἀεὶ γεννώμενος υἱὸς θεοῦ ἐν Χριστῷ Ἰησοῦ·

to imply a more concrete content to the eternal existence of creation. He applies to the title "almighty" a similar argument to the one he used for the fatherhood of God, that it is impossible for God to be almighty "if there are none over whom he can exercise his power," and that if it is better for God to be almighty than not, then those things by virtue of which he is almighty must always have existed (*FP* 1.2.10). This seems to suggest that creation must in some sense be eternally actualized for God to be eternally the Almighty. Stated in such a manner, it rests upon the premise that true statements about God must hold eternally, and the (mistaken) inference from this that anything standing in relation to God must also exist eternally. However, Origen's concern here is not so much the status of creation itself, but that this creative activity of God must be understood in terms of his existence already as Father. If Wisdom is said to be "a pure effluence of the glory of the Almighty," it is nevertheless "in Wisdom" that God has made all things (Ps 103:24, LXX) and by the Word that all things were made (Jn 1:3), so that "the title of 'almighty' cannot be older in God than that of Father, for it is through the Son that the Father is almighty" (*FP* 1.2.10). God's creative act, just as his salvific act of adoption, is grounded in the eternal relationship between Father and Son. More specifically, the dominion which the Father holds over all things and by virtue of which he is called "the Almighty," is exercised through his Son, who is thus also called "Almighty" (cf. Rev 1:8), for "at the name of Jesus every knee bows" (Phil 2:10). So, Origen concludes, "it is undoubtedly Jesus to whom all things have been subjected, and it is he who wields dominion over all things, and all things have been subjected to the Father through him" (*FP* 1.2.10). Not only does the attribute of omnipotence which calls creation into being derive from the relationship between the Father and the Son, but the "glory of omnipotence" is found nowhere else but on the Cross.[89]

As for the scriptural assertion that Wisdom was "created" (ἔκτισεν) by God (Prov 8:22), it is almost certain that at one point in the original text of *On First Principles* Origen did describe the Son as a "creature" (κτίσμα, *FP* 4.4.1). However, what he might have meant by this word

---

89 Cf. *ComJn.* 1.278, where Origen asserts in passing that "the Son became king through suffering the Cross" (ἐβασίλευσε γὰρ διὰ τοῦ πεπονθέναι τὸν σταυρόν).

is difficult to ascertain. Harl points out that Origen seems to make a distinction between the various words used to describe different aspects of "creation."[90] In the *Commentary on John*, for instance, Origen indicates a descending gradation of "create" (κτίζειν), "make" (ποιεῖν) and "mold" (πλάσσειν): The first man, by falling way from the superior life, became the beginning, not of that which is created or made, but of what is molded by the Lord to be mocked by the angels (Job 40:19, LXX); thus "our superior substance" (ἡ προηγουμένη ὑπόστασις) is being in the image of the Creator, while the substance deriving "from a cause" (ἡ ἐξ αἰτίας) is that which is molded from the dust of the earth (*ComJn*. 20.182). In various passages of *On First Principles*, Origen attempts to explain the diversity of the world in terms which do not implicate God in the arbitrariness attributed to him by the Gnostics, who taught that there are different kinds of human beings, each destined to their own fate.[91] He suggests instead that when, "'in the beginning' he created what he wished to create," God created "rational spirits," or intellects, for no other reason than his own goodness (*FP* 2.9.6). Being himself without variation or change, God "created all his creatures equal and alike, for the simple reason that there was in him no cause that could give rise to variety and diversity" (ibid.). The world as we know it, with its irrational diversity, results from the freedom with which God endowed his creatures. God, however, "arranged his creation according to merit," gathering the diversities of intellects "into the harmony of a single world," as "one house" in which there are vessels of gold and silver and also those of wood and earth, each placed in a position appropriate for their education (ibid.). Origen certainly believed the common teaching that the soul was not created with the body but introduced from without (cf. *ComJn*. 2.182), and therefore in a sense "anterior." But rather than imagining a host of eternally existing intellects who through some pre-cosmic fall descend into bodies,[92] it seems more probable that the "anterior causes" invoked by Origen to reconcile the inequality of human fate

---

90 M. Harl, "La Préexistence des âmes dans l'oeuvre d'Origène," in L. Lies (ed.), *Origeniana Quarta*, 238-58.

91 Cf. *FP* 1.6.2; 1.8.1; 2.1.1-2, etc.

92 This was how Methodios of Olympus interpreted Origen (cf. Photius, *Bibl.*, 234), a charge which was then taken up by Epiphanius, *Panarion*, 64.

with an affirmation of the justice of God (e.g., *FP* 2.9.7; 3.1.22) refers to the anteriority of the foreknowledge of God, who knows all things for each from their womb.[93] Either way, for Origen the "arrangement" of the cosmos cannot really be described as "creation" (κτίσις), for it does not express perfectly the will of God. Creation proper, as Williams puts it, "is strictly only the unimpeded expression of God's rational will."[94] But the will of God is most perfectly expressed in the Son, and so it is not implausible that Origen described him as "created," though by this Origen clearly meant something other than what was later understood as "creation."

Having examined his "divine nature," when Origen "resumes" his "inquiry into the Incarnation of our Lord and Savior," he turns to consider how Christ is the "mediator" between God and man (*FP* 2.6.1; 1 Tim 2:5). Though "what is related in the Holy Scriptures of his majesty" is so immense that "it is impossible to put into writing all that belongs to the Savior's glory," Origen contends that all this serves, in fact, to render his abasement all the more amazing: "When, therefore, we consider these great and marvelous truths about the nature of the Son of God, we are lost in the deepest amazement that such a being, towering high above all, should have 'emptied himself' of his majestic condition and become man and dwelt among men" (*FP* 2.6.1). Of all the splendid things about the Son, the one which "utterly transcends the limits of human wonder and is beyond the capacity of our weak

93 As argued by Harl, "La Préexistence des âmes." Thus the distinction described in *ComJn.* 20.182, cited above, should not be taken in a chronological sense ("Préexistence," 246). In his later writings, Origen no longer refers to "anterior causes," but only divine foreknowledge, which he always holds together with personal freedom. See especially *Phil.* 25, where, referring to Paul's describing of his election in Rom 1:1 and Gal 1:15, Origen comments that "any one who is predestined through the foreknowledge of God is the cause of the events known," rather than being "saved by nature" as he charges his opponents with teaching. Origen also consistently dissociates himself from any kind of metempsychosis, claiming that the story of Adam gives a teaching "superior to the Platonic doctrine of the descent of the soul" (*CC* 4.40). Nevertheless, Origen did inhabit a universe in which superior spirits descended into bodies, such as John the Baptist (cf. *ComJn.* 2.175-88), a teaching he found stated clearly in the apocryphal Jewish text, *The Prayer of Joseph*. For the Jewish background of this form of the "preexistence" of souls, see G. Bostock, "The Sources of Origen's Doctrine of Pre-Existence," in L. Lies (ed.), *Origeniana Quarta* (Innsbruck-Vienna: Tyrolia, 1987), 259-64.

94 Williams, *Arius*, 141.

mortal intelligence to think of or understand" is how the very Word of God "existed within the compass of the man who appeared in Judaea," how the Wisdom of God was born as a child, how he was "troubled" and finally led to a shameful death, rising again on the third day (*FP* 2.6.2). The bewilderment felt by Origen evokes one of the most poetic passages in *On First Principles*:

> When, therefore, we see in him some things so human that they appear in no way to differ from the common frailty of mortals, and some things so divine that they are appropriate to nothing else but the primal and ineffable nature of divinity, the human understanding with its narrow limits is baffled, and, struck with amazement at so mighty a wonder, knows not which way to turn, what to hold to, or whither to take itself. If it thinks of God, it sees a man; if it thinks of a man, it beholds one returning from the dead with spoils after vanquishing the kingdom of death. For this reason we must pursue our contemplation with all fear and reverence, as we seek to prove how the truth of each nature exists in one and the same [subject], in such a way that nothing unworthy or unfitting may be thought to reside in that divine and ineffable existence, nor on the other hand may the events of his life be supposed to be the illusion caused by deceptive fantasies. (*FP* 2.6.2)

Origen's contemplation of Christ does not proceed by analyzing the constituent parts of his being. Rather, it develops by looking at how Christ is described in Scripture, where a single subject is spoken of in both divine and human terms. This demonstrates the "truth of each nature" and that they both exist in one and the same subject. But again this must not be taken in materialistic terms, as if the "natures" were locatable parts within the being of Christ. It is, rather, a matter of predication, that one and the same Christ is the subject of two different, contrary even, sets of predicates. Moreover, although these "natures" can be differentiated conceptually, in Christ they exist together: "if it thinks of God, it sees a man; it if thinks of a man, it beholds one returning from the dead." In Christ, God and man have become one, without undermining either the divinity, by attributing anything unworthy to it, or the humanity, rendering it an illusion. Jesus Christ is thus truly "the Mediator" between God and man, not by having some lower, mediating form of divinity, but by being both, reconciling God and man together in himself.

The completeness of this unity of God and man in Christ is

emphasized by Origen through the use of what would later be referred to as the *communicatio idiomatum*, the "exchange of properties." According to Origen, although the Son of God granted to all rational creatures a participation in himself proportionate to the love by which they clung to him, all the souls, in their freedom, turned aside in varying degrees with the exception of the soul of which Jesus said "no man takes my soul from me" (Jn 10:18). This soul cleaved to God "from the beginning of creation and ever after in a union inseparable and indissoluble, as being the soul of the Wisdom and Word of God," such that "it was made one spirit with him" (*FP* 2.6.3). This soul, moreover, acts "as a medium" between God and the flesh, so that through its activity, tenaciously adhering to God, "there is born the God-man," whose being embraces the opposite extremes of divinity and humanity (ibid.). That it is through the activity of the one devoted to the Word that the God-man is born, echoes Origen's point noted earlier, that it is through the Cross, remaining steadfast in the will of the Father, that Jesus becomes one with the Word of God (cf. *ComJn.* 32.325), and that it is through him that the Father, as the Almighty, exercises dominion over a creation eternally subject to Jesus (*FP* 1.2.10). As the Word and the soul, and through it the flesh, of Jesus have become completely one, what is predicated of the Son in respect of one nature, can also be said of him in respect to the other nature: "throughout the whole of Scripture, while the divine nature is spoken of in human terms, the human nature is in its turn adorned with the marks that belong to the divine prerogative" (*FP* 2.6.3). The very human soul and flesh assumed by the Son of God can be called the Wisdom and the Power of God, while in reverse, the Son of God is said to have died, by virtue of that nature which is susceptible to death.

Finally, in response to those who find it difficult to accept the existence in Christ of a rational soul, with its free will and thus inherent mutability, Origen exploits the Stoic image of iron and fire (*FP* 2.6.5-6). Iron is capable of being both cold and hot, yet when it is placed in a furnace it is changed into fire, so that nothing can be perceived in it except the fire. Likewise, the soul which "was for ever placed in the Word, for ever in the Wisdom, for ever in God, is God in all its acts and feelings and thoughts" (*FP* 2.6.6). The soul which has cleaved to Christ is by nature the same as all other souls, but in its case, "what formerly depended upon the will was by the influence of long custom changed into nature" (*FP* 2.6.5). So, Origen asserts, there was a rational soul in Christ "that had neither any thoughts nor any possibility of sin" (*FP* 2.6.5). This sounds somewhat docetic, and similar formulae would be repeated throughout the centuries with a more certain docetic intent. It is central to the apostolic witness that Christ was tempted as are all other human beings, but that he stood firm in obedience to God (esp. Heb 2:10-18; 4:15; 5:5-10). Origen seems to want to affirm the same, when he describes how the soul of Jesus alone among all the other souls stood firm in its adherence to God, even unto death on the Cross. Yet what is achieved in this way, the complete identification of Jesus with the divine Word, is then assumed as a given in the description of Christ as he takes flesh in the letters of the Gospels. Jesus Christ, the crucified and exalted Lord, is the very Word of God from the beginning, from all eternity, present to the patriarchs and prophets of old and thereafter to those who understand their writings. So, for Origen, it is impossible to think that Christ, whose human soul and flesh is changed into the Word and who now appears in the pages of the four Gospels, though subject to temptations and agony, was able to sin. Whether it is actually possible to depict Christ as genuinely subject to temptation yet without the possibility of succumbing to it, is not a question Origen addressed, nor, for that matter, would it have made any sense to him, for the primary purpose of the Gospel accounts is not to recount historical events but to effect the coming of the Word into the hearts of its hearers.

From this brief sketch of Origen's theological reflection, it can readily be seen how many points of later developments he anticipates For instance, his strong affirmation of the transcendence of the Father and the impossibility of there being two first principles, are points which are important for Arius. So also is Origen's emphasis on the concrete and distinct subsistence of three divine hypostases and his rejection of the term *homoousios* to describe their relationship. Finally, his avoidance of any terms or imagery which might occasion a materialistic understanding, such as describing the Son as being an "emanation" from the Father or his being "begotten from the essence of the Father," would also find an echo in Arius. Yet, on the other hand, Origen's insistence on the eternity of the Son, related to the existence of God as Father, rather than Creator, firmly anticipates the key points of Nicaea. With regard to the person of Christ, Origen already has a sense of the need to affirm that there is only one subject, but two natures, and does so in a manner that enables him to deploy the principle of *communicatio idiomatum*. Moreover, he recognizes the need to affirm the completeness of Christ's human nature, including a rational soul which, at least in its own definition, is mutable, and he is also aware of difficulties that this might pose. However, to see Origen simply as a collection of anticipated positions is not satisfactory. None of the points just mentioned are, with Origen, isolable dogmatic formula. Removed from their own proper context and nuanced role in Origen's theological vision, they become mere formulae which can be aligned with contradictory positions (Arian and Nicene). The context for Origen was always the pedagogy of Scripture and its exegesis.[95] Even when the flesh and bones of Origen's works were deemed heretical, the spirit of his theological enterprise endured. According to the Byzantine *Suidae Lexicon*, Gregory the Theologian declared that "Origen is the whetstone of us all."[96]

The Immediate Legacy of Origen in Alexandria

The legacy of Origen is extremely complex, not least because of the difficulties of specifying the relation between his works and the "origenism" condemned in Alexandria by Theophilus at the end of the fourth century, and the "origenism" condemned by Justinian and the Second Council of Constantinople in the sixth century. Initially in Alexandria it seems that Heraclas maintained Demetrius' hostility towards Origen. Later, however, although they were critical of some ideas, primarily concerning cosmology and anthropology, reputed

---

95 R. Williams suggests that "[i]n short, Origen's sense of what orthodoxy requires, because it is based upon a close connection between orthodoxy and the practice of systematic spiritual exegesis considered as, in the strictest sense, a spiritual exercise, is almost bound to appear heterodox in an age when the dominant discourse of theology is moulded by the pressure to agree formularies that can be communicated economically and authoritatively." ("Origen: Between Orthodoxy and Heresy," 13).

96 *Suidae Lexicon*, ed. A. Adler, 3.619.

to be Origen's, Dionysius the Great (d. c. 264) and Peter (d. 311) were by no means "anti-origenist," and indeed the influence of Origen's theology on Dionysius at least is readily evident.[97] In fact, even as late as the middle of the fourth century Origen's reputation was such that Athanasius could respectfully call upon "the labor-loving Origen" in support of his defense of the Nicene Creed.[98]

The case of Dionysius is particularly interesting, and becomes important in the controversies of the following century when certain statements of his were appealed to by the opponents of Nicaea in support of their position, provoking a full defense from Athanasius. According to Athanasius, the passage in question came from a letter sent by Dionysius, in the middle of the third century, to Euphranor and Ammonius concerning an outbreak of Sabellianism currently affecting the churches of the Libyan Pentapolis.[99] Concerned to counter Sabellian teaching by emphasizing the real distinction between the Father and the Son, Dionysius described the Son as "a creature and something come into being" (ποίημα καὶ γενητὸν), claiming that the Son is not "proper" (ἴδιον) by nature to God, but "alien in substance" (ξένον κατ᾽ οὐσίαν) to the Father, as a vinedresser is different from a vine and a shipwright from a boat, and, though this is possibly a corollary deduced by his opponents, that "being a creature, he was not before he came to be."[100] Athanasius admitted that these words were indeed written by Dionysius, but that they were taken out of context, and that his position, as exemplified in his

---

97 Cf. W. A. Bienert, *Dionysius von Alexandrien: Zur Frage des Origenismus im dritten Jahrhundert*, PTS 21 (Berlin: De Gruyter, 1978); T. Vivian, *St Peter of Alexandria: Bishop and Martyr* (Philadelphia: Fortress Press, 1988), 87-138.

98 Athanasius, *On the Decrees of Nicaea*, 27.

99 Athanasius, *On the Opinion of Dionysius*, 5, 9-10. Eusebius (*EH* 7.26) mentions that Dionysius wrote letters against Sabellius to "Ammon bishop of the church at Berenice" and to Telesphorus, Euphranor and Euporus, and also to Basilides, "bishop of the communities in the Pentapolis."

100 Athanasius, *Opinion*, 4 (Opitz, 48.22-3): ὡς ποίημα ὢν οὐκ ἦν πρὶν γένηται. That this statement, which does not square with anything else that we know of Dionysius' teaching, might be a conclusion drawn by his opponents, is suggested by Williams, *Arius*, 152-3. The authenticity of the passages from Dionysius, quoted by Athanasius in *On the Opinion of Dionysius*, called into question by Luise Abramowski, has recently been challenged again by Uta Heil in *Athanasius von Alexandrien: De Sententia Dionysii*, PTS 52 (Berlin: De Gruyter, 1999).

other writings, vindicates his orthodoxy; Basil of Caesarea, on the other hand, more candidly admits that the desire to resist Sabellius had driven Dionysius into the opposite error, laying the seeds for further deviations.[101]

Objecting to the extreme manner in which he had emphasized the distinctness of the Son from the Father, some brethren, who otherwise "thought correctly," went to Rome, without consulting Dionysius of Alexandria, to complain to his namesake there.[102] Dionysius of Rome (d. 268) replied with a letter in which he lambasted not only Sabellius but certain "catechists and teachers of the divine Word" for falling into the opposite error, in which they destroy the divine monarchy, splitting it into "three powers or separate hypostases or divinities" so that "in some way they preach three Gods, dividing the sacred Monad into three hypostases completely alien to each other and utterly separate."[103] It is important to note how Dionysius of Rome indicates that his real concern with the language of three hypostases is that he suspects that behind it lies the error of Rome's oldest enemy, "for it is the teaching of the presumptuous Marcion to sever and divide the divine monarchy into three [independent, first] principles (ἀρχάς)."[104] As Williams points out, if the *bête noir* of Rome was Marcionism, in Alexandria it was Valentinianism, so that while both Origen and Dionysius, and later Arius, want to stress that the Son is not simply a manifestation of an essentially remote yet divisible divine life, the concern in Rome was to avoid any hint of a gap between the creator and the redeemer.[105] Drawing a distinction perhaps similar to Origen's but certainly not derived from him, Dionysius of Rome explained Proverbs 8:22 by claiming that it is possible to speak of the Son as "created" (ἔκτισεν), but not made (ἐποίησε), by God, in the sense that he has been placed over all things which were made by him; other than this, one must not speak of the Son as being a "handiwork" (χειροποίητον) or something "made" (ποίημα).[106] Nor is one to speak of the Son as "coming into being," as

101 Basil of Caesarea, *Epistle*, 9.2.
102 Athanasius, *Opinion*, 13.
103 Athanasius, *Decrees*, 26 (Opitz, 22.1-9).
104 Ibid. (Opitz, 22.12-13).
105 Williams, *Arius*, 150-1.
106 Athanasius, *Decrees*, 26 (Opitz, 22.19-23.10).

this would imply the "absurdity" that "he once was not," and if Christ is in the Father and is the Word, Wisdom and Power of God, then the Son always exists.[107] Throughout "the divine oracles," Dionysius of Rome claims, the Father is said to "beget" the Son (referring to Prov 8:25), so that his origin is not an act of creation but a "divine and ineffable generation."[108] Insisting in this way that the almighty God of all, the Father, is never without his Word or his Spirit, who are always united with him, gathered up and brought together in him, Dionysius is satisfied that both the divine Trinity and the preaching of the monarchy can be preserved.[109]

Dionysius of Rome also sent a personal letter to the Alexandrian, informing him of the accusations made against him. Dionysius of Alexandria replied immediately, composing his *Refutation and Defense*, which he then sent to Rome.[110] In the fragments of this work preserved by Athanasius, Dionysius defends the propriety of calling the Son a "creature" or "something made" on the grounds that human beings can be described as the creators or makers of their own utterances or discourses (λόγοι), though Athanasius, embarrassed by this elastic usage, adds his own characteristic, and continual, refrain that Dionysius intended that all such statements be taken as referring to the created flesh of Christ.[111] More importantly, Dionysius points out that if he had indulged in such language, he had nevertheless previously specified that God is the Father, not of things created, but of the Son.[112] In explaining himself further, Dionysius draws on ideas and imagery that are redolent of Origen. He is emphatic that the Father, Son and Spirit cannot be separated, for the names of each are "inseparable and

---

107 Ibid. (Opitz, 22.20-22): εἰ γὰρ γέγονεν υἱός, ἦν ὅτε οὐκ ἦν· ἀεὶ δὲ ἦν, εἴ γε "ἐν τῷ πατρί" ἐστιν, ὡς αὐτός φησι, καὶ εἰ λόγος καὶ σοφία καὶ δύναμις ὁ Χριστός.
108 Ibid. (Opitz, 23.7-10).
109 Ibid. (Opitz, 22.9-12; 23.12-16).
110 Cf. Athanasius, *Opinion*, 13. Eusebius refers to four treatises (συγγράμματα) of Dionysius addressed to his namesake at Rome (*EH* 7.26), and Athanasius also refers to a "third" (*Opinion*, 18) and "fourth" book (*Opinion*, 23), but the integrity of the title, *Refutation and Defense*, covering all volumes (cf. esp. *Opinion*, 14, Opitz 56.33), seems to stand.
111 Athanasius, *Opinion*, 20-1; cf. ibid. 10-11, and the desperate measures taken by Athanasius in *Opinion*, 12, where he imagines what Dionysius would have said.
112 Ibid. 20 (Opitz, 61.19-25).

indivisible" from the others, so that the names of Father and Son imply each other, while the Spirit is designated by reference to the one from whom and the one through whom he proceeds.[113] As such Dionysius also affirmed unambiguously that as "there never was a time when God was not Father," so Christ is eternal, being the Wisdom, Word and Power of God, not having his being from himself, as would an independent first principle, but from the Father.[114] Applying the imagery of light to God, Dionysius described the Son as being the "brightness (τὸ ἀπαύγασμα) of light eternal," being with God "without beginning and ever-begotten" (ἄναρχον καὶ ἀειγενὲς), shining in his presence and being that Wisdom in which God takes delight.[115] Dealing with the charge that he did not state that Christ is "of one essence" (ὁμοούσιος) with God, Dionysius pointed out that the term is not found in Scripture.[116] However, he continued, the examples he had given, of a parent and child, who are "homogenous" (ὁμογενεῖς), belonging to the same genus yet other than each other, and a plant and its root, which are different but of the same nature (ὁμοφυεῖς), as are a river and its source, indicate that he accepts the meaning of the term *homoousios*.[117] Dionysius was thus prepared to accept the term *homoousios* only in a loose, generic sense, so that it did not carry any materialistic overtones nor threaten the distinct subsistence of each of the Trinity. By his various arguments, such as the eternal correlativity of Father and Son, and images, Dionysius wanted to make it clear to his Roman namesake that this concrete distinctiveness does not undermine the basis structure of a monotheistic confession. Holding both sides together, Dionysius declared that "we extend the Monad indivisibly into the Trinity and conversely gather together the Trinity without diminution into the Monad,"[118] that is, contemplating the one God, the Father, leads inevitably to the Son and the Spirit, without dividing the uniqueness of this one God in any way, while the very thought of the Son and the Spirit

---

113 Ibid. 17.
114 Ibid. 15 (Opitz, 57.1-3).
115 Ibid. 15 (Opitz, 57.4-13), citing Wis 7:26 and Prov 8:30.
116 On the question of who introduced the term *homoousios* into the debate, see Hanson, *Search for the Christian Doctrine*, 192-3.
117 Ibid. 18.
118 Ibid. 17 (Opitz, 58.24-5): οὕτω μὲν ἡμεῖς εἴς τε τὴν τριάδα τὴν μονάδα πλατύνομεν ἀδιαίρετον, καὶ τὴν τριάδα πάλιν ἀμείωτον εἰς τὴν μονάδα συγκεφαλαιούμεθα.

brings one back to the Father, without undermining the concrete and distinct subsistence of each of the three.

Later Alexandrian teachers, such as Theognostus (d.c. 282) and Pierius (d.c. 300), seem to have followed in a similar theological vein.[119] While the general lineaments of Origen's theology brought Alexandria into controversy with Rome in the third century, positions which he had held together, when the focus of theological reflection was on the pedagogy of Scripture and its exegesis, lost their cohesion and appeared as irresolvable tensions in a theological discourse increasingly concentrated on precise dogmatic formulae. As we have seen, it is possible to trace key aspects of both the Arian and the Nicene positions back to Origen. This ambiguity, together with a lingering uneasiness about role of the episcopacy in Alexandria, made it almost inevitable that controversy would explode within the city, over issues so fundamental to the Christian faith, primarily of course the true divinity of Jesus Christ, that the whole of the Christian world would be drawn into the debate.

---

119 Along with Origen and Dionysius, Athanasius also cites a passage of Theognostus in defense of the Nicene Creed (*Decrees*, 25); otherwise their teaching is only known through the biased summaries provided by Photius (*Bibl.* 106, 119). Cf. Vivian, *Peter*, 115-16.

8

Paul of Samosata and the
Council of Antioch

Towards the end of his life, Dionysius of Alexandria (d. c. 264) was invited to Antioch to investigate the teaching of Paul of Samosata, who had succeeded Demetrian to the episcopacy at Antioch around the year 260. We know very little about Paul and his teaching, despite the fact that he is one of the most notorious figures of the early centuries, whose name is used from his deposition onwards to blacken almost every theological opponent, so that he was associated in polemical literature with figures as diverse as Artemon (or Artemas), Sabellius, Mani, Origen, Arius, Marcellus, Photinus, Diodore of Tarsus, Theodore of Mopsuestia, and Nestorius. The affair concerning Paul, entangled in politics as much as matters of theology, is difficult to reconstruct. With regard to its doctrinal dimensions, Paul's teaching is known only through the reports of his opponents, and the attempt to establish his theological position is made all the more difficult by the fact that the various sources present his errors differently, reflecting the issues of their own contemporary debates. The earliest source concerning Paul, and the only one whose authenticity has never been questioned, is the "Synodal Letter," passages of which are preserved by Eusebius (*EH* 7.30), though his extracts are only minimally concerned with theology. Eusebius was, however, familiar with the primary source material, and so his comments elsewhere are of importance: his basic charge against Paul, which is echoed in other fourth-century writers, in the context of the Trinitarian debates, is that Paul denied the "preexistence" of Christ, or, alternatively, that he denied the substantial existence of the Word as the Son of God. A similar charge is raised by the "Letter of the Six Bishops," a document purporting, plausibly, to have been composed by those assembled in Antioch, though the authenticity of this source is less secure. Finally, from the time of Apollinarius of Laodicea onwards, and particularly in the quotations from the *Acta* of the Council of Antioch which appear in the fifth century, in the context of the Christological debates, Paul is criticized for having divided the one Christ into two distinct beings. Despite the differing charges raised against Paul, the positions developed in response indicate that the basic issue was how best to understand the "identity" of the Son of God: while it seems that Paul emphasized the identity of the Son of God as proclaimed in the kerygma, his opponents tended to take the identity of the Son of God as that of the Word who took the place of the soul in the composite, though unified, being of the one Jesus Christ, a position which later generations found as problematic as those who condemned Paul had found his.

The Council of Antioch and the "Synodal Letter"

The "Synodal Letter" was written by sixteen named figures together with "all the others who dwell with us in the neighboring cities and nations, bishops, presbyters and deacons and the churches of God," and addressed to Dionysius of Rome and Maximus of Alexandria "and to all our fellow-ministers throughout the world, bishops, presbyters and deacons and to the whole Catholic Church under heaven" (*EH* 7.30.2). The authors of this letter describe how they had requested the presence of many bishops, some even from a great distance, "to heal the deadly doctrine" of Paul.[1] Two distinguished bishops are singled out for specific mention in the Letter: Dionysius of Alexandria, whose theology and ecclesiastical activity were discussed in the previous chapter; and Firmilian of Caesarea in Cappadocia, who had invited Origen to Cappadocia for the benefit of the churches there and had himself journeyed to Caesarea in Palestine to study with the great master (*EH* 6.27). Dionysius did not accept the invitation, but expressed his opinion by a letter addressed to the whole community in Antioch, which

---

1   *EH* 7.30.3. Eusebius (*EH* 7.28.2), after naming various bishops and noting the presence of presbyters and deacons, comments: "When all of these assembled at different times and frequently to consider these matters, the arguments and questions were discussed at every meeting: the adherents of the Samosatene endeavoring to cover and conceal his heterodoxy, and the others striving zealously to lay bare and make manifest his heresy and blasphemy against Christ."

was appended to the "Synodal Letter" and was still extant in Eusebius' day but is so no longer. Firmilian, on the other hand, came to Antioch twice and condemned Paul's teaching, though as Paul promised to change his position Firmilian took no further action. When Firmilian learned of Paul's deceit, he set off for Antioch again, but died en route in Tarsus (*EH* 7.30.3-5). Paul was finally unmasked and condemned for heresy at an assembly held in 268/9.[2] According to Eusebius this meeting consisted of a great number of bishops, though he further notes that the only person able to unmask "that crafty and deceitful man" was Malchion, the learned head of a Greek rhetorical school in Antioch and also a presbyter of the community (*EH* 7.29.2). Eusebius also adds that Malchion "had stenographers taking notes as he held his disputation (ζήτησιν)" with Paul, and that these records are extant in his own times (*EH* 7.29.2). The "Synodal Letter" issued by the assembly concludes by relating how its authors felt themselves obliged to excommunicate Paul and to appoint in his place Domnus, the son of the former bishop, Demetrian (*EH* 7.30.17). Paul refused to surrender the church building, and according to a later report there ensued "schisms among the people, revolt among the priests and confusion among the pastors."[3] Eventually the Emperor Aurelian was approached, probably after 272 when he had regained control of Antioch, and he decided, "most equitably" in Eusebius' opinion, that the building should be given to those with whom the bishops in Italy and Rome would communicate in writing (*EH* 7.30.19). Paul is not heard of again thereafter, though his name continually haunted later heresiologists.

The Council of Antioch in 268/9 was one of the most significant events of its kind in the third century. The letter issued by the Council, excommunicating Paul and announcing their decisions to Rome and Alexandria and to "the whole Catholic Church under heaven," is the earliest such document known, and the Council itself became an important reference point for later synodal activity. Although Tertullian had earlier referred to councils being held, the form of such

---

2   *EH* 7.29.1. On the date, cf. F. Millar, "Paul of Samosata, Zenobia and Aurelian: The Church, Local Culture and Political Allegiance in Third-Century Syria," *JRS* 61 (1971), 11.

3   Basil the deacon at the Council of Ephesus (431), *ACO* 1.1.5, 8.

ecclesiastical activity is obscure.[4] Eusebius also refers to many "synods of bishops" being held at the end of the second century concerning the proper date for celebrating Pascha, though his account is certainly anachronistic.[5] However, the form of the Council of Antioch, as described by Eusebius, corresponds to a type of ecclesiastical assembly which is otherwise well documented during the third century—the doctrinal disputation with a teacher of the church.[6] The most notable example in the third century of a teacher engaged in such activity is Origen, who was invited many times to investigate doctrinal problems in diverse places. Most interesting, in view of the charges raised against Paul of Samosata, is the case of Beryllus of Bostra in Arabia sometime between 238 and 244. According to Eusebius, Beryllus was charged with "daring to say that our Savior and Lord did not preexist in an individual existence of his own before his sojourn among men, nor had he a divinity of his own, but only the Father's dwelling in him."[7] After various bishops had held "questionings and debates" (ζητήσεις καὶ διαλόγους) with Beryllus, Origen, at this point a presbyter in Caesarea in Palestine, was invited to enter into discussion (εἰς ὁμιλίαν) with him, and once he understood the position of Beryllus "he corrected what was unorthodox, and, persuading by reasoning (λογισμῷ τε πείσας), established him in the truth concerning the doctrine."[8] Around the same time Origen was called to another "synod of no small dimensions" in Arabia (*EH* 6.37).

About the proceedings of such assemblies we are exceptionally, and fortuitously, informed, due to the discovery (in 1941) of the *Dialogue of Origen with Heraclides and his Fellow Bishops on the Father, the Son*

---

4 Tertullian, *On Modesty* 10; *On Fasting* 13. Cf. H. J. Sieben, *Die Konzilsidee der Alten Kirche*, Konziliengeschichte, B, Untersuchungen (Paderborn *et al*: Schöningh, 1979), 467.

5 Eusebius, *EH* 5.23.2. Cf. W. L. Petersen, "Eusebius and the Paschal Controversy," in H. W. Attridge and G. Hata (eds.), *Eusebius, Christianity, and Judaism* (Leiden: Brill, 1992), 311-25; Brent, *Hippolytus*, 412-15.

6 Cf. Sieben, *Konzilsidee*, 466-76; U. M. Lang, "The Christological Controversy at the Synod of Antioch in 268/9," *JTS* ns 51.1 (2000), 61-5.

7 *EH* 6.33.1: τὸν σωτῆρα καὶ κύριον ἡμῶν λέγειν τολμῶν μὴ προϋφεστάναι κατ᾽ ἰδίαν οὐσίας περιγραφὴν πρὸ τῆς εἰς ἀνθρώπους ἐπιδημίας μηδὲ μὴν θεότητα ἰδίαν ἔχειν, ἀλλ᾽ ἐμπολιτευομένην αὐτῷ μόνην τὴν πατρικήν.

8 *EH* 6.33.2-3. Eusebius claims that written records of this meeting were extant in his day; Jerome also claims that they were extant, though his account is probably derived from Eusebius (*On Famous Men*, 60).

and the Soul, which records a meeting of this kind held somewhere in Arabia between 244 and 249. The account begins by noting that the bishops in attendance had expressed their concerns about the faith of the bishop Heraclides, followed by a short statement of faith given by Heraclides. After this prefatory material, the inquiry proper begins with Origen engaging Heraclides in dialogue and leading him to the correct faith. The bulk of the work, however, follows this brief exchange and consists of long homilies given by Origen. It is clear that Origen's role in this assembly was understood, even by the bishops, as didactic.[9] He spoke on a variety of topics concerning the canon of faith and the correct interpretation of Scripture, sometimes in response to questions but always addressing all those present.[10] Such evidence for third-century conciliar activity in matters of doctrine, suggests that the most important role in the proceedings did not belong to the episcopacy but to the teacher, who by reason and rational discourse investigated the matter at hand and corrected any erroneous beliefs, or at least refuted the errors in a manner convincing to the assembly, and who thus led all those present to a deeper understanding of the faith. Unity in faith was preserved or regained through the ability of the teacher, and the process was most successful when this role was filled by an outstanding figure such as Origen.[11]

This seems to have been the general format of the meetings held in Antioch. Various renowned theologians, in this case the bishops Dionysius and Firmilian, had been invited to Antioch to investigate the teaching of Paul of Samosata, yet in the final meeting it was the *presbyter* Malchion who conducted the investigation of the *bishop* Paul in the presence of a number of other bishops, presbyters, deacons and others. The purpose of this disputation was to bring to light the errors of Paul's teachings, which only Malchion, the head of a Greek rhetorical school, was able to accomplish, and to effect his correction, though in this respect the outcome was not successful. Clearly laymen and presbyters took an active role in developing and teaching theology in this period.

9 Cf. *Dialogue with Heraclides*, 24.25-6: "When bishop Phillip had entered, Demetrius, another bishop, said: 'Our brother Origen teaches (διδάσκει) that the soul is immortal.'"
10 Cf. *Dialogue*, 10.18-19: [Origen] "If there is anything remaining concerning the canon, mention it; otherwise we will speak still further on Scripture."
11 Cf. Sieben, *Konzilsidee*, 476.

As this role became associated, increasingly exclusively, with the episcopacy such a state of affairs began to seem anomalous, so that the bishops assembled at Antioch some fifty years later repudiated the charge of Arianism by indignantly asking how it was possible to think that they, as bishops, had followed a presbyter, referring to Arius.[12]

Despite the extensive efforts made to reveal the error of Paul's teaching, doctrinal considerations figure relatively little in the extant passages of the "Synodal Letter." The authors state that as Paul has turned aside from the canon it is unnecessary to consider his conduct, but the passages of the "Synodal Letter" preserved by Eusebius are almost exclusively concerned with what they considered to be Paul's haughty attitude and dubious activities, which they recount fulsomely: the way that he strutted through the marketplace, conducting his business as he walked, attended by bodyguards and adoring crowds; his preference for the title of *ducenarius* to bishop; his acquisition of abundant wealth through extortion, plunder and other iniquities; his chicanery in ecclesiastical assemblies, and his decision to build a tribunal and lofty throne, and a *secretum*; his habit of slapping his thigh and stomping on the tribunal, and his threats to those who did not applaud him; and his potentially scandalous association with women.[13] No doubt when selecting these passages Eusebius was less interested in issues of doctrine than the history and governance of the Church, and perhaps particularly those affairs which would interest a possible pagan audience.[14] However, the sheer effort expended in condemning Paul suggests that his doctrinal errors were not at all self-evident, and the overall impression given by Eusebius is that other issues were at least as important, casting a shadow over the appointment of the previous bishop's son to the episcopacy in Paul's stead.

As for Paul's theology, the "Synodal Letter" considers it to be a revival of the error of Artemas (*EH* 7.30.16-17). Paul is apparently quoted, from "the records" attached to the Letter, as having said that

12 In the First Creed of the Council of Antioch in 341, recorded in Athanasius, *On the Synods*, 22.3 (Opitz, 248.29-30). Cf. Lang, "The Christological Controversy," 65, who argues that this change in the form of conciliar activity indicates that the extant fragments claiming to derive from the Acts of the Council of Antioch in 268/9 do indeed belong to the third century.

13 Eusebius, *EH* 7.30.7-16. Cf. F. W. Norris, "Paul of Samosata: *Procurator Ducenarius*," *JTS* ns 35.1 (1984), 50-70.

14 Cf. Lang, "The Christological Controversy," 58.

"Jesus Christ is from below ('Ιησοῦν Χριστὸν κάτωθεν)," which the authors of the Letter take as a refusal to acknowledge that "the Son of God has come down from heaven" (*EH* 7.30.11). Perhaps along the same lines, the Letter charges Paul with having stopped the singing of certain hymns to the Lord Jesus Christ, hymns which were probably Paschal as it is further alleged that Paul had women sing songs to him on the great day of Pascha (*EH* 7.30.10). Eusebius, who had read the whole Letter and probably also the appended synodal records,[15] introduces the whole account by stating that Paul "held low and degraded views of Christ, namely that in his nature he was a common man" (ὡς κοινοῦ τὴν φύσιν ἀνθρώπου γενομένου, *EH* 7.27.2). Elsewhere in his *History*, Eusebius concurs with the Letter's assessment that Paul was simply reviving the heresy of Artemon, which held that the Savior was "a mere man" (ψιλὸν ἄνθρωπον, *EH* 5.28.1-2).

Paul in the Context of the Trinitarian Debates

Given that Eusebius was acquainted with the primary source material concerning Paul, his comments in the *Ecclesiastical Theology*, written a while later (around 337), are also important. At one point in this work Eusebius attributes to Marcellus of Ancyra the position that Christ was "a mere man, composed of body and soul, as if he differed in no way from the common nature of man," and so, Eusebius continues, Marcellus follows the Ebionites and Paul of Samosata.[16] Eusebius' alternative to this is to regard the Logos as taking the place of the soul in Christ, dwelling in and animating a human body.[17] His reasoning depends upon a "compositional" approach to understanding Jesus Christ, arguing that unless the Logos took the place of the soul, there is no "part" of Christ that is divine and so he is no different from any other human being—he is a "mere man." However, there is no direct evidence that Marcellus did recognize the presence of a human soul in Christ. It is possible that this charge actually derives from Eusebius' earlier controversy with Eustathius of Antioch who most certainly did,

15 Cf. H. de Riedmatten, *Les Acts du Procès de Paul de Samosate: Étude sur la Christologie du IIIe au IVe siècle*, Paradosis 6 (Fribourg en Suisse: St Paul, 1952), 17-23.
16 Eusebius, *Ecclesiastical Theology*, 1.20.7 (43).
17 Ibid. 1.20.7 (40-1).

and that this had prompted Eusebius to re-read the Acts of the Council of 268/9.[18] If so, this might be taken to suggest that the Council's accusation that Paul held Christ to be a "mere man" turned upon Paul's recognition of the presence of a human soul in Christ. However, as the focus of Eusebius' polemic is Marcellus, it is not certain that he intends to attribute to Paul a deliberate affirmation of both the human body *and soul* of Christ. It seems more likely that Eusebius' attempt to ascribe this position to Marcellus resulted in his charge that Marcellus taught that Christ was a "mere man" and that this was the basis for the association with Paul.[19] A similar train of reasoning appears to be at work in various charges made against Origen that are dealt with by Pamphilus early in the fourth century. Certain critics of Origen alleged that he preached "two Christs," apparently on the grounds that as he taught that Christ had a human soul, he must have regarded the Word of God and Jesus Christ as being two different entities.[20] This is the most likely basis for another charge made against Origen, that he taught that Jesus Christ was "merely a man," as had Artemas and Paul of Samosata.[21] Again, Paul is invoked as one who taught that Christ is merely human, rather than for any more sophisticated assertion concerning the relation between Christ and the Word.[22] As for the content of the charge that Paul taught that Christ was a "mere man," the most that can be drawn from this is that he did not recognize the divinity of Christ in the same manner as did his opponents, while their position is not necessarily that of Eusebius fifty years later.

18 As suggested by C. Stead, "Marcel Richard on Malchion and Paul of Samosata," H. C. Brennecke, E. L. Grasmück, C. Markschies (eds.), *Logos: Festschrift für Luise Abramowski zum 8 Juli 1993* (Berlin-New York, 1993), 149-50. Cf. Socrates, *Ecclesiastical History*, 1.23; Eustathius, frag. 17, in M. Spanneut, *Recherches sur les Écrits d'Eustathe d'Antioche, avec une édition nouvelle des fragments dogmatiques et exégétiques* (Lille: Facultés Catholiques, 1948).

19 In his *Prophetic Extracts*, 3.19 (PG 22.1144b), which antedates the controversy with Eustathius and Marcellus, Eusebius gives no indication that the presence of a human soul in Christ was an issue in the case of Paul; Paul was rather counted among those who denied the "preexistence" of Christ.

20 Pamphilus, *Apology for Origen*, PG 17.588-90.

21 Ibid. PG 17.578-9.

22 Even in the fragments deriving from a later era, the term "Word" does not play a significant role in Paul's understanding of Jesus Christ. For a brave attempt to explicate Paul's theology against the background of Luke-Acts rather than John, see R. L. Sample, "The Messiah as Prophet: The Christology of Paul of Samosata" (Ph.D. Diss., Northwestern University, Evanston, Ill. 1977), though note the comments of Norris ("Paul of Samosata," 56-8).

More certain information concerning Paul is given by Eusebius in an earlier passage from his *Ecclesiastical Theology*. Here Eusebius mentions four different heresies, distinguishing Paul from, first, Sabellius, who taught one God, but called the Father "Son"; second, the Ebionites, who confess one God and acknowledge the bodily reality of the Savior, but do not recognize the divinity of the Son; and lastly Marcellus, who defines God and the Logos in him to be one, while granting him the two titles of "Father" and "Son." Of Paul, Eusebius says that "although he teaches that Jesus is the Christ of God, and, like Marcellus, confesses one God of all, the Church fathers declared that the Samosatene was alien to the Church of God because he does not confess that Christ is the Son of God and God before his generation in the flesh."[23] Paul, just like Beryllus of Bostra before him, is accused of denying Christ's "preexistence." It seems, according to this report, that Paul taught that Jesus was indeed the Christ, the expected Messiah of God, who makes his appearance at the fullness of time, but who therefore does not "preexist" this definitive moment. Paul's Christ is indeed a man, as the earliest reports, in the "Synodal Letter" and Pamphilus, charge him with teaching, but Eusebius, nearing the middle of the fourth century, now differentiates the Ebionites, who also hold such a position, from Paul, whose error is more specifically related to the question of Christ's "preexistence." The two issues, of course, are not unrelated. It is possible that the charge of denying Christ's preexistence is an implication which fourth-century writers, given the nature of the debates they were engaged in, were eager to attribute to Paul.[24] Of Paul himself, it seems very likely that an emphasis on the revelation of Christ at a determinate time is an original part of his teaching. There is a highly suggestive report of Paul's teaching given in the work *On the Incarnation of our Lord Jesus Christ, against Apollinarius* falsely attributed to Athanasius, which emphasizes precisely the point that God was born from the virgin, revealed out of Nazareth, and that this is the beginning of his existence; he is from all eternity "in predetermination," but in actual existence known only as the one from Nazareth. It is also noteworthy

---

23 Eusebius, *Ecclesiastical Theology*, 1.14: ὅτι μὴ καὶ υἱὸν θεοῦ καὶ θεὸν πρὸ τῆς ἐνσάρκου γενέσεως ὄντα τὸν Χριστὸν ὡμολόγει.

24 Cf. e.g., Athanasius, *On the Synods*, 45.

that this report suggests that Paul's motivation was to preserve the uniqueness of the Father as the one God of all.[25] A work attributed to Epiphanius, the *Anakephalaiosis*, also records a tradition that Paul claimed that although Christ has things said about him, prophetically, in the Scriptures, he does not actually exist until incarnate from Mary.[26] A similar indication is given in the sixth century by Leontius of Byzantium, who quotes a saying of Paul (from the *Acta* of the Council of 268/9, which will be considered later) that seems to be a variation of the apparent quotation given in the "Synodal Letter," that "Jesus Christ is from below (κάτωθεν)." According to Leontius, Paul asserted that "The Word is from the beginning (ἄνωθεν); Jesus Christ, a man, is thenceforth (ἐντεῦθεν)."[27] The different adverb suggests that the contrast intended by Paul is temporal, referring to the fulfillment of the predetermined plans of God, rather than spatial, attempting to describe the "descent" of the Logos.

Among the other fourth-century references to Paul, of particular interest is the report given in a letter written by George of Laodicea, usually associated with the "Dated Creed" issued by the Council at Sirmium on May 22, 359.[28] According to this report, Paul of Samosata and Marcellus, both motivated by the opening verse of the Gospel of John, refused to acknowledge "that the Son of God is truly a Son," but claimed instead that the Word of God must be understood in terms of "the word and utterance (ῥῆμα καὶ φθέγμα) from

25 Ps.-Athanasius, *On the Incarnation of our Lord Jesus Christ, against Apollinarius*, 2.3 (PG 26.1136b): "Paul of Samosata confesses that God is from the virgin, that God was seen from Nazareth, and has thence (ἐντεῦθεν) the beginning of his existence (ὑπάρξεως) and received the beginning of his rule. He confesses that the active Word from heaven and Wisdom were in him; being before the ages in predetermination (τῷ μὲν προορισμῷ πρὸ αἰώνων ὄντα), but revealed from Nazareth in existence (τῇ δὲ ὑπάρξει ἐκ Ναζαρὲτ ἀναδειχθέντα); so that, he says, there might be one God of all, the Father."

26 Ps.-Epiphanius, *Anakephalaiosis*, 2.2.1 (PG 42.868c): προκαταγγελτικῶς μὲν τὰ περὶ αὐτοῦ ἐν ταῖς θείαις γραφαῖς εἰρημένα ἔχοντος, μὴ ὄντος δὲ, ἀλλ᾽ ἀπὸ Μαρίας καὶ δεῦρο διὰ τῆς ἐνσάρκου παρουσίας.

27 Following the text as edited by de Riedmatten, *Les Acts du Procès*, 153.

28 Cf. Hanson, *The Search for the Christian Doctrine of God*, 365-6. That the circle from which this letter emanated knew the Acts of the Council of Antioch 268/9 is argued by M. Simonetti, "Per la rivalutazione di al cune testimonianze su Paolo di Samosata," *Rivista di Storia e Letteratura Religiosa*, 24 (1988), 182.

the mouth." To emphasize that the Son of God "has subsistence, is existing and is being, and is not a spoken word (ῥῆμα)," the report continues, the fathers who condemned Paul used the terms "essence and Son" for the Word, "indicating by the term 'essence' the difference between that which has no independent existence and the One who exists."[29] There is no direct indication that Paul utilized the Gospel of John, let alone that he took his starting point from its prologue; this interpretation of his motivation results from the assimilation of Paul to the polemics of a later age. However, it is clear that Paul's insistence on the historically specific revelation of Jesus the Christ seemed to his opponents to be a denial of their understanding of the eternal, distinct and concrete existence of the Word of God as the Son of God. Hence their insistence that the Word of God is an "essence," this term here being used to designate a concrete being, who is properly called "Son." Epiphanius also claims that Paul held the Word to be a nonsubstantial, nonpersonal utterance of God, or thought existing in God like "reason in the heart of man," perhaps echoing the distinction between an "immanent" and an "uttered" logos taught in Antioch a century earlier by Theophilus.[30]

But, rather than attributing to Paul simply the opposite of what his critics would maintain, that is, a nonpersonal and nonsubstantial Word instead of a personal and substantial Word, there are indications that Paul himself understood the expression "Word of God" in a manner quite different to his opponents. According to a sixth-century writer, "Paul did not say that the self-subsisting Word was in Christ, but called the order and the commandment [of God] 'Word' (λόγον ἔλεγε τὴν κέλευσιν καὶ τὸ πρόσταγμα), that is, God ordered through that man what he willed, and did it."[31] That is, Paul's understanding of the Word of God is set within the broader context of God's will, so that the Word is, as it were, the intent of God for his Christ and his people.[32] This report also connects this perspective of Paul with a desire to maintain the uniqueness of God; the account continues, "he did not say that the

29 Epiphanius, *Panarion*, 73.12.2-3.
30 Theophilus of Antioch, *To Autolycus*, 2.22. For a fourth-century interpretation of Paul along these lines, see Epiphanius, *Panarion*, 65.1.5.
31 Ps.-Leontius, *On the Sects*, 3.3 (PG 86.1216a).
32 Cf. Sample, *The Messiah as Prophet*, 109.

Father, Son and Holy Spirit are one and the same, but he calls the God who created all things 'Father,' the mere man 'Son,' and the grace which inspired the apostles the 'Spirit.'"[33] Whether Paul, as Origen earlier, was sensitive to the distinction between calling the Father "*the* God" (ὁ θεός) and the Son "God" (θεός) is not indicated, but his hesitation certainly led some critics, just as in the case of Origen,[34] to conclude that Paul regarded Christ as a mere man rather than God. Eusebius, on the other hand, in at least one place, considered above, differentiated the Ebionites, who do not acknowledge the divinity of Christ, from Paul, whose error was having failed to accept his "preexistence."[35] A more positive indication that Paul, in his own terms, did recognize Christ as divine is given by the Macrostich Creed (345 AD), which claims that the disciples of Paul said that "after the incarnation, he was by advance made God (ἐκ προκοπῆς τεθεοποιῆσθαι), though by nature a mere man."[36] If Paul did indeed recognize the divinity of the man Jesus, it is as the Christ of God, the one who accomplishes the will of God at the fullness of time, rather than as a being divine "by nature."[37]

The letter of George of Laodicea reported that the fathers who condemned Paul used the term "essence" (οὐσία) to describe the concrete existence of the Word, so emphasizing the Son's distinct subsistence alongside the Father. The implication of this affirmation is drawn out in a letter referred to by Athanasius, but which he had not seen, which alleged that the bishops who condemned the Samosatene also stated in writing that "the Son is not consubstantial (ὁμοούσιος) with the Father."[38] The authenticity of the report went unchallenged, and

---

33 Ps.-Leontius, *On the Sects*, 3.3 (PG 86.1216b).
34 Cf. Pamphilus, *Apology*, third charge, PG 17.578-9.
35 Eusebius, *Ecclesiastical Theology*, 1.14.
36 Athanasius, *On the Synods*, 26 (4), (Opitz, 252, 28-30); cf. Athanasius, *Orations against the Arians*, 3.51, where this "advance" is related to Luke 2:52.
37 For other reports along these lines, see Athanasius, *Orations against the Arians* 2.13, and Nestorius, *The Bazaar of Heracleides*, 1.1.53 (trans. G. R. Driver and L. Hodgson, *Nestorius, the Bazaar of Heracleides* [Oxford: Clarendon, 1925], 44). This thrust of Paul's teaching is certainly akin to the fragments from the *Discourse to Sabinus*, though Sample's attempt to argue for their authenticity (*Messiah*, 56-63) is not successful (cf. Norris, "Paul of Samosata," 57).
38 Athanasius, *On the Synods*, 43 (Opitz, 268.16-18).

Athanasius, Hilary and Basil of Caesarea each felt obliged to explain why the Council of Antioch had condemned the application of the term "consubstantial" to the relation between Father and Son, and also to justify its use by the Council of Nicaea. According to Athanasius, Paul had argued that, if one did not accept that Christ is a man who has become God, then one must accept that he is "consubstantial" with the Father, but that this necessarily leads to the supposition that there is a third "essence" prior to the Father and the Son, from which they are both derived. It was to guard against any such misunderstandings, Athanasius claimed, that the fathers of the Council of Antioch asserted that Christ was not "consubstantial" with the Father. Athanasius also argued that the repudiation of the term extends only to the "bodily sense" in which it was used in Antioch, so that nothing prevents the fathers of Nicaea from using it in a different manner.[39] The credibility of Athanasius' account, however, is severely undermined by the fact that he attributes exactly the same argument as he puts on Paul's lips to his own opponents.[40] Basil's account is similar, though he does not mention any objection raised by Paul.[41] Hilary, on the other hand, mentions the concern of some that using the term "consubstantial" suggests that there was a substance prior to the Father and Son, but claims that the reason for its rejection at the Council of Antioch was that Paul "by this declaration of a single essence, taught that God was single and unitary (*solitarum atque unicum*), and at once Father and Son to himself."[42] Given Paul's insistence on the human character of Christ's existence, it is unthinkable that he could have taught a unitary God existing as both Father and Son. It is possible that Hilary has based his report on an account, such as that given in the letter of George of Laodicea, where Paul and Marcellus are classified together.[43] Alternatively, the sharp distinction between Father and Son that Paul's critics themselves suggest by describing the Word as an "essence" in its own right, may well have prompted Paul, perhaps even recalling the recent controversy between Dionysius of Rome and Dionysius of

39 Ibid. 45 (Opitz, 269.37-270.4).
40 Cf. Ibid. 51 (274.35-275.4).
41 Basil, *Epistle*, 52.1.
42 Hilary, *On the Councils*, 81 (PL 10.534).
43 Cf. G. L. Prestige, *God in Patristic Thought* (London: SPCK, 1959), 206-8.

Alexandria, to respond with the assertion that the Word, as Paul understood this term, is in fact "consubstantial" with the Father, which to his opponents would have confused the very distinction they were trying to secure.[44] It is not possible to ascertain from these echoes how Paul or his critics used the term "consubstantial," but it does seem quite probable that the Council of Antioch did condemn the term, though their repudiation must have been heavily qualified given that they sent their "Synodal Letter" together with a copy of the Acts of the Council to none other than Dionysius of Rome![45]

The Letter of the Six Bishops

The brief description of Paul's teaching given in the "Synodal Letter," together with the other accounts given by Eusebius, suggests that Paul held that the man Jesus was the Christ of God, appearing at the fullness of time, fulfilling the will of God, and in this way is God. While the earliest documented charge is that Paul taught that Christ was a "mere man," the concern comes to focus more precisely on the issue of the "preexistence" of Christ, though according to George of Laodicea, who may have had access to the primary documentation, this was already tackled at the Council of Antioch by the application of the terms "essence" and "Son" to the Word to affirm the personal and concrete existence of the eternal Word of God. The picture thus described is exactly the context which the next source to be considered, the "Letter of the Six Bishops," presupposes.[46] Although doubts have been raised about the authenticity of this text, the points it makes (and those it does not), the manner in which develops its affirmations and the texts it utilizes, all indicate that it is genuine.[47] The names of the six bishops to whom this letter is attributed appear among the names given in the "Synodal Letter," and it is possible that this letter was composed at one of the earlier meetings and sent to Paul prior to the final assembly in

---

44 Cf. De Riedmatten, *Les Acts du Procès*, 106-7.

45 A point made by de Riedmatten, ibid.

46 For the text of the Letter of the Six Bishops, see G. Bardy, *Paul de Samosate: Étude historique*, rev. edn. (Louvain: Spicilegium Sacrum Lovaniense, 1929), 13-19.

47 Cf. De Riedmatten, *Les Acts du Procès*, 121-34; R. L. Sample, *Messiah*, 63-76; *idem*, "The Christology of the Council of Antioch (268 C.E.) Reconsidered," *CH*, 48 (1979), 18-26, esp. 22-3.

268/9. Given that at least two of the bishops invited to these meetings, Dionysius of Alexandria and Firmilian of Caesarea, were schooled in Origen's theology, it is to be expected that the critics of Paul based themselves on Origen, and thus not surprising that characteristic elements of Origen's theology are reflected in this letter.

The letter asserts in unambiguous terms the very points regarding which Paul's teaching was considered deficient. In the opening statement of faith, after noting that "no man has seen or is able to see" the unbegotten God (1 Tim 6:16) but that "no one has known the Father except the Son and anyone to whom the Son reveals him" (Matt 11:27), the bishops conclude that "this one, having known [him] in both the Old and the New Testaments, we confess and proclaim [to be] the begotten Son, the only-begotten Son, being 'the image of the invisible God, the First-born of all creation,' Wisdom, Word, and Power of God, being God before the ages, not in foreknowledge but in essence and subsistence (πρὸ αἰώνων ὄντα οὐ προγνώσει ἀλλ᾽ οὐσίᾳ καὶ ὑποστάσει θεὸν), Son of God."[48] The six bishops are in no doubt that Christ, the one by whom alone the Father is made known, is not a man who has been deified, but is God "in essence and subsistence," and as such is God from all eternity. It is interesting to note that this position is not supported by an appeal to the eternal correlativity of Father and Son (that if God is eternally Father, then the Son is also eternal). Rather, the framework and content of the assertion, as indicated in the preceding quotation, is exegetical, it is what has been learnt from the Scriptures—that Christ is present in both the Old and the New Testaments. The letter acknowledges the concern that Paul seems to have raised, that if one were to accept that the Son is to be proclaimed as God, and God before the creation of the world, then two Gods would be proclaimed, but it points out that both the Old and New Testament Scriptures acknowledge one God and yet at the same time "all the Scriptures inspired by God reveal that the Son of God is God."[49] Again, the argument proceeds by exegetical considerations rather than abstract theological or philosophical principles. The greater part of the letter is concerned with such exegetical issues, especially the Old

48 Letter, 2, citing Col 1:15.
49 Letter, 3.

Testament theophanies, arguing, for instance, that the one who appeared to Abraham was the angel of the Father, the Son who is both Lord and God.[50] Finally the letter concludes on a similar note by stating that "Christ, before the Incarnation, was named 'Christ' in the divine Scriptures."[51] Moreover, as it is *Christ* who is spoken of by the Scriptures,[52] it is not simply as the Power and Wisdom of God that Christ is "before the ages," but *as Christ himself,* an affirmation made by utilizing a distinction drawn by Origen, that although Christ is "one and the same in essence, for the most part he is known by many aspects (πολλαῖς ἐπινοίαις ἐπινοεῖται)"[53]—Christ himself is the subject. It is Christ who is "God before the ages," and while he is spoken of and known by many different names—Image, First-born, Word, Wisdom, and Power of God—these do not refer to different entities, but are aspects of the one Christ who is thus "confessed and proclaimed to be God before the ages." Regarding these names of Christ, it is interesting to note how little the title "Word" figures in the letter;[54] the bishops, as had Origen, understood Christ in a manner too multifaceted to permit being reduced to a single term.

This insistence on Christ's eternal existence as God by nature, defended within the matrix of Scripture, is held in balance with two other important points. First, that though he is "God in essence and subsistence," he is not himself "the unbegotten, beginningless, invisible and unchanging God."[55] He is, rather, the Son of this God, and the letter has no hesitation in declaring that the Son has a "measured knowledge" of him.[56] Similarly, the letter explains the eternal existence of the Son "with the Father" in terms of the Son as the Father's agent in creation, the one who responds to the Father's commandments (referring to Ps 148:5), "fulfilling the paternal will concerning the creation of all things."[57] Citing the Prologue of John (1:3) and Paul (Col 1:16),

---

50 Letter, 5.
51 Letter, 9.
52 Citing here Lam 4:20; 2 Cor 3:17; 1 Cor 10:4; 1 Cor 10:9; Heb 11:26; 1 Pet 1:10-11; 1 Cor 1:24.
53 Letter, 9.
54 The term "Word" is used three times: Letter, 1 (citing Lk 1:2), 2, 4.
55 Letter, 2.
56 Ibid.
57 Letter, 4.

the letter argues that as God has made all things through him, he "truly exists and is active as both Word and God," and that even if the Son is the agent of the Father, he is not "a mere instrument or an insubstantial (ἀνυποστάτου) wisdom," for "the Father has begotten the Son as a living and subsistent (ἐνυπόστατον) energy, working all things in all."[58] The second important point is that the natural or essential divinity of Christ is not asserted in a manner that would impair the humanity of Christ. It does not approach the matter by analyzing the constituent "parts" of Christ, suggesting, for instance, that the Logos took the place of the human soul in Christ. Picking up again on Johannine imagery, the letter speaks of "the Son, being with the Father, God and Lord of all things, and sent by the Father from heaven, taking flesh and becoming man (σαρκωθέντα ἐνηνθρωπηκέναι)."[59] In this way, the letter continues, "the body from the virgin, containing 'the whole fullness of divinity bodily,' was united immutably to the divinity and was deified (τῇ θεότητι ἀτρέπτως ἥνωται καὶ τεθεοποίηται)."[60] Though the body of Christ is "deified" in this way, Christ is definitely not a man become God, but the Son of God, himself God by nature, become man. The soteriological necessity that it is God who works from above to save man below, in the Gospel from God not from man (cf. Rom 1:1; Gal 1:11-12), is respectfully maintained. Yet the resulting confession, which follows immediately, is strictly parallel: "on account of this, he, the same, is both God and man, Jesus Christ, prophesied in the Law and the Prophets and believed in by the whole Church under heaven."[61] One and the same subject, Jesus Christ, the object of their confession from the beginning, is what it is to be both God and man. Their theological affirmations concern what is to be predicated of this subject, rather than providing an analysis of the composition or structure of his being. That he is both God and man is shown, the letter continues, in his activity, that, on the one hand, the Gospels record that he, as God, accomplished miracles, while, on the other hand, as sharing in flesh and blood, he was also subject to

58 Ibid.
59 Letter, 8.
60 Ibid., citing Col 2:9.
61 Ibid.

temptation in every respect, yet without sin.[62] As an episcopal, perhaps even synodal, statement of theology, the letter of the six bishops is a major signpost for future theological reflection. It indicates elements of theology that come to be accepted as essential: the affirmation of the divinity and humanity of the one subject, Jesus Christ, yet with the priority being ascribed to the divine, and the affirmation of his eternal existence demonstrated within the matrix of scripture.

Paul in the Context of the Christological Debates

Paul's notoriety for having regarded Christ as a "mere man" and denying his "preexistence," the charges raised against him until the middle of the fourth century, was overshadowed thereafter by the even more infamous "distinction" or "separation" he was perceived to have made between Jesus Christ and the Word of God as two entities. An early reference to this is found in the first letter of Apollinarius of Laodicea (d.c. 390) to Dionysius, which begins,

> I am astonished hearing about those who confess the Lord as God incarnate and yet fall into the separation (διαιρέσει) wickedly introduced by those thinking like Paul. Slavishly following Paul of Samosata, they assert that the one is from heaven, whom they confess to be God, and the other is a man from the earth, saying that one is uncreated the other created, one eternal the other from yesterday.[63]

The transition to a more focused analysis of the relationship between Christ and the Word can also be seen in the difference between, on the one hand, the three books of the *Orations against the Arians* by Athanasius, where the references to Paul concern issues of preexistence and the priority of the divine in Christ (that he is God-made-man, not man-made-God), and on the other hand, the fourth *Oration against the Arians* ascribed to Athanasius, where "some of the followers of the Samosatene" are criticized for "distinguishing the Word from the Son" and saying that the Son is Christ while the Word is another.[64] In the

---

62 Ibid., referring to Heb 2:14, and citing Heb 4:15.
63 Apollinarius of Laodicea, First Letter to Dionysius, 1 (ed. Lietzmann, 256-7).
64 Cf. Athanasius, *Orations against the Arians*, 2.13; 3.51; and 4.30. On the mention of Paul and the concern with a "divisive" Christology in Athanasius' letter to Maximus, see Sample (*Messiah*, 41-2).

debates of the late fourth century, concerning the completeness of Christ's human nature and the manner in which it is united to the Word, Apollinarius and his circle attacked their opponents, principally Diodore of Tarsus, by claiming that they follow the Samosatene, even if the pertinent aspects of Paul's teaching had not previously been noted, and, indeed, they even forged works such as the "Symbol of Antioch" and the "Letter of Felix to Maximus," in which the characteristic ideas and words of their opponents appear as those of Paul, only to be condemned.[65]

In arguing his case, Apollinarius appealed to certain "synodal decrees" (δόγματα συνοδικά) issued against Paul of Samosata, though what these were is not clear.[66] Further references soon materialized, however, and these are the final, and most debated, group of testimonies concerning Paul of Samosata to be considered, that is, the so-called *Acta* of the Council of Antioch in 268/9, referring to a dialogue between Paul and Malchion and a letter issued by the council (which should probably be differentiated from the "Synodal Letter" from which Eusebius extracted various passages).[67] References to this material first appear in 428/9, when Eusebius, later bishop of Dorylaeum but at that point a zealous rhetor, skilled in jurisprudence and perhaps a court official,[68] raised his placard against Nestorius, listing a series of statements from Nestorius juxtaposed with ones claiming to derive from Paul, to demonstrate the similarity of their thought and thus damn the bishop of Constantinople by association.[69] Further extracts in Greek from the *Acta* are given in the sixth century by Leontius of Byzantium and the emperor Justinian, both of whom also utilized the passages they cite to demonstrate the source of Nestorius' teaching in the infamous Samosatene. In addition, a number

---

65 On these two texts see G. Bardy, *Paul de Samosate*, 133-44.

66 Cf. Gregory of Nyssa, *Reply to Apollinarius* (GNO 3.1, p.142); cf, Bardy, *Paul*, 91-2.

67 For the text of these fragments, see de Riedmatten, *Les Acts du Procès*, 135-58; references to these fragments follow the numeration of de Riedmatten, using as he does the prefix "S."

68 Evagrius, *Ecclesiastical History*, 1.9; Leontius of Byzantium, *Three Books against the Nestorians and Eutychians*, 3 (PG 86.1389b, reprinted in de Reidmatten, 151-2); Theophanes, *Chronography*, AM 5923 (ed. C. de Boor, 88).

69 The "Declaration" is preserved, anonymously, in the Acts of the Council of Ephesus (ACO 1.1.1, pp.101-2); Leontius of Byzantium, who reproduces the text and supplies further passages from the *Acta*, mentions that "they say" that the document was placarded by Eusebius of Dorylaeum (PG 86.1389b, de Riedmatten, 151-2).

of extracts are provided by the non-Chalcedonian writers, Timothy Aelurus in the fifth century and Severus of Antioch in the sixth, but this time used to argue for the dubious heritage of the Chalcedonian position, and an untitled non-Chalcedonian dossier of texts, no doubt compiled for the same purpose, preserves a number of other fragments.[70] Thus, despite being used against different opponents, the extracts are preserved by writers who all lay claim to the theological tradition of Athanasius and Cyril of Alexandria (and Apollinarius), and are consistently deployed against a common error, that of distinguishing between the Word and Jesus Christ.

However, the collections of testimonies compiled in these quarters for polemical purposes are known to contain, alongside genuine fragments, passages that are undoubtedly Apollinarian forgeries.[71] Given this provenance, it is not surprising that the authenticity of these fragments has been hotly debated.[72] It is possible that the earlier silence regarding these *Acta*, with perhaps the exception of Eusebius, when writing his *Ecclesiastical Theology*, and the Letter of George of Laodicaea, is because prior to the outbreak of the Nestorian controversy it was not common practice to substantiate a position by extensive and detailed quotations from earlier authorities. Likewise, it is also possible that the reason why the testimonies concerning Paul given in

70 There is also a passage preserved in Latin by Petrus Diaconus (S 25), and the important dialogue preserved in ms Jan. gr. 27 (S 36).

71 Cf. M. Richard, "Les Florilèges diphysites du Ve et VIe siècle," in *Das Konzil von Chalkedon*, ed. A. Grillmeier and H. Bracht, vol. 1 (Würzburg: Echter Verlag, 1959), 721-48.

72 G. Bardy took the opportunity of reviewing de Riedmatten's book to announce publicly his retraction of his former endorsement of the *Acta*, and his suspicion that they are in fact Apollinarian forgeries (*RSR* 26 [1952], 294-6). From the following decades, Stead lists J. N. D. Kelly, A. Grillmeier, R. L. Sample, F. W. Norris, H. C. Brennecke and R. P. C. Hanson as accepting Richard's arguments and rejecting the *Acta*, and R. Lorenz, T. D. Barnes, W. H. C. Frend, R. D. Williams as accepting them as genuine ("Marcel Richard on Malchion and Paul of Samosata," 141, n. 4 for references); to which can be added M. Simonetti ("Paolo di Samosata e Malchione. Riesame di alcune testimonianze," *Hestíasis: Studi di tarda antichità offerti a Salvatore Calderone*, Studi Tardoantichi 1 [Messina, 1986], 7-25, and "Per la rivalutzione di alcune testimonianze su Paolo di Samosata"), Stead ("Marcel Richard"), L. Perrone ("L'enigma di Paolo di Samosata. Dogma, chiesa e società nella Siria del III secolo: prospettive di un ventennio di studi," *Cristianesimo nella Storia*, 13 [1992], 253-327), and U. M. Lang ("The Christological Controversy") as supporting their authenticity.

the fifth and sixth centuries deal with very different issues than those raised during the fourth century is because the focus of the contemporary debates themselves had changed, from the fourth century debate about the eternal and substantial existence of the Word of God, to the later concern with the mode of union between the Word and his body. It is also true that the character of the exchanges between Malchion and Paul suggest a third century "doctrinal disputation with a teacher of the Church," as discussed earlier, and that while the fragments do employ some of the words and phrases characteristic of later Apollinarian writings, the absence of other key technical terms is even more significant.[73] Nevertheless, even if they do indeed date to the third century, it remains very likely that the *Acta* were subject to some "editing" when summoned into service for a theological debate whose terms and framework had considerably developed since its own times.[74]

The basic criticism of Paul in the *Acta* is that he differentiated between Jesus Christ and the Word of God as two distinct entities: "he says that the one is Jesus Christ and the other is the Word" (S 7). The debate seems initially to have been exegetical in character, concerned with the identity of the one anointed by God (probably referring to Ps 44:8, LXX) and the way in which Paul applied this title to the Savior, "the anointed one from David" (ὁ ἐκ Δαβὶδ χρισθείς).[75] Paul apparently argued that "the Word is not anointed" (perhaps, if he thought of the Word of God in this way at all, on the common assumption that the divine and immutable Word could not be a passive recipient of an action of God), but that rather "a man is anointed": "the Nazarene our Lord is anointed" (S 26). The Word, he continued, is in fact "greater than Christ," and is "from the beginning" (or "from above"), while "Jesus Christ, a man, is from henceforth" (or "from below") and "became great through Wisdom" (S 26). The logic employed here is then extended to the matter of the birth of Christ, resulting in the

73 For all these arguments, see the articles of Simonetti and Lang noted above.
74 Even Simonetti concedes that the wording of the fragments may have undergone some alteration ("Per la rivalutzione," 208).
75 See the fragments preserved in Eusebius of Dorylaeum (S 1-6), Timothy (S 8, 9, 12) and Leontius (S 26-28), usefully printed in parallel by de Riedmatten (*Les Acts du Procès*, 31-2). For the exegetical basis of the debate, and the legacy of Origen, see Williams, *Arius*, 160-1.

statements which Eusebius of Dorylaeum found so useful against Nestorius: that "Mary did not bear the Word," as "she was not before the ages" (S 1, 2, 26); that "she received the Word and is not older than the Word" (S 3, 26). Instead, while apparently accepting that "the Word is begotten from God" (S 18), Paul was emphatic that "Mary bore a man like us" (S 4, 26). Although "a man like us," Jesus Christ is nevertheless "better with respect to all things," specifically, Paul continued, in that "the grace upon him was from the Holy Spirit and from the promises and the Scriptures" (S 5, 26). Thus "the anointed one from David," Paul concluded, so far from being a stranger to Wisdom, in fact has Wisdom dwelling in him in a unique manner: "for Wisdom was also in the Prophets, and more so in Moses, and in many lords, but even more so in Christ, as in a temple" (S 6, 8-9, 27). Yet while having Wisdom dwelling in him in a superlative manner, Christ, "the one revealed" or "brought to light" (ὁ φαινόμενος), is not himself Wisdom, for Wisdom can neither be confined to a particular form nor be seen by human vision, being greater than all visible phenomena (S 12, 28).

Despite the changed polemical context for these reports of Paul's teaching, echoes of the characteristic emphases of earlier reports are still heard: Jesus of Nazareth, a man like us, is the Christ of God, the one who has finally been made manifest. However, further facets of this basic position are now brought to light. Of particular interest is the specification that the grace upon Christ is "from the Spirit and the promises and the Scriptures" (S 5). This rather unusual assertion, the peculiarity of which suggests that it is authentic, points to the exegetical context of Paul's theological reflection, something also seen in the Letter of the Six Bishops, but otherwise absent from the *Acta*. The statement seems to indicate that for Paul the grace of the Spirit upon Christ, the anointed one, is understood in terms of the fulfillment of the Scriptures when interpreted, under the inspiration of the same Spirit, as promises concerning the Christ.[76] Also noteworthy and new are the claims that Paul taught that Wisdom, or alternatively the

---

76 The Lukan background of Paul argued for by Sample (*The Messiah as Prophet*) would seem to be the best setting for this statement (cf. esp. Lk 4:16-21). It is worth noting, as mentioned above, that according to a sixth-century report Paul identified the Spirit as "the grace which inspired the apostles" (*On the Sects*, 3.3; PG 86.1216b); for the apostolic reading of Scripture as speaking of Christ, see Chapter One above.

Word, having previously dwelt in the Prophets, Moses and "many lords" (perhaps the patriarchs and righteous of the Old Testament), now resides in Christ in a superlative manner, "as in a temple."[77] It is possible that these words do go back to Paul, where they might simply have indicated where the Wisdom of God is now to be found, that is, in Christ and his Gospel rather than in the Law and the Prophets, but it is also possible that the charge results from an attempt to depict Paul as anticipating Diodore and Theodore of Mopsuestia. Either way, the point of these claims is to emphasize the sharp distinction that Paul was believed to have made between the Wisdom or Word of God and Jesus Christ, for that which "dwells" is clearly other than that in which it dwells.

It is also claimed, though acknowledging that this is an implication not actually drawn by Paul, that such teaching leads to a belief in two sons of God: "they say that there are not two sons, but if Jesus Christ is the Son of God, and if Wisdom also is the Son of God, and if Wisdom is one thing and Jesus Christ another, then there are two sons."[78] That the Wisdom or Word of God is to be designated as a "son" is a position that Paul would almost certainly not have accepted; the argument is based upon his opponents' premises and proceeds by a *reductio ad absurdam*. In fact, a statement of Paul recorded in a Syriac florilegium indicates that he consciously tried to avoid asserting two sons, and, moreover, that this was a conclusion he believed to be implied by his opponents' position:

> Jesus Christ, he who was born of Mary, was united with Wisdom, was one with her and through her was "Son" and "Christ." For one says that he who suffered, who endured stripes and blows, who was buried and descended into Hell, who is risen from the dead, is Jesus Christ, the Son of God. For one must not separate him who is before the ages from him who was born at the end of days; as for me, I dread to maintain two sons, I dread to maintain two Christs. (S 21)

Here Paul appeals to what is probably a traditional, confessional statement,[79] to explain how he understands Jesus being united with

77 See also S 14, 25, 31.
78 S 32. Cf. S 17.
79 On the "one says" see Bardy, *Paul*, 51, n. 2.

Wisdom to the point of becoming "one" with Wisdom, and thus being the Son and Christ of God—that is, as the one who has undergone the Passion and Resurrection.[80] It is this identity, in the sense of defining properties, that Paul is here concerned to maintain, an identity that he feels would be sacrificed if a distinction were to be made between one who is from all eternity and another who is revealed at the fullness of time. Even if his opponents were to claim that the one who is from all eternity as the Word and Wisdom of God is the very same one who was born of Mary, Paul would argue that on their own terms a distinction has been made in which what is said of the one born of Mary, that he was crucified and rose again, is not said of the Word in his eternal state with God and thus does not pertain to the actual identity of the eternal Word; the defining characteristics of the one are not the defining characteristics of the other, and so two sons are proclaimed. Such reasoning would also explain the perception, which characterized the earlier reports of his teachings, that Paul denied the "preexistence" of Christ; Paul was prepared to speak of Christ as existing "prophetically" before his human sojourn, but did not understand this "preexistence" as a different stage in a biography of the Word, whose identity at this earlier time would have been otherwise described.[81] Whatever Paul himself might have meant by speaking of Wisdom dwelling in Christ, rather than what his opponents understood by this, Paul's theological reflection turns upon the identical identity, as it were, of the beginning and the end, the alpha and the omega, Jesus Christ, rather than the structure or composition of his being.

The issues that Paul attempts to address here do not seem to have troubled his critics. They were, however, very disturbed by the way he seemed to them to introduce a radical distinction between the Word or Wisdom of God and Jesus Christ. It appeared to them that Paul only allowed for a "conjunction (συνάφεια) of goodwill" between the man Jesus and the divine Wisdom (S 24), or for a "participation" in

---

80　Cf. Athanasius, *Against the Arians*, 2.13: "If they [the Arians] suppose that the Savior was not Lord and King even before he became man and endured the Cross, but then began to be Lord, let them know that they are openly reviving the statements of the Samosatene."

81　Cf. the passages from Epiphanius (*Ecclesiastical Theology*, 1.14), Ps.-Epiphanius (*Anakephalaiosis*, 2.2.1) and Ps.-Athanasius (*On the Incarnation of our Lord Jesus Christ against Apollinarius*, 2.3) discussed above.

Wisdom (S 25, 36). In contrast, Paul's critics argued for a very strong conception of the absolute unity of the Word of God and the body he assumed. According to Malchion, the Word and his body have been "compounded" together, so that "the Son of God is substantiated (οὐσιῶσθαι) in his body."[82] Malchion allows the description of the union between Wisdom and the body as a "conjunction," so long as it is not taken as being "according to instruction and participation," as Paul takes it, but rather "according to substance, substantiated in the body."[83] The Word is "substantially" (οὐσιωδῶς) united with his body, and the result is a "composition" (σύνθεσις) or "substantial union" (ἕνωσις οὐσιώδης), all crucial terms for Paul's opponents.[84] In this way, Malchion thinks he has secured that "the only-begotten Son, who is from all eternity before every creature, was substantiated in the whole Savior," something not accepted by Paul.[85] While affirming that the Word and his body have been "substantially united" in such a manner that there is no longer any "division" between the two,[86] Malchion and the Council of Antioch do nevertheless distinguish between what is said of Jesus Christ, in the first instance, as man, and in the second, as God.[87]

What Malchion means by asserting a "substantial unity" between the Word and his body is made clear in an important fragment that preserves part of a lively verbal exchange between Malchion and Paul. The passage is incomplete, but it seems that Malchion is replying to a question posed by Paul:

MALCHION: This Word, thus subsisting (ὑφεστηκὼς), was himself born in that body, as you also admitted in the expression "from Mary,"

---

82 S 22, preserved in Syriac; the Greek is supplied by de Riedmatten (*Les Actes*, 147).

83 S 33: τὴν δὲ συνάφειαν ἑτέρως πρὸς τὴν σοφίαν νοεῖ [i.e. Paul], κατὰ μάθησιν καὶ μετουσίαν, οὐχὶ οὐσίαν οὐσιωμένην ἐν σώματι.

84 S 23. Cf. Lang, "The Christological Controversy," 66.

85 S 35: οὐ πάλαι τοῦτο ἔλεγον ὅτι οὐ δίδως οὐσιῶσθαι ἐν τῷ ὅλῳ σωτῆρι τὸν υἱὸν τὸν μονογενῆ, τὸν πρὸ πάσης κτίσεως αἰδίως ὑπάρχοντα.

86 Cf. S 25: "The composite is surely made up of simple elements, even as in the case of Christ Jesus, who was made one out of God the Word and a human body from the seed of David, who subsists without any manner of division between the two, but in unity."

87 E.g., S 34: "He was formed, in the first instance, as man in the womb, and, in the second instance, God was in the womb united essentially with the human" (θεὸς ἦν ἐν γαστρὶ συνουσιωμένος τῷ ἀνθρωπίνῳ). Cf. S 15, 20.

since the Scriptures say that he shared our nature, as we participate in it and since "children"—says Scripture—"have shared flesh and blood," for this reason the Son of God did so too [Heb 2:14]. I inquire therefore if, just as we human beings, this composite living being, possess a coming together of flesh and of something dwelling in the flesh, even so the Word himself, Wisdom herself, was in that body as life is in us while on earth? Even as in our case we are complete from the conjunction, so too it is in his case from the concurrence in the same of the Word of God and that which came from the Virgin (ἐκ τοῦ συνδεδραμηκέναι ἐν ταὐτῷ τόν τε θεὸν λόγον καὶ τὸ ἐκ τῆς παρθένου).

PAUL: You answered, I think, for us as well, as you supposed.

MALCHION: I asked—since you speak of Wisdom and Word, one man is said to participate in word and wisdom, while another lacks them, but do you say that (in the case of Christ) it is by participation in these or by the Word itself and Wisdom coming down upon him? Substance and participation are not alike. For the substantial is as a part of the whole, of the one who became our Lord by the intermingling of God and man (τὸ μὲν γὰρ οὐσιῶδες ὡς μέρος τοῦ ὅλου, τοῦ κατὰ συμπλοκὴν θεοῦ καὶ ἀνθρώπου γενομένου κυρίου ἡμῶν), but participation does not mean being part of the one in whom it is.

PAUL: All those here agree with what I say. Now *you* tell me—I am asking first (this time): your argument has tried to put forward as an illustration something in no way analogous. The human organism has a different constitution (ἑτεροίαν... τὴν κατασκευήν). We were talking about Word and Wisdom. And all... [talk about the analogy of a human being that you have introduced is irrelevant].[88]

By using the term "substantial," Malchion wants to emphasize that the relationship between Jesus Christ and the Word is more than a union of "participation," in which the participants retain their own identity and merely acquire an additional, accidental or non-essential, property in varying degrees (a man is still a man whether wise or not). But rather than asserting their total identity, that Jesus Christ *is* the Word of God, Malchion argues instead for their unity in terms of composition: that Jesus Christ is composed of, or constituted from, the Word and the body from Mary. As "parts of the whole," these elements are designated

88 S 36; modifying the translation given by J. Stevenson, *A New Eusebius* (London: SPCK, 1963), 278-9.

by Malchion as "substantial," which when combined, or intertwined
(κατὰ συμπλοκήν), result in the one Lord Jesus Christ, who thus is not
a man participating in Wisdom but Wisdom "substantiated in a
body." As noted earlier, Malchion asserts that the unity thus achieved
is absolute, so that there is no longer any division between the Word
and the body.[89] This of course stands in contrast to Paul, who is continually charged with having separated the Word or Wisdom from
Jesus Christ. However, Malchion's insistence that Jesus Christ is composed of the Word and a body, bound together in a substantial union,
has the consequence, somewhat paradoxically, that he seems reluctant,
or even unable, to call Jesus Christ the Word of God.[90]

In the above passage Malchion further explains how he understands
this "substantial union" between the Word and his body by the analogy
of the human constitution: that the Word is in Jesus Christ in the same
way as that which dwells in the flesh is in human beings. Although, as in
the above passage, Malchion is prepared to use the term "man" to
describe the human "part" united to the Word, the terminology he more
frequently employs is restricted to "the body" or "that which is from the
Virgin."[91] And the reason for this is evident, that for Malchion, the Word
was in the body of Jesus Christ in the same way as that which animates
the flesh dwells in human beings. The point is made even more explicitly
in a passage from the letter written by the Council preserved by
Leontius, when it picks up on Paul's objection that this anthropological
paradigm is not applicable as the human constitution is so different that
it does not permit such an analogy to be drawn:

---

89 Cf. S 25, cited above.

90 Cf. e.g., S 18, recording a statement of the Council of 268/9: "Thus it is the Word,
    whose origin is from the days of old, who is prophesied as going forth from Bethlehem
    [cf. Mic 5:1]—all things which the teacher of heresy contradicts. And again [he says] that
    Jesus Christ is from Mary, but the Word is begotten of God. But it is written—this time
    again, to give only one saying as evidence—that God is the Father of Jesus Christ [cf. 2
    Cor 1:3 etc.]; for according to this, the Father of the Word is also Father of the whole
    Jesus Christ, who is composed of the Word and the body [born] of Mary." I have found
    no instances in the *Acta* where the critics of Paul state, tout court, that Jesus Christ *is* the
    Word of God.

91 Cf. S 14, 15, 16, 18, 20, 22, 23, 25, 31. For "man," see S 20 and 34, both of which are
    concerned with the distinction between what Christ does as man and as God (the third
    passage employing this distinction, S 15, only speaks of "the human body").

What is the meaning of asserting the different constitution (ἑτεϱοίαν... τὴν κατασκευὴν) of Jesus Christ compared to ours? We consider that his composition (σύστασιν) differs from ours in but one respect, though of greatest import, that God the Word is in him what the inner man is in us. (S 30).

It is hard to take the comments of Malchion and the Council of Antioch in any other sense than as implying that the Word took the place of the soul in the composite being of Jesus Christ.[92] That those present at the Council of Antioch should have held such a position is not necessarily anachronistic, nor should it be surprising. It was noted earlier in this chapter how Origen's teaching concerning the human soul of Jesus Christ came under attack in the late third and early fourth century. The point of concern there was not the myth of "preexistent souls" criticized by Methodius, but the conviction that if Christ possessed a human soul, then there was no "part" of him that was divine and, as such, he was "merely human." The logic of this argument depends upon an approach to understanding Jesus Christ which reduces the multifaceted and complex reflections, examined in the previous chapters, to a fairly crude, materialistic even, compositional analysis of the "parts" of Christ. Such an approach is clearly reflected in the arguments advanced by those who condemned Paul of Samosata. However, their indirect way of speaking, and the fact that Paul's complaint, admittedly recorded in an incomplete fragment, concerned the proposed analogy, rather than any denial of a part of the human constitution, suggests that those assembled to condemn Paul were taking hesitant steps in uncharted territory rather than advocating a fully developed and well-known theory. Similarly, a few decades later, Pamphilus and Eusebius defended Origen by simply referring to the passages of Scripture which mention the soul of Christ rather than addressing involved questions of Christology. Only in later writings does Eusebius assert explicitly that he takes the Word as

---

92 Both F. Loofs (*Paul von Samosata. Eine Untersuchung zur altkirchlichen Literatur und Dogmengeschichte*, TU 3/14, 5 [Leipzig, 1924], 262) and G. Bardy (*Paul de Samoste*, 482-7) denied the identification, though de Riedmatten (*Les Actes du Procès*, 52-3), and most scholars since, have accepted it. For a more considered investigation of the background for these statements in Origen's interpretation of the phrase "the inner man" from Rom 7:22, see Lang, "The Christological Controversy," 72-9.

animating flesh that is "soulless and nonrational" (ἄψυχον... καὶ ἄλογον), and, in fact, it is the ability of the Word to do this that demonstrates, for Eusebius, the individual subsistence of the Word.[93] The condemnation of the infamous Paul of Samosata, together with the criticisms raised against him by the Council of Antioch, encouraged the position that treated the Incarnation of the Word as the "ensouling" of a body, a dubious legacy that contributed significantly to the controversies of the following century.[94]

93 Eusebius, *Ecclesiastical Theology*, 1.20.7 (ed. Klostermann, 87.34-5). Eusebius' *Commentary on the Psalms*, which contains references to the soul of Christ, should probably be dated to the pre-Nicene period.
94 Cf. Williams, *Arius*, 170.

Epilogue

The way to Nicaea is charted by theological reflection and debates focused on the identity of Jesus Christ. Indeed, contemplation of the person and work of Christ is the unchanging heart of Christian theology. The apostles, in their proclamation of the crucified and risen Christ, initiated this task, and the Gospel they proclaimed continues to demand engagement. The basis upon which Christ is proclaimed, and the framework for engaging in the interpretative task of theology, was established by the end of the second century in terms of the canon and tradition of the Gospel according to Scripture—the Law, the Psalms and the Prophets—a foundation accepted as normative, at least in the period covered by this series. Here, the subject of theological reflection is not the "historical Jesus," nor the "meaning" of the scriptural and apostolic texts as established by a variety of historical-critical methodologies, but the Scriptural Christ, the Christ contemplated through the medium of Scripture, for he alone is the Word of God. The crucified and risen Christ is the subject throughout Scripture, "the same yesterday, today and forever" (Heb 13:8), becoming flesh in the Gospel that recapitulates Scripture in a concise Word. Yet he remains the Coming One, who directs our attention back to the Scriptures to contemplate his true identity (cf. Matt 11:2-5), and who continues to be "incarnate" in those who devote themselves to the Word, learning Christ (cf. Eph 4:20), dying with Christ (Rom 6:3-11) and finally reaching the stature of the fullness of Christ (Eph 4:13).

The canon of truth thus facilitates the meaningful engagement with Scripture, an interpretative engagement carried out from the perspective of the Cross, so maintaining the tradition of the Gospel preached, from the beginning, "according to the Scriptures." While accepted in principle, the details of this canon were, nevertheless, the subject of intense reflection and debate. And these debates again revolved around the person of Jesus Christ: How is the divinity of Jesus Christ related to that of God, and his sonship to that of the fatherhood of God? How does he relate to us? Is he truly human as we are, and if so, how can he also be divine and yet still be "one Lord" (1 Cor 8:6)? The manner in which various pre-Nicene figures dealt with such issues, each in their own way, has been extensively discussed in the preceding pages and does not need to be rehearsed here.

However, there are certain aspects and issues that recur in the theological reflection of the period prior to Nicaea, simmering, as it were, ready to erupt dramatically in the controversies of the following centuries. The most important nexus of issues concerns not simply the identity of Christ, but the manner in which identity as such is construed. One possibility is to understand the identity of Christ in terms of a "personal subject," whose personal identity remains the same while acting in various ways along a temporal axis. This approach was found in Justin Martyr, for whom it seems that existence "as" Jesus Christ is but one phase in a biography of the Word, and was adopted much more explicitly by Malchion, at the Council of Antioch, when he suggests that the "Incarnation" should be understood in terms of the "ensouling" of an inanimate body by the Word. Both of these were found to be problematic: For Justin, the Word, as an intermediary, does not so much reveal the Father, bringing us into communion with God, but reveals his own lower divinity; for the critics of Paul of Samosata, Jesus Christ is no longer himself the Word of God, but a compound of which one element is the Word. There is, moreover, one common element which indicates a more profound modification: in these cases, as also with the author of the *Refutation of all Heresies* attributed to Hippolytus, the subject of reflection has changed, from Jesus Christ to the Word, the latter understood as an independent, divine or semi-divine, agent. This shift of focus effectively turns theology into mythology, an attempt to recount, from an unspecified vantage point, the biography of this Word and to explain, in a crude materialistic manner, the structure or composition of the being of Christ, the Incarnate Word. Here, furthermore, the "preexistence" of Christ is not taken, strictly speak, as the preexistence *of Christ*, but as the eternity, understood in a chronological manner, of a subject whose identity, as subject, remains continuous, while appearing in diverse forms and acting in diverse manners; what is said of the Word as Incarnate, as Jesus Christ, is not what is said of the Word prior to this episode and certainly not from all eternity.

An alternative approach to understanding the identity of Jesus Christ is exemplified, each in their own manner, by Ignatius, Irenaeus, Hippolytus, and Origen, and even, judging from the clues which remain, by Paul of Samosata. Here identity is best understood in a predicative sense, so that the identity of Christ is revealed in those properties that mark him out, those, that is, which are proclaimed in the Gospel. As such, theology here retains its confessional and kerygmatic character. The subject for their theological reflection remains the crucified and risen Christ, and his identity is understood in terms of the confession made, through the interpretative engagement with Scripture, regarding him: He it is who is the Word of God and the Son of the Father. A consequence of this confessional approach, within the matrix of Scripture, is that the eternity of Christ is not temporalized, nor is his preexistence understood in terms of a continuity of personal subject who is identified by other characteristics prior to the Passion. Rather his preexistence and eternity is scriptural: Christ, and the Gospel proclaiming him, is the subject of Scripture from the beginning. Moreover, at least for Ignatius and Irenaeus, there is no question that as Son he does indeed reveal his Father, the one true God, so bringing us into communion with God himself.

It was noted that the contrast between Justin and Irenaeus regarding the relationship between the Word and God in many ways parallels that between Arius and the Creed of Nicaea (325). The affirmation that the Son is consubstantial with the Father excludes any conception of the Son as an intermediary being, mediating between the true God and created reality, a position which ultimately only serves to keep God and creation separate. Rather than acting as a buffer, as it were, between God and creation, the Son, being true God of true God, as Nicaea insists, is in fact the locus for the revelation of the Father in the world and thus the guarantee that God has indeed entered into communion with his handiwork. Similarly, the refusal to consider the generation of the Word in temporal categories corrects any attempt to temporalize God, and mythologize theology, but focuses attention uniquely on Christ himself. The same point is made, after the first round of christological controversy, by the definition of Chalcedon (451), when it asserts that it is one and the same Lord Jesus Christ who is the subject of divine and human predication, in such a manner that both natures are preserved intact in the one hypostasis, the one subject of predication, Jesus Christ—he it is who is the Son, the only-begotten God, the Word and Lord, as was taught by the prophets from the beginning.

The understanding of Incarnation as "ensouling," tentatively suggested by the Council of Antioch in 268, became a common position in the following century. It can be found in Eusebius of Caesarea, it is claimed to be an Arian position, and, of course, it is best known as the position of Apollinarius of Laodicea, whose employment of the idea led to controversy and condemnation. It is also an understanding of Incarnation often attributed to Athanasius, though as we will see, when he writes his early treatise on this very topic, *On the Incarnation*, he does not attempt to analyze the composition of the being of Christ, nor does he assume the results of the fourth century Trinitarian controversies, abstracted from the discussion that led to them, to describe how one of the Trinity became man. Instead he opens his work by specifying that the treatise is meant as an apology for the Cross; the "Incarnation," for Athanasius, cannot be separated, as a distinct event, from the Passion, for it is the crucified and risen One who is the Incarnate Word of God. There are clearly many implications that follow on from such a position. We have seen how some pre-Nicene theologians explored this point; further consideration of Athanasius must wait for the next volume of this series.

A further important aspect of the reflections traced in this volume is that the theological positions and formulae encountered here were largely developed within a scriptural matrix: the native context for theological formulae is the engagement with Scripture. This is especially clear in the case of Origen. He is aware, for example, of the fact that the affirmation of the distinct and eternal subsistence of the Son is bound up with the necessity that theological reflection should not stay at the level of the flesh, either that of Jesus himself or that of Scripture, its letters and their literal sense, but should penetrate these veils to discern the very Word of God. And the basic dynamic of this exegetical framework, to which he devotes the introduction to his *Commentary on John*, is the relation between the Scriptures and the Gospel, which takes the exegete right to the heart of theological reflection, in the canon and tradition of the Gospel according to Scripture. In the writings of Origen one can indeed find many of the theological positions and formulae that reappear in later generations, both Arian, Nicene and Chalcedonian—such as an affirmation of three hypostases, a rejection of the term homoousios in preference for a participatory schema, the idea of an eternal generation, related to God as Father rather than as Creator, and the affirmation that one and the same Christ is the subject of two different, contrary even, sets of predication, so demonstrating the reality of the two natures in Christ, which retain their integrity while undergoing an "exchange of properties"—all positions which will be encountered in subsequent volumes. All of these theological insights emerge from the contemplation of Christ through the engagement with Scripture. They do not stand independently, as the building blocks of a dogmatic system built according to its own hypothesis. Although the debates of later ages tend to focus on the formulae themselves, so as to be able to reach universal agreement regarding the substance of faith, and therefore economically and authoritatively, the formulae discussed belong no less to the fundamental context of the engagement with Scripture in the contemplation of Christ. Histories of dogma that only look to the pre-Nicene period for anticipations of the theological formulae of the Nicene and post-Nicene era, run the risk of overlooking the context which gives meaning to those formulae. As was noted in the introduction, conclusions without the arguments that lead to them are at best ambiguous. The way to Nicaea is, thus, not a pre-history of Nicaea, but the necessary background for understanding the theological debates of subsequent ages.

Bibliography

The following includes only the texts and studies directly referred to in this work, and does not aim to be a comprehensive guide to the vast, and growing, body of literature; the bibliographies given in the major studies listed here provide valuable further references.

Primary Material

Acta Conciliorum Oecumenicorum, ed. E. Schwartz (Berlin and Leipzig: De Gruyter, 1927-44).

Apollinarius of Laodicea, *Letter to Dionysius*, ed. H. Lietzmann, *Apollinaris von Laodicea und seine Schule* (Tübingen: Mohr, 1904), 25-62.

Aristotle, *Eudemian Ethics*, ed. and trans. H. Rackham, LCL Aristotle, 20 (Cambridge, Mass.: Harvard University Press, 1935).

— *Metaphysics*, ed. and trans. H. Tredennick, LCL Aristotle, 17-18 (Cambridge, Mass.: Harvard University Press, 1933).

— *On the Soul*, ed. and trans. W. S. Hett, LCL Aristotle, 8 (Cambridge, Mass.: Harvard University Press, 1936).

Athanasius, *On the Decrees of Nicaea*, ed. H. G. Opitz, Athanasius Werke, II.1 (Berlin: De Gruyter, 1935-41), 1-45; trans. in NPNF, second series, 4 (1891; repr. Grand Rapids, Mich.: Eerdmans, 1980), 150-72.

— *On the Incarnation. Contra Gentes and De Incarnatione*, ed. and trans. R. W. Thomson, OECT (Oxford: Clarendon Press, 1971).

— *On the Opinion of Dionysius*, ed. H. G. Opitz, Athanasius Werke, II.1 (Berlin: De Gruyter, 1935-41), 46-67; trans. in NPNF, second series, 4 (1891; repr. Grand Rapids, Mich.: Eerdmans, 1980), 173-87.

— *Orations against the Arians*, ed. W. Bright (Oxford: Clarendon Press, 1884); trans. in NPNF, second series, 4 (1891; repr. Grand Rapids, Mich.: Eerdmans, 1980), 303-431.

— *On the Synods*, ed. H. G. Opitz, Athanasius Werke, II.1 (Berlin: De Gruyter, 1935-41), 231-78; trans. in NPNF, second series, 4 (1891; repr. Grand Rapids, Mich.: Eerdmans, 1980), 448-81.

Ps.-Athanasius, *On the Incarnation of our Lord Jesus Christ, against Apollinarius*, PG 26.1093-1165.

Augustine, *The Trinity*, trans. E. Hill, The Works of Saint Augustine, Part 1, vol. 5, ed. J. E. Rotelle (Brooklyn: New City Press, 1991).

Basil of Caesarea, *Epistles. Saint Basile: Lettres*, ed. and French trans. Y. Courtonne, 3 vols. (Paris: Belles Lettres, 1957-66); trans. in NPNF, second series, 8 (1894; repr. Grand Rapids, Mich.: Eerdmans, 1955), 109-327.

— *On the Holy Spirit. Basile de Césarée: Sur le Saint-Esprit*, ed. and French trans. B. Pruche, SC 17 bis (Paris: Cerf, 1968); trans. D. Anderson (New York: SVS, 1980).

Clement of Alexandria, *Stromata I-VI*, ed. O. Stählin, 3rd edn., rev. L. Früchtel, GCS 52 (Berlin: Akademie Verlag, 1972); trans. in ANF 2 (1887: repr. Grand Rapids, Mich.: Eerdmans, 1989), 299-520.

— *Stromata VII, VIII, Excerpta ex Theodoto, Eclogae Propheticae, Quis Dives Salvetur, Fragmente*, ed. O. Stählin, 2nd edn., rev. L. Früchtel and U. Treu, GCS 17 (Berlin: Akademie Verlag, 1970); trans. in ANF 2 (1887: repr. Grand Rapids, Mich.: Eerdmans, 1989), 523-67 (*Strom.* 7-8); 591-604 (*Who is the Rich Man that shall be Saved?*).

Clement of Rome, *First Letter*, ed. J. B. Lightfoot, *The Apostolic Fathers* (Macmillan, 1889; repr. Peabody, Mass.: Hendrickson, 1989), Pt. 1, vols. 1-2; ed. and trans. K. Lake, LCL Apostolic Fathers, 1 (Cambridge, Mass.: Harvard University Press, 1985).

Cyprian, *Epistles*, ed. and French trans. L. Bayard, 2 vols. (Paris: Collection des Universités de France, 1925); trans. in ANF 5 (1868-9; repr. Grand Rapids, Mich.: Eerdmans, 1986), 275-409.

Diogenes Laertius, *Lives of Eminent Philosophers*, ed. and trans. R. D. Hick, LCL, 2 vols. (Cambridge, Mass.: Harvard University Press, 1925).

Epiphanius, *Panarion*, ed. K. Holl: Epiphanius I (heresies 1-33), GCS 25 (Leipzig: Hinrichs Verlag, 1915); Epiphanius II (heresies 34-64), rev. J. Dummer, GCS 31 (Berlin: Akademie Verlag, 1980); Epiphanius III (heresies 65-80), rev. J. Dummer, GCS 37 (Berlin: Akademie Verlag, 1985). Selective English trans. P. R. Amidon, *The* Panarion *of Epiphanius of Salamis: Selected Passages* (Oxford: Oxford University Press, 1990).

Ps.-Epiphanius, *Anakephalaiosis*, PG 42.833-85.

Eusebius of Caesarea, *Ecclesiastical History*, ed. and trans. K. Lake, LCL, 2 vols. (Cambridge, Mass: Harvard University Press, 1989).

— *Ecclesiastical Theology*, ed. E. Klostermann, 3rd edn., rev. G. C. Hansen, GCS 14, Eusebius Werke, 4 (Berlin: Akademie Verlag, 1972).

— *Prophetic Extracts*, PG 22.1017-1261.

Evagrius Scholasticus, *Ecclesiastical History*, ed. J. Bidez and L. Parmentier (Amsterdam: Adolf M. Hakkert, 1964); trans. (London: Samuel Bagster and Sons, 1846).

Gregory of Nazianzus, *Letter 101*. *Grégoire de Nazianze: Lettres Théologiques*, ed. and French trans. P. Gallay, SC 208 (Paris: Cerf, 1974); trans. in NPNF, second series, 7 (1894; repr. Grand Rapids, Mich.: Eerdmans, 1987), 439-43.

— *Panegyric on St Basil* (Oration 43). *Grégoire de Nazianze: Discourse 42-43*, ed. and French trans. J. Bernardi, SC 384 (Paris: Cerf, 1992); trans. in NPNF, second series, 7 (1894; repr. Grand Rapids, Mich.: Eerdmans, 1987), 395-422.

Gregory of Nyssa, *Reply to Apollinarius. Antirrheticus adversus Apolinarium*, ed. W. Jaeger, GNO 3.1 (Leiden: Brill, 1958), 131-233.

— *On the Three Day Period. De Tridui Spatio*, ed. E. Gebhardt, GNO 9 (Leiden: Brill, 1967), 273-306; trans. S. G. Hall, in A. Spira and C. Klock (eds.), *The Easter Sermons of Gregory of Nyssa*, Patristic Monograph Series, 9 (Philadelphia: Philadelphia Patristic Foundation, 1981), 31-50.

Gregory Palamas, *The One Hundred and Fifty Chapters*, ed. and trans. R. E. Sinkewicz, Studies and Texts, 83 (Toronto: Pontifical Institute of Mediaeval Studies, 1988).

Hermas, *The Shepherd*, ed. and trans. K. Lake, LCL Apostolic Fathers, 2 (Cambridge, Mass.: Harvard University Press, 1976).

Hilary of Poitiers, *On the Councils*, PL 10.471-546; trans. in NPNF, second series, 9 (1898; repr. Grand Rapids, Mich.: Eerdmans, 1973), 4-29.

Hippolytus, *On the Christ and the Antichrist*, ed. H. Achelis, GCS 1.2 (Leipzig: Hinrichs Verlag, 1897), 1-47; trans. in ANF 5 (1887; repr. Grand Rapids, Mich.: Eerdmans, 1986), 204-19.

— *Contra Noetum*, ed. and trans. R. Butterworth (London: Heythrop Monographs, 1977).

"Hippolytus," *Refutation of all Heresies. Refutatio omnium haeresium*, ed. P. Wendland, GCS 26 (Leipzig: Hinrichs Verlag, 1916); ed. M. Marcovich, PTS 25 (Berlin: De Gruyter, 1986); trans. in ANF 5 (1887; repr. Grand Rapids, Mich.: Eerdmans, 1986), 9-153; trans. of *Ref.* 9.7-12, in C. Osborne, *Rethinking Early Greek Philosophy* (London: Duckworth, 1987), 326-49.

Ignatius of Antioch, *Epistles*, ed. J. B. Lightfoot, *The Apostolic Fathers* (Macmillan, 1889; repr. Peabody, Mass.: Hendrickson, 1989), Pt. 2, vols. 1-3; ed. and trans. K. Lake, LCL Apostolic Fathers, 1 (Cambridge, Mass.: Harvard University Press, 1985).

Irenaeus of Lyons, *Against the Heresies. Sancti Irenaei episcopi Lugdunensis libros quinque adversus haereses*, ed. W. W. Harvey, 2 vols. (Cambridge, 1857); *Irénée de Lyon: Contre les Hérésies, Livre I, Livre II*, and *Livre III*, ed. and French trans. A. Rousseau and L. Doutreleau, SC 263-4, 293-4, 210-11 (Paris: Cerf, 1979, 1982, 1974); *Livre IV*, ed. and French trans. A. Rousseau, B. Hemmerdinger, L. Doutreleau and C. Mercier, SC 100 (Paris: Cerf, 1965); *Livre V*, ed. and French trans. A. Rousseau, L. Doutreleau and C. Mercier SC 152-3 (Paris: Cerf, 1969); English trans. ANF 1 (1885; repr. Grand Rapids, Mich.: Eerdmans, 1987).

— *Demonstration of the Apostolic Preaching. Εἰς ἐπίδειξιν τοῦ ἀποστολιχοῦ χηρύγματος. The Proof of the Apostolic Preaching, with Seven Fragments*, K. Ter-Mekerttschian, and S. G. Wilson, with Prince Maxe of Saxony, eds. and English trans., French trans. J. Barthoulot, PO 12.5 (Paris, 1917; repr. Turnhout: Brepols, 1989). *Irénée de Lyon: Démonstration de la Prédication Apostolique*, trans. and annotations A. Rousseau, SC 406 (Paris: Cerf, 1995); *St Irenaeus of Lyons: On the Apostolic Preaching*, trans. J. Behr (New York: Saint Vladimir's Seminary Press, 1997).

Isaac of Syria, *Isaac of Nineveh (Isaac the Syrian): "The Second Part," Chapters IV-XLI*, ed. and trans. S. Brock, CSCO 555, scriptores syri 225 (Louvain: Peeters, 1995).

Jerome, *Epistles. Saint Jérôme, Lettres*, ed. and French trans. J. Labourt, 8 vols. (Paris: Belles Lettres, 1949-63); trans in NPNF, second series, 6 (1892: repr. Grand Rapids, Mich.: Eerdmans, 1954), 1-295.

— *On Famous Men*, PL 33.601-720; trans. in NPNF, second series, 3 (1892: repr. Grand Rapids, Mich.: Eerdmans, 1953), 359-84.

Acts of John. Acta Iohannis, ed. E. Junod and J. D. Kaestli, 2 vols., Corpus Christianorum; Series Apocryphorum, 1-2 (Turnhout: Brepols, 1983); trans. in J. K. Elliot, *The Apocryphal New Testament* (Oxford: Clarendon Press, 1993), 303-49.

John Chrysostom, *Homilies on John*, in *Sancti Patris Nostri Joannis Chrysostomi ... Opera Omnia Quae Exstant*, ed. B. de Montfaucon, vol. 8 (Paris: 1836); trans. in NPNF, first series, 14 (1852; repr. Grand Rapid, Mich.: Eerdmans, 1956).

Justin Martyr, *Apologies. Iustini martyris apologiae pro christianis*, ed. M. Marcovich, PTS 38 (Berlin, New York: De Gruyter, 1994); trans. in ANF 1 (Edinburgh, 1887; repr. Grand Rapids, Mich.: Eerdmans, 1987), 163-93, and trans. L. W. Barnard, *St Justin Martyr: The First and Second Apologies*, ACW 56 (New York: Paulist Press, 1997).

— *Dialogue with Trypho. Iustini martyris dialogus cum Tryphone*, ed. M. Marcovich, PTS 47 (Berlin, New York: De Gruyter, 1997); trans. in ANF 1 (1887; repr. Grand Rapids, Mich.: Eerdmans, 1987), 194-270.

— *The Martyrdom of Justin*, in *The Acts of the Christian Martyrs*, ed. and trans. H. Musurillo, OECT (Oxford: Clarendon Press, 1972).

Leontius of Byzantium, *Three Books against the Nestorians and the Eutychians*, PG 86.1267-1396.

Ps.-Leontius, *On the Sects*, PG 86.1193-1268.

The Letter of the Six Bishops, ed. in G. Bardy, *Paul de Samosate: Étude historique*, rev. edn. (Louvain: Spicilegium Sacrum Lovaniense, 1929), 13-19.

Melito of Sardis, *On Pascha*, ed. and trans. S. G. Hall, OECT (Oxford: Clarendon Press, 1979).

Nestorius, *The Bazaar of Heracleides*, trans. G. R. Driver and L. Hodgson (Oxford: Clarendon Press, 1925).

Novatian, *On the Trinity*, PL 3.861-970; trans. in ANF 5 (1887; repr. Grand Rapids, Mich.: Eerdmans, 1986), 611-44.

Origen, *Commentary on John. Origène: Commentaire sur saint Jean*, ed. and French trans. C. Blanc, SC 120, 157, 222, 290, 385 (Paris: Cerf, 1966, 1970, 1975, 1982, 1992); English trans. R. E. Heine, *Origen: Commentary on the Gospel according to Saint John*, FC 80, 89 (Washington: Catholic University of America, 1989, 1993).

— *Commentary on Matthew. Origenes Matthäuserklärung*, I, *Die griechisch erhaltenen Tomoi*, ed. E. Benz and E. Klostermann, GCS 40, Origenes Werke, 10, two parts (Leipzig: Hinrichs Verlag, 1935, 1937); partial trans. in ANF 10 (1887; repr. Grand Rapids: Eerdmans, 1986), 413-512.

Commentariorum in Matth. series, ed. E. Klosterman, 2nd edn., rev. U. Treu, GCS 38, Origenes Werke, 11.2 (Berlin: Akademie Verlag, 1976).

— *Contra Celsum. Origène: Contre Celse*, ed. and French trans. M. Borret, SC 132, 136, 147, 150, 227 (Paris: Cerf, 1967, 1968, 1969 [2], 1976); English trans. H. Chadwick (Cambridge: Cambridge University Press, 1953).

— *Dialogue with Heraclides. Entretien d'Origène avec Héraclide et les évêques ses collègues sur le Père, le Fils et l'âme*, ed. J. Scherer, Publications de la Société Fouad I de Papyrologi; Textes et Documents, 9 (Cairo: Institue Français d'Archéologie Orientale, 1949); English trans. R. J. Daly, *Origen: Treatise on Passover and Dialogue with Heraclides and his Fellow Bishops on the Father, the Son and the Soul*, ACW 54 (New York: Paulist Press, 1992).

— *On First Principles. Origenes: Vier Bücher von den Prinzipien*, ed. and German trans. by H. Görgemanns and H. Karpp, 3rd edn. (Darmstadt: Wissenschaftliche Buchgesellschaft, 1992); English trans. G. W. Butterworth (Gloucester, Mass.: Peter Smith, 1973).

— *Homilies on Genesis. Origène: Homélies sur la Genèse*, ed. and French trans. H. de Lubac and L. Doutreleau, SC 7, 3rd edn. (Paris: Cerf, 1966); English trans. R. E. Heine, *Origen: Homilies on Genesis and Exodus*, FC 71 (Washington: Catholic University of America, 1982).

— *Homilies on Jeremiah. Origène: Homélies sur Jérémie*, ed. P. Nautin, French trans. P. Husson and P. Nautin, SC 232, 238 (Paris: Cerf, 1976, 1977); English trans. J. C. Smith, *Origen: Homilies on Jeremiah; Homily on 1 Kings 28*, FC 97 (Washington: Catholic University of America, 1998).

— *Homilies on Leviticus. Origène: Homélies sur le Lévitique*, ed. and French trans. M. Borret, SC 286-7, (Paris: Cerf, 1981); English trans. G. W. Barkley, *Origen: Homilies on Leviticus, 1-16*, FC 83 (Washington: Catholic University of America, 1990).

— *Homilies on Luke. Die Homilien zu Lukas in der Übersetzung des Hieronymus und die griechischen Reste der Homilien und des Lukas-Kommentars*, ed. Max Rauer, GCS 49, Origenes Werke, 9 (Berlin: Akademie Verlag, 1959); English trans. J. T. Lienhard, *Origen: Homilies on Luke: Fragments on Luke*, FC 94 (Washington: Catholic University of America, 1996).

— *Philokalia. The Philocalia of Origen*, ed. J. A. Robinson (Cambridge: Cambridge University Press, 1893); ed., French trans., introduction and notes M. Harl, *Origène: Philocalie, 1-20; Sur les Écritures*, SC 302 (Paris: Cerf, 1983); trans. G. Lewis (Edinburgh: T. and T. Clark, 1911).

— *On Prayer. Die Schrift vom Gebet*, ed. P. Koetschau, GCS 3, Origenes Werke, 2 (Leipzig: Hinrichs Verlag, 1899); English trans. R. A. Greer, *Origen: An Exhortation to Martyrdom, Prayer ...*, Classics of Western Spirituality (New York: Paulist Press, 1979).

Pamphilus, *Apology for Origen*, PG 17.521-616.

Philo, *On Dreams*, ed. and trans. F. H. Colson and G. H. Whitaker, LCL Philo, 5 (Cambridge, Mass.: Harvard University Press, 1958).

Photius, *Bibliotheca*, ed. and French trans. R. Henry, 8 vols. (Paris: Belles Lettres, 1959-77); trans. (to chap. 145) J. H. Freese (London: SPCK, 1920).

Plato, *Republic*, ed. and trans. P. Shorey, LCL Plato, 5-6 (Cambridge, Mass.: Harvard University Press, 1963).

— *Timaeus*, ed. and trans. R. G. Bury, LCL Plato, 9 (Cambridge, Mass.: Harvard University Press, 1981).

Polycarp, *Letter to the Philippians*, ed. and trans. K. Lake, LCL Apostolic Fathers, 1 (Cambridge, Mass.: Harvard University Press, 1985).

Ptolemy, *Letter to Flora*. Text from Epiphanius, *Panarion 33.3-7. Ptolémée: Lettre à Flora*, ed. and trans. G. Quispel, SC 24 bis, (Paris: Cerf, 1966); English trans. in P. R. Amidon, *The Panarion of Epiphanius of Salamis: Selected Passages* (Oxford: Oxford University Press, 1990), 119-23, and in R. Grant, *Second-Century Christianity: A Collection of Fragments* (London: SPCK, 1946), 30-7.

Quintilian, *Institutio Oratoria*, ed. and trans. H. E. Butler, LCL 4 vols. (Cambridge, Mass.: Harvard University Press, 1976-85).

The Second Treatise of the Great Seth, in *The Nag Hammadi Library in English*, ed. J. M. Robinson, (Leiden: Brill, 1988), 362-71.

Sextus Empiricus, *Against the Grammarians*, ed. and trans. R. G. Bury, LCL Sextus Empiricus, 4 (Cambridge Mass.: Harvard University Press, 1937).

Socrates, *Ecclesiastical History*, ed. G. C. Hansen with M. Sirinjan, GCS, NF 1 (Berlin: Akademie Verlag, 1995); trans. in NPNF second series, 2 (1890: repr. Grand Rapids, Mich.: Eerdmans, 1952), 1-178.

Stoicorum Veterum Fragmenta, ed. J. von Arnim (Leipzig: Teubner, 1903-1924).

Suidae Lexicon, ed. A. Adler, 5 vols., Lexicographi Graeci, 1 (Leipzig: Teubner, 1928-38).

Tertullian, *On Fasting. De ieiunio adversus psychicos*, ed. A. Reifferscheid and G. Wissowa, Corpus Scriptorum Ecclesiasticorum Latinorum, 20 (1890), 274-97; trans. in ANF 4 (1885: repr. Grand Rapids, Mich.: Eerdmans, 1975), 102-14.

— *Against Marcion*, ed. and trans. E. Evans, OECT (Oxford: Clarendon Press, 1972).

— *On Modesty. Tertullien: La Pudicité*, ed. and French trans. C. Munier, SC 394-5 (Paris: Cerf, 1993); trans. in ANF 4 (1885: repr. Grand Rapids, Mich.: Eerdmans, 1975), 74-101.

— *Against Praxeas*, ed. and trans. E. Evans (London: SPCK, 1948).

The Gospel according to Thomas, ed. B. Layton, trans. T. O. Lambdin, in *Nag Hammadi Codex II, 2-7*, vol. 1, ed. B. Layton, Nag Hammadi Studies, 20 (Leiden: Brill, 1989).

Theodoret of Cyrus, *Compendium of Heretical Fables*, PG 83.335-556.

Theophanes, *Chonography*, ed. C. de Boor (Leipzig: Teubner, 1883; repr. Hildesheim: Olms, 1963).

Theophilus of Antioch, *To Autolycus*, ed. and trans. R. M. Grant, OECT (Oxford: Clarendon, 1970).

Secondary Material

Abraham, W. J., *Canon and Criterion in Christian Theology* (Oxford: Clarendon Press, 1998).

Andresen, C., "Justin und der mittlere Platonismus," *ZNTW* 44 (1952/3), 157-95.

Aune, D. E., *Prophecy in Early Christianity and the Ancient Mediterranean World* (Grand Rapids, Mich.: Eerdmans, 1983).

Bacq, P., *De l'ancienne à la nouvelle Alliance selon S. Irénée: Unité du livre IV de l'Adversus Haereses* (Paris: Éditions Lethielleux, Presses Universitaires de Namur, 1978).

Bammel, C. P., "Ignatian Problems," *JTS* ns 33 (1982), 62-97.

— "The State of Play with regard to Hippolytus and the *Contra Noetum*," *Heythrop Journal*, 31 (1990), 195-9.

Bardy, G., *Paul de Samosate: Étude historique*, rev. edn. (Louvain: Spicilegium Sacrum Lovaniense, 1929).

— "Aux origenes de l'école d'Alexandrie," *RSR* 27 (1937), 65-90.

— review (of H. de Riedmatten, *Les Acts du Procès de Paul de Samosate: Étude sur la Christologie du IIIe au IVe siècle*), *RSR* 26 (1952), 294-6.

Barr, J., *Old and New in Interpretation: A Study of the Two Testaments* (New York: Harper and Row, 1966).

— *Holy Scripture: Canon, Authority, Criticism* (Philadelphia: Westminster Press, 1983).

— *The Garden of Eden and the Hope of Immortality* (Minneapolis: Fortress Press, 1993).

Barton, J., *Holy Writings, Sacred Text: The Canon in Early Christianity* (Louisville, KY: John Knox Press, 1997).

Bauer, W., *Rechtglaübigkeit und Ketzerei im ältesten Christentum* (Tübingen: Mohr, 1934); trans. of 2nd edn. (1964, ed. by G. Strecker) by R. Kraft et al., *Orthodoxy and Heresy in Earliest Christianity* (Philadelphia: Fortress Press, 1971).

Behr, J., *Asceticism and Anthropology in Irenaeus and Clement* (Oxford: Oxford University Press, 2000).

Bienert, W. A., *Dionysius von Alexandrien: Zur Frage des Origenismus im dritten Jahrhundert*, PTS 21 (Berlin: De Gruyter, 1978).

Blowers, P. M., "The *Regula Fidei* and the Narrative Character of Early Christian Faith," *Pro Ecclesia*, 6.2 (1997), 199-228.

Bostock, G., "The Sources of Origen's Doctrine of Pre-Existence," in L. Lies (ed.), *Origeniana Quarta* (Innsbruck-Vienna: Tyrolia, 1987), 259-64.

Bousset, W., *Kyrios Christos: A History of Belief in Christ from the Beginnings of Christianity to Irenaeus*, trans. of the 2ⁿᵈ German edn. (1921) by J. E. Steely (New York and Nashville, Tenn.: Abingdon Press, 1970).

Brent, A., "The Relations between Ignatius and the Didascalia," *Second Century*, 8.3 (1991), 129-56.

— "Diogenes Laertius and the Apostolic Succession," *JEH* 44.3 (1993), 367-89.

— *Hippolytus and the Roman Church in the Third Century: Communities in Tension before the Emergence of a Monarch-Bishop* (Leiden: Brill, 1995).

Brown, C. T., *The Gospel and Ignatius of Antioch*, Studies in Biblical Literature, 12 (New York: Peter Lang, 2000).

Brown, R. E., "Does the New Testament call Jesus God," in idem, *Jesus, God and Man* (Milwaukee: Bruce, 1967), 1-38.

— *The Community of the Beloved Disciple: The Life, Loves, and Hates of an Individual Church in New Testament Times* (Mahwah, N.Y.: Paulist Press, 1979).

— *The Epistles of John*, The Anchor Bible (New York: Doubleday, 1982).

— *An Adult Christ at Christmas: Essays on the Three Biblical Christmas Stories* (Collegeville: Liturgical Press, 1978).

— *The Birth of the Messiah: A Commentary on the Infancy Narratives in the Gospels of Matthew and Luke* (New York: Doubleday, 1993).

Campenhausen, H. von, *The Formation of the Bible*, trans. J. A. Baker (Philadelphia: Fortress Press, 1972).

Chadwick, H., "Eucharist and Christology in the Nestorian Controversy," *JTS* ns 2.2 (1951), 145-64.

— review (of H. de Riedmatten, *Les Acts du Procès de Paul de Samosate: Étude sur la Christologie du IIIe au IVe siècle*), *JTS* ns 4 (1953), 91-4.

— *Early Christian Thought and the Classical Tradition* (Oxford: Clarendon Press, 1987 [1966]).

Clark, E. A., *The Origenist Controversy: The Cultural Construction of an Early Christian Debate* (Princeton: Princeton University Press, 1992).

Congar, Y. M.-J., *Tradition and Traditions: An Historical and a Theological Essay* (New York: Macmillan, 1967).

Cosgrove, C. H., "Justin Martyr and the Emerging Christian Canon: Observations on the Purpose and Destination of the Dialogue with Trypho," *VC* 36 (1982), 209-32.

Crouzel, H., *Origène et la "connaissance mystique"* (Bruges/Paris: Desclée de Brouwer, 1961).

— *Origen*, trans. A. S. Worrall (Edinburgh: T. and T. Clark, 1989).

Dawson, D., *Allegorical Readers and Cultural Revision in Ancient Alexandria* (Berkeley: University of California Press, 1992).

Dillon, J., *The Middle Platonists: 80 B.C. to A.D. 220*, rev. edn. (Ithaca, N.Y.: Cornell University Press, 1996).

Döllinger, J. J. I. von, *Hippolytus and Callistus*, trans. A. Plummer (Edinburgh: T. and T. Clark, 1876).

Droge, A. J., *Homer or Moses? Early Christian Interpretation of the History of Culture* (Tübingen: Mohr, 1989).

Edwards, M. J., "On the Platonic Schooling of Justin Martyr," *JTS* ns 42.1 (1991), 17-34.

— "Justin's Logos and the Word of God," *JECS* 3.3 (1995), 261-80.

— "Ignatius and the Second Century. An Answer to R. Hübner," *ZAC* 2 (1998), 214-26.

— "Did Origen Apply the Word *Homoousios* to the Son?" *JTS* ns 49.2 (1998), 658-70.

Ehrman, B., *The Orthodox Corruption of Scripture: The Effect of Early Christological Controversies on the Text of the New Testament* (New York and Oxford: Oxford University Press, 1993).

Ellis, P. F., *The Genius of John: A Composition-Critical Commentary on the Fourth Gospel* (Collegeville: Liturgical Press, 1984).

— "Inclusion, Chiasm, and the Division of the Fourth Gospel," *SVTQ* 43.3-4 (1999), 269-338.

Elster, J., "Belief, Bias and Ideology," in M. Hollis and S. Lukes (eds.), *Rationality and Relativism* (Cambridge, Mass.: MIT Press, 1982), 123-48.

Eynde, D. van den, *Les normes de l'enseignement Chrétien dans la littérature patristique des trois premiers siècles* (Paris: Gabalda, 1933).

Fishbane, M., *Biblical Interpretation in Ancient Israel* (Oxford: Clarendon Press, 1985).

Flesseman-van Leer, E., *Tradition and Scripture in the Early Church* (Assen: Van Gorcum, 1954).

Florovsky, G., "The Function of Tradition in the Ancient Church," *GOTR* 9.2 (1963-4), 181-200; repr. in idem, *Bible, Church, Tradition* (Vaduz, Büchervertriebsanstalt, 1987), 73-92.

Frye, N., *The Great Code: The Bible and Literature* (New York: Harcourt Brace Jovanovich, 1982).

Gadamer, H. G., *Wahrheit und Methode*, 5th edn. (Tübingen: Mohr, 1986); trans. J. Weinsheimer and D. G. Marshall, *Truth and Method* (New York: Continuum, 1997).

Gamble, H. Y., *Books and Readers in the Early Church: A History of Early Christian Texts* (New Haven and London: Yale University Press, 1995).

Gögler, R., *Zur Theologie des biblischen Wortes bei Origenes* (Düsseldorf: Patmos Verlag, 1963).

Grant, R. M., *Second-Century Christianity: A Collection of Fragments* (London: SPCK, 1946).

— "Early Alexandrian Christianity," *CH* 40 (1971), 133-44.

— *Heresy and Criticism: The Search for Authenticity in Early Christian Literature* (Louisville, KY: Westminster-John Knox Press, 1993).

— *Irenaeus of Lyons* (New York: Routledge, 1997).

Greer, R. A., "The Christian Bible and Its Interpretation," in J. L. Kugel and R. A. Greer, *Early Biblical Interpretation* (Philadelphia: Westminster Press, 1986), 107-208.

Grillmeier, A., *Christ in Christian Tradition*, vol. 1, trans. of the 2nd rev. German edn. by J. Bowden (London: Mowbrays, 1975).

Hanson, R. P. C., "The Passage marked 'Unde?' in Robinson's *Philocalia* XV,19," in H. Crouzel and A. Quacquarelli (eds.), *Origeniana Secunda* (Rome: Ateneo, 1980), 293-303.

— *The Search for the Christian Doctrine of God* (Edinburgh: T. and T. Clark, 1988).

Harl, M., *Origène et la fonction révélatrice du Verbe Incarné* (Paris: Seuil, 1958).

—"La Préexistence des âmes dans l'oeuvre d'Origène," in L. Lies (ed.), *Origeniana Quarta* (Innsbruck-Vienna: Tyrolia, 1987), 238-58.

Harnack, A. von, *History of Dogma*, trans. of 3rd German edn. (1894), 7 vols. (London: Williams and Norgate, 1894-9).

— *Marcion: Das Evangelium vom fremden Gott*, 2nd edn. (Leipzig: Hinrichs Verlag, 1924); partial trans. by J. E. Steely and L. D. Bierma, *Marcion: The Gospel of an Alien God* (Durham, N.C.: Labyrinth Press, 1990).

Hays, R., *Echoes of Scripture in the Letters of Paul* (New Haven and London: Yale University Press, 1989).

Heine, R. E., "The Christology of Callistus," *JTS* ns 49.1 (1998), 56-91.

Heil, U., *Athanasius von Alexandrien: De Sententia Dionysii*, PTS 52 (Berlin: De Gruyter, 1999).

Hill, C. E., "Justin and the New Testament Writings," *St. Patr.* 30 (Leuven: Peeters, 1997), 42-8.

— "Ignatius and the Apostolate: The Witness of Ignatius to the Emergence of Christian Scripture," forthcoming in *St. Patr.*

Hoeck, A. van den, "The 'Catechetical School' of Early Christian Alexandria and Its Philonic Heritage," *HTR* 90.1 (1997), 59-87.

Holte, R., "Logos Spermatikos: Christianity and Ancient Philosophy according to St Justin's *Apologies*," *Studia Theologica*, 12 (1958), 109-68.

Hoskyns, E. C., *The Fourth Gospel*, 2nd rev. edn., ed. F. N. Davey (London: Faber and Faber, 1947).

Hübner, R., "Thesen zur Echtheit und Datierung der sieben Briefe des Ignatius von Antiochen," *ZAC* 1 (1997), 44-72.

Huby P. and G. Neal (eds.), *The Criterion of Truth* (Liverpool: Liverpool University Press, 1989).

Johnson, L. Timothy, *The Real Jesus: The Misguided Quest for the Historical Jesus and the Truth of the Traditional Gospels* (San Francisco: Harper, 1997).

Kelly, J. N. D., *Early Christian Creeds*, 3rd edn. (London: Longman, 1972).

— *Early Christian Doctrines*, 5th edn. (San Francisco: Harper, 1978).

Kinzig, W. and M. Vinzent, "Recent Research on the Origin of the Creed," *JTS* ns 50.2 (1999), 535-59.

Kittel, G., *Theological Dictionary of the New Testament*, trans. and ed. G. W. Bromiley (Grand Rapids, Mich.: Eerdmans, 1966).

Klijn, A. F. L. and G. J. Reinink, *Patristic Evidence for Jewish-Christian Sects*, Supplements to *Novum Testamentum*, 36 (Leiden: Brill, 1973).

Koester, H., *Ancient Christian Gospels: Their History and Development* (London: SCM Press; Philadelphia, Trinity Press, 1990).

Kugel, J. L., "Early Interpretation: The Common Background of Late Forms in Biblical Exegesis," in J. L. Kugel and R. A. Greer, *Early Biblical Interpretation* (Philadelphia: Westminster Press, 1986), 9-106.

— *Traditions of the Bible: A Guide to the Bible As It Was at the Start of the Common Era* (Cambridge Mass.: Harvard University Press, 1998).

Lampe, P. *Die stadtrömischen Christen in den ersten beiden Jahrhunderten*, 2nd rev. edn. (Tübingen: Mohr, 1989).

Lang, U. M., "The Christological Controversy at the Synod of Antioch in 268/9," *JTS* ns 51.1 (2000), 54-80.

Layton, B., *The Gnostic Scriptures: Ancient Wisdom for the New Age* (New York: Doubleday, 1987).

Levenson, J. D., "The Eighth Principle of Judaism and the Literary Simultaneity of Scripture," *Journal of Religion*, 68 (1988), 205-25.

Liddle, H. G. and R. Scott (eds.), *A Greek-English Lexicon*, 9th edn., rev. H. S. Jones and R. McKenzie (Oxford: Clarendon Press, 1996).

Lilla, S. R. C., *Clement of Alexandria: A Study in Christian Platonism and Gnosticism* (Oxford: Oxford University Press, 1971).

Lindars, B., *The Gospel of John*, New Century Bible Commentary (Grand Rapids, Mich.: Eerdmans, 1972).

Lindemann, A., "Antworf auf die 'Thesen zum Echtheit und Datierung der sieben Briefe des Ignatius von Antiochen,'" *ZAC* 1 (1997), 185-94.

Logan, A., "Origen and the Development of Trinitarian Theology," in L. Lies (ed.), *Origeniana Quarta* (Innsbruck-Vienna: Tyrolia, 1987), 424-9.

Loofs, F., *Paul von Samosata. Eine Untersuchung zur altkirchlichen Literatur und Dogmengeschichte*, TU 3/14, 5 (Leipzig: Hinrichs Verlag, 1924).

— *Leitfaden zum Studium der Dogmengeschichte*, 5th edn., rev. K. Aland (Halle-Saale: Max Niemeyer Verlag, 1950-3).

Louth, A., *Discerning the Mystery: An Essay on the Nature of Theology* (Oxford: Clarendon Press, 1983).

Lubac, H. de, *Histoire et Esprit: L'intelligence de l'Écriture d'après Origène* (Paris: Aubier, 1950).

Markschies, C., *Valentinus Gnosticus?* (Tübingen: Mohr, 1992).

McGrath, A. E., *The Genesis of Doctrine: A Study in the Foundation of Doctrinal Criticism* (Grand Rapids, Mich.: Eerdmans, 1990).

McGuckin, J. A., "The Changing Forms of Jesus," in L. Lies (ed.), *Origeniana Quarta* (Innsbruck-Vienna: Tyrolia, 1987), 215-22.

— "Structural Design and Apologetic Intent in Origen's *Commentary on John*," in G. Dorival and A. Le Boulluec (eds.), *Origeniana Sexta* (Leuven: Peeters, 1995), 441-57.

Meeks, W. A., "The Man from Heaven in Johannine Sectarianism," *JBL* 91 (1972), 44-72.

Meijering, R., *Literary and Rhetorical Theories in Greek Scholia* (Groningen: Egbert Forsten, 1987).

Metzger, B. M., *A Textual Commentary on the Greek New Testament* (New York: UBS, 1971).

— *The Canon of the New Testament: Its Origin, Development, and Significance* (Oxford: Clarendon Press, 1989).

Millar, F., "Paul of Samosata, Zenobia and Aurelian: The Church, Local Culture and Political Allegiance in Third-Century Syria," *JRS* 61 (1971), 1-17.

Minns, D., *Irenaeus* (London: Geoffrey Chapman, 1994).

Moody, D., "God's Only Son," *JBL* 72.4 (1953), 213-19.

Nahm, C., "The Debate on the 'Platonism' of Justin Martyr," *Second Century*, 9.3 (1992), 129-51.

Nautin, P., *Hippolyte et Josipe: Contribution à l'histoire de la littérature chrétienne du troisième siècle* (Paris: Cerf, 1947).

— *Lettres et écrivains chrétiens des IIe et IIIe siècles* (Paris: Cerf, 1961).

— *Origène: Sa vie et son œuvre* (Paris: Beauchesne, 1977).

Noormann, R., *Irenäus als Paulusinterpret* (Tübingen: Mohr, 1994).

Norris, F. W., "Paul of Samosata: *Procurator Ducenarius*," *JTS* ns 35.1 (1984), 50-70.

Norris, R. A., "Theology and Language in Irenaeus of Lyons," *Anglican Theological Review*, 76.3 (1994), 285-95.

Osborn, E., "Reason and Rule of Faith in the Second Century AD," in R. Williams (ed.), *The Making of Orthodoxy: Essays in Honour of Henry Chadwick* (Cambridge: Cambridge University Press, 1989), 40-61.

— "Origen: The Twentieth Century Quarrel and Its Recovery," in R. Daly (ed.), *Origeniana Quinta* (Leuven: Peeters, 1992), 26-39.

— "Arguments for Faith in Clement of Alexandria," *VC* 48 (1994), 1-24.

— *Tertullian: First Theologian of the West* (Cambridge: Cambridge University Press, 1997).

Osborne, C., *Rethinking Early Greek Philosophy* (London: Duckworth, 1987).

Perrone, L., "L'enigma di Paolo di Samosata. Dogma, chiesa e società nella Siria del III secolo: prospettive di un ventennio di studi," *Cristianesimo nella Storia*, 13 (1992), 253-327.

Petersen, W. L., "Eusebius and the Paschal Controversy," in H. W. Attridge and G. Hata (eds.), *Eusebius, Christianity, and Judaism* (Leiden: Brill, 1992), 311-25.

Pétrement, S., *A Separate God: The Origins and Teachings of Gnosticism*, trans. C. Harrison (San Francisco: Harper, 1990).

Pfeiffer, R., *History of Classical Scholarship: From the Beginnings to the End of the Hellenistic Age* (Oxford: Clarendon Press, 1968).

Pollard, T. E., *Johannine Christology and the Early Church* (Cambridge: Cambridge University Press, 1970).

Prestige, G. L., *God in Patristic Thought* (London: SPCK, 1959).

Rahner, K., "Theos in the New Testament," in idem, *God, Christ, Mary and Grace*, Theological Investigations, 1, trans. by C. Ernst (Baltimore: Helicon, 1965), 79-148.

Reynders, B., "Paradosis: Le progress de l'idée de tradition jusqu' à saint Irénée," *Recherches de Théologie Ancienne et Médiévale*, 5 (1933), 155-91.

Richard, M., "Les Florilèges diphysites du Ve et VIe siècle," in *Das Konzil von Chalkedon*, ed. A. Grillmeier and H. Bracht, vol. 1 (Würzburg: Echter Verlag, 1959), 721-48.

— "Malchion et Paul de Samosate: Le témoignage d'Eusèbe de Césarée," *Ephemerides Theologicae Lovanienses*, 35 (1959), 325-38.

Ricoeur, P., *Essays on Biblical Interpretation* (Philadelphia: Fortress Press, 1980).

Riedmatten, H. de, *Les Acts du Procès de Paul de Samosate: Étude sur la Christologie du IIIe au IVe siècle*, Paradosis 6 (Fribourg en Suisse: St. Paul, 1952).

Robbins, G. A., "Eusebius' Lexicon of 'Canonicity,'" *St. Patr.* 25 (Leuven: Peeters, 1993), 134-41.

Roberts, C. H., *Manuscript, Society and Belief in Early Christian Egypt* (London: Oxford University Press, 1979).

Rousseau, P., *Basil of Caesarea* (Berkeley: University of California Press, 1994).

Sample, R. L. "The Messiah as Prophet: The Christology of Paul of Samosata" (Ph.D. Diss., Northwestern University, Evanston, Ill., 1977).

— "The Christology of the Council of Antioch (268 C.E.) Reconsidered," *CH* 48 (1979), 18-26.

Schmid, U., *Marcion und sein Apostolos* (Berlin: De Gruyter, 1995).

Schnackenburg, R., *The Johannine Epistles: Introduction and Commentary*, trans. R. and I. Fuller (New York: Crossroad, 1992).

Schoedel, W. R., *Ignatius of Antioch*, Hermenia (Philadelphia: Fortress Press, 1985).

Schofield, M., M. Burnyeat, and J. Barnes (eds.), *Doubt and Dogmatism: Studies in Hellenistic Epistemology* (Oxford: Oxford University Press, 1980).

Schöllgen, G., "Die Ignatian als pseudepigraphisches Brief-corpus. Anmerkung zu den Thesen von Reinhard M. Hübner," *ZAC* 2 (1998), 16-25.

Sieben, H. J., *Die Konzilsidee der Alten Kirche*, Konziliengeschichte, B, Untersuchungen (Paderborn *et al.*: Schöningh, 1979).

Simonetti, M., "Paolo di Samosata e Malchione. Riesame di alcune testimonianze," in *Hestíasis: Studi di tarda antichità offerti a Salvatore Calderone*, Studi Tardoantichi, 1 (Messina, 1986), 7-25.

— "Per la rivalutazione di alcune testimonianze su Paolo di Samosata," *Rivista di Storia e Letteratura Religiosa*, 24 (1988), 177-210.

Skarsaune, O., *The Proof From Prophecy: A Study in Justin Martyr's Proof-Text Tradition: Text-Type, Provenance, Theological Profile* (Leiden: Brill, 1987).

Skeat, T. C., "The Oldest Manuscript of the Four Gospels?" *NTS* 43 (1997), 1-34.

Spanneut, M., *Recherches sur les Écrits d'Eustathe d'Antioche, avec une édition nouvelle des fragments dogmatiques et exégétiques* (Lille: Facultés Catholiques, 1948).

Stanton, G. N., "The Fourfold Gospel," *NTS* 43 (1997), 317-46.

Stark, R., *The Rise of Christianity: A Sociologist Reconsiders History* (Princeton: Princeton University Press, 1996).

Stead, C., "Marcel Richard on Malchion and Paul of Samosata," in H. C. Brennecke, E. L. Grasmück, C. Markschies (eds.), *Logos: Festschrift für Luise Abramowski zum 8 Juli 1993* (Berlin-New York: De Gruyter, 1993), 140-50.

Stevenson, J., *A New Eusebius: Documents Illustrative of the History of the Church to A.D. 337* (London: SPCK, 1963).

Striker, G., "Κριτήριον τῆς ἀληθείας," *Nachrichten der Akademie der Wissenschaften in Göttingen*, I. Phil.-hist. Kl. (1974), 2:47-110.

Torjesen, K. J., *Hermeneutical Procedure and Theological Method in Origen's Exegesis*, PTS 28 (Berlin: De Gruyter, 1986).

— "Hermeneutics and Soteriology in Origen's *Peri Archon*," *St. Patr.* 21 (Leuven, 1989), 333-48.

Torrance, T. F., *Divine Meaning: Studies in Patristic Hermeneutics* (Edinburgh: T. and T. Clark, 1995).

Tremblay, R., *La Manifestation et la vision de Dieu selon saint Irénée de Lyon* (Münster: Aschendorff, 1978).

Trigg, J. W., "The Charismatic Intellectual: Origen's Understanding of Religious Leadership," *CH* 50 (1981), 5-19.

Valantasis, R., *The Gospel of Thomas* (London and New York: Routledge, 1997).

Vivian, T., *St Peter of Alexandria: Bishop and Martyr* (Philadelphia: Fortress Press, 1988).

Widdicombe, P., *The Fatherhood of God from Origen to Athanasius* (Oxford: Clarendon Press, 1994).

Wilken, R. L., "Alexandria: A School for Training in Virtue," in P. Henry (ed.), *Schools of Thought in the Christian Tradition* (Philadelphia: Fortress Press, 1984), 15-30.

Williams, M. A., *Rethinking "Gnosticism": An Argument for Dismantling a Dubious Category* (Princeton: Princeton University Press, 1996).

Williams, R. D., *Arius: Heresy and Tradition* (London: Darton, Longman and Todd, 1987).

— "Origen: Between Orthodoxy and Heresy," in W. A. Bienert and U. Kühneweg (eds.), *Origeniana Septima* (Leuven: Peeters, 1996), 3-14.

Young, F., *The Art of Performance: Towards a Theology of Holy Scripture* (London: Darton, Longman and Todd, 1990).

— *Biblical Exegesis and the Formation of Christian Culture* (Cambridge: Cambridge University Press, 1997).

Zahn-Harnack, A. von, *Adolf von Harnack* (Berlin: De Gruyter, 1951).

Index